THE
LONG
JOURNEY
TO
JAKE
PALMER

OTHER BOOKS BY JAMES L. RUBART

The Five Times I Met Myself

Book of Days

The Chair

Rooms

THE WELL SPRING NOVELS

Soul's Gate

Memory's Door

Spirit Bridge

THE

LONG
JOURNEY

TO

JAKE
PALMER

JAMES L. RUBART

THOMAS NELSON
Since 1798

Published in Nashville, Tennessee, by Thomas Nelson. Thomas Nelson is a registered trademark of HarperCollins Christian Publishing, Inc.

The author is represented by the literary agency of Alive Communications, Inc., 7680 Goddard Sreet, Suite 200, Colorado Springs, CO, 80920. www. alivecommunications.com.

Thomas Nelson titles may be purchased in bulk for educational, business, fund-raising, or sales promotional use. For information, please e-mail SpecialMarkets@ThomasNelson.com.

Scripture quotations are taken from the New American Standard Bible®. Copyright © 1960, 1962, 1963, 1968, 1971, 1972, 1973, 1975, 1977, 1995 by The Lockman Foundation. Used by permission. (www.Lockman.org)

Publisher's Note: This novel is a work of fiction. Names, characters, places, and incidents are either products of the author's imagination or used fictitiously. All characters are fictional, and any similarity to people living or dead is purely coincidental.

Library of Congress Cataloging-in-Publication Data

Names: Rubart, James L., author.
Title: The long journey to Jake Palmer / James L. Rubart.
Description: Nashville : Thomas Nelson, 2016.
Identifiers: LCCN 2016006264 | ISBN 9781401686130 (softcover)
Subjects: LCSH: Life change events--Fiction. | Loss (Psychology)--Fiction. | Self-realization--Fiction. | Self-actualization (Psychology)--Fiction. | GSAFD: Christian fiction.
Classification: LCC PS3618.U2326 L66 2016 | DDC 813/.6--dc23 LC record available at http://lccn.loc.gov/2016006264

Printed in the United States of America

16 17 18 19 20 21 RRD 6 5 4 3

For Jamie, I'll never forget you.

And for you, dear reader, I pray you're willing
to take the long journey for yourself.

"And you? When will you begin
that long journey into yourself?"

—RUMI

1

If Jake Palmer had only kept the mundane promise he'd made to himself, his life wouldn't be headed down a dead-end road at the speed of light. He'd vowed there'd be no more late-night flights. No more trips stacked on top of each other. No more landings at Seattle's Sea-Tac Airport after midnight, which pushed him to physical and emotional exhaustion. But there he'd been for the third time in eight days.

His phone rang as he pulled out of the parking garage, and Jake glanced at the time before he picked up. Twelve thirty-five a.m. Sienna should be asleep.

"What are you still doing up?"

"I miss you. I've hardly seen you for the past three months."

"I know. Not fun. But Italy will be here in six short weeks. Then fourteen days of cruising where you'll have to put up with me 24/7."

"Maybe I *should* get some rest."

Jake laughed.

"How far away are you, Adonis?" Sienna asked.

He smiled at her pet name for him. "Forty minutes."

"Get here now. I'll wait up."

"And sacrifice your beauty rest?" Jake tapped on his steering wheel and grinned.

"Yes, even though it'll make me look horrible tomorrow."

"Impossible. You'd win every beauty contest known to man even if you stayed up for a month."

"If I'm asleep when you get home, wake me up. Promise."

"Absolutely."

Sienna blew a kiss through the phone and hung up.

Jake glanced at his gas gauge as he headed up I-5. The yellow warning light glared at him, red needle on the wrong side of the empty line. Problem. Wouldn't be good to run out before getting back to Bothell. He glanced at the exits coming up. Probably not the greatest section of Seattle to get gas this late at night, but running out here would be worse. Why hadn't he filled up before the trip? Because his schedule was insane and there hadn't been time.

Jake pulled off I-5 at the next exit. Quick fill and he'd be back on the asphalt river, home to Sienna before one twenty. He pulled up to the outside gas island and snatched his wallet out of his coat at the same time. As he stepped outside into the October chill, odors of pot and gas filled his nose.

As he stepped to the pump, a battered Honda Civic with peeling dark blue paint lurched into the station and stopped behind his Jeep. A young woman got out, her black hair streaked with red and purple, her denim coat marred with grime and amateur images of dragons drawn with blue and red Sharpies.

She swiped a credit card and as she pumped her gas glanced furtively past Jake at the street to his back, then at the street in front of them. She jiggled her nozzle up and down as if to try to make the gas flow faster.

"You okay?"

She flinched and glanced at Jake as if she hadn't seen him during her scans of the street and was shocked to find someone standing nearby. "No, I'm . . . yeah, I'm fine."

"I didn't mean to startle you."

"No, I . . . uh . . . just thinking about . . . stuff."

Her eyes continued to dart in a quick circle, and before her gaze had made it back to the starting point, the screech of tires filled the night air. The agitation on her face turned to fear as a gray Dodge Neon with a spoiler and white racing stripes sped into the station, then skidded to a stop behind the girl's car, brakes squealing.

She dropped her nozzle and turned to run past Jake, but a beat-up Toyota appeared in front of Jake's Jeep and she froze.

The passenger window of the Neon came down and a kid, couldn't be more than twenty, adjusted his unneeded sunglasses and called out to her.

"Hey, sugar. We gotta talk. We're running a business and you're the product, see. And when the product goes missing, our clients aren't happy. So we're not happy. And it's a trickle-down economy, which means you're not going to be happy."

The girl held out her palms as if they could keep the cars and the men inside them at bay. "I told you, I'm out of the game. You promised you'd leave me alone. You promised!"

"Don't jam me." The man swore, then flicked a cigarette toward the garbage can that sat between Jake's pump and the girl's. "Five more. That was the deal. Five. More. Don't test me, girl."

"No. I'm out now. Please!"

"You will be, baby. All the way out. Just five more. But right now, we gotta getcha all cleaned up. Nice and fresh, then we can start again, get it done, a week tops, then you're free." The man climbed out of his car and extended a completely tattooed arm toward her and wiggled his fingers. "Now come here, sugar. Now!"

Jake debated whether to move away or stay. But only for a moment. He left the nozzle stuck in the gas line and eased over next to the girl, his palms raised.

"What do you think you're doing?" The man sneered at Jake. "You looking for a party? Or to get yourself totally messed up?"

"Neither."

"Then bounce!" The kid took a step toward Jake and swore so hard spittle flew out his mouth.

Jake glanced at the kid in the driver's seat of the Neon, then behind him. Two more in the front seat of the Toyota. Four against one. Jake was in good shape and knew how to handle himself in a fight, but these weren't great odds. And the likelihood of one of these punks carrying a gun was high.

Jake kept his hands raised and shook his head. "I am not looking for any kind of trouble."

"Good. That means you're going to get in your Jeep right now, jam down hard on the gas pedal, and be back on your way to your castle. Go!" The kid stabbed his finger toward Jake's Jeep, then eased toward the girl, a sick grin on his face.

"Tell you what. Let's say I am looking for a party. Five parties. Why don't I give you some money for your party supplies and you can let your friend here get back to filling up her car."

He pointed to his back pocket. "Right now, I'm just going to grab my wallet."

Jake took all his cash and held it out. The kid took the bills and spun through them. "Two hundred eighty-five. You're a real hero, aren't you, pokey?"

"No. Not a hero. I'm just thinking this will end better for you, for me, for her, and for the cameras on the pumps if you take that and we all head out of here."

The kid grinned, then nodded at the driver of the Neon and toward the Toyota behind Jake.

"Oh, yeah, okay, I like that." The kid strutted back and forth in front of Jake. "You're a real Mr. Entertainment. Seriously funny guy. But I'm not laughing. You threaten me like I'm too stupid to think about the cameras?

"See this place?" The kid laughed and swept his finger toward the store in a tight circle. "We come here, hang out sometimes. So we've adjusted the cameras to our liking. The clerks all like us too."

The kid stepped forward and jabbed Jake in the chest. "Nobody's gonna see what goes on here. Nobody. Which means you're going to jump in your shiny new Jeep right now and pull away and pretend you didn't see nothing. Got it?"

"Take the money, let her go."

"Wait, am I hearing you right?" The kid yanked on his earlobe.

"Yeah, you heard right. Let her go."

The kid's face grew red. He whipped off his sunglasses and got within inches of Jake, his voice a hiss now. "Last chance, hero."

"Let her go."

The kid hopped back and jerked up and down in a spastic

dance. "Wow. This is crazy. You're not asking anymore? You're telling? You don't do that. I gave you a chance. Gave you two. But you're breaking all the rules, Mr. Entertainment. You break our rules, we always get to have a little fun. And you get to take a bath."

The kid pulled out a matchbook at the same moment something wet hit the small of Jake's back, then his legs. He spun. One of the kids from the other car had a grin on his face, and Jake's nozzle in his hand, gas streaming toward him in a lazy rainbow. Now his stomach and all the way down to his shoes were covered. He twisted back to glance at the first kid even though he knew exactly what was about to happen. He started to run, but he was far too late.

The last thing he remembered was a matchbook on fire, looping through the air toward his silver belt buckle.

2

ONE AND A HALF YEARS LATER

Jake took a deep breath as he rode the elevator to the eleventh floor of Chicago's Willis Tower. He forced a smile for his own benefit and tried to ignore the churning in his stomach. He could do this; he'd given this talk a million times. Written a book about it. Nothing to it. Like riding a bike.

He smoothed his suit coat and tightened his grip on his briefcase. When the doors finally parted, Jaclyn Thurman was waiting for him.

The woman's style was business casual, but something about the way she adjusted her glasses told him she was all work and no play. Fine by him. She gave his hand a quick shake, then folded hers in front of her as she led him toward the staff training center.

"Your first training session in a year and a half, right?" she asked.

"Right."

"Glad you came out of retirement."

"I wasn't retired, I was . . . taking some time off."

"A sabbatical?"

"Something like that."

A forced leave of absence was more like it. A complete reset of life as he knew it. Learning to walk again. Learning to live alone. Pretending he was completely healed. Climbing back on the horse that was his consulting business.

"Well, good to have you back in the game," Jaclyn said.

"Thanks."

"If the things my business associates say about your talks are true, you're going to take hold of my team, knock 'em dead, and bring them back to life again."

If his horse didn't buck him off into the cheap seats first.

"I didn't realize you'd hired me to kill people." Jake raised his eyebrows. "But I do appreciate the compliment. Hope I can live up to it."

"I'm counting on it."

Jaclyn's company was high-tech and the office reflected it. Sixty-inch monitors were built into the walls, and Jaclyn commented that the entire office was voice activated. The motif was stark but well designed. White walls and glass dominated the workspace. As she led Jake toward the auditorium where he'd spend the next six and a half hours, he spotted creatively decorated workstations. Individuality. Good. Stark was fine, sterile wasn't.

Jaclyn glanced at her watch as they clipped along the slate floor at a pace just above comfortable. "I told my team to be ready to go at ten o'clock. That gives you nineteen minutes to set up. Is that enough time?"

"Plenty. Thanks."

They reached a small auditorium filled with two hundred–plus seats, and Jaclyn excused herself. "I'll be back just before ten. I'll send one of my techs in to make sure your laptop is liking our systems. Anything else?"

"I'm good."

Jaclyn strode away and Jake walked stiffly to the center of the room. He stared at the empty seats and decided there wouldn't be any mingling with the audience as he'd always done. His gait was improving—he worked on it daily—but he didn't want to risk an ill-timed stumble.

By nine fifty-one, Jake was ready, and he moved into a corner of the room to watch Jaclyn's team as they ambled in. He studied the interesting mix of sharply dressed men and women, along with ones who appeared to have just jumped off the all-nighter wagon, and the rest somewhere in between. Again, good. It wasn't a company of clones.

Jaclyn had said she expected thirty-five of the company's staff to show up—as the training was optional—but as Jake studied the men and women seated in the eight or nine semicircle rows, it looked closer to seventy-five. Jake had hoped for the smaller crowd—it created a safer atmosphere for people to tell their stories at the end—but it was an element he couldn't control.

Jaclyn gave a quick introduction, motioned to Jake, and he approached the podium. He studied his fingertips as he tapped them together, then looked back up at Jaclyn's expectant team.

"We"—Jake motioned at the group, then at himself—"have a significant problem."

He stooped and picked up a large dark green bottle from behind the podium. Its label was blank. Jake lifted it high in the air to his left, then spun on his heel 180 degrees, stopping as he faced the right-hand side of the audience. Then he strode to a small table and smacked the bottle down hard enough to make the table wobble. A smattering of nervous laughter came from the group.

"Yes, we indeed have a serious problem." Jake steepled his hands, his profile to the audience as he stared at the bottle. He waited another second, then pointed at the crowd. "You . . . have a problem."

He brought his fingers up to point at himself as he leaned in toward Jaclyn's team. "*I* have a problem. Today I'm going to show you how to fix the problem. But it's your choice whether you want to take action and apply the solution to your life. If you're willing, you will never be the same again."

He pointed at the green bottle on the table. "Our situation? We are the bottle. Each of us."

Jake clicked to the first slide of his presentation and a quote filled the sixty-inch screen behind him. He read it slowly, taking time to emphasize each word. "It's extremely difficult to read the label when you're standing inside the bottle."

He bent slightly at the waist as a smattering of laughter skittered through the crowd. "Hear it once more: it is extremely difficult to read the label when you're standing inside the bottle."

He scanned the group. "And we are all standing inside our own bottles."

Jake waited as he always did for realization and small murmurs of acknowledgment to move through the crowd. He let the nods and quick whispers fade, then picked up the bottle and took two steps forward.

"You get it, don't you?" He laughed. "I see it in your eyes." He smiled and pointed at the bottle. "For each of us, the label is blank. We don't know the life-changing words that are written there. No clue, believe me. But we need to. How desperately we need to."

Jake looked around the room, pausing to make eye contact every few seconds.

"And I promise you, what is written on every single one of your bottles are words and phrases and truths more powerful than you can imagine. If you knew what was written there, right there on your label, if you truly knew what other people think of you, if you truly knew the impact you have on them, you would be stunned.

"I know exactly what some of you are thinking. 'He doesn't know the dark parts of me.' You're right, I don't. Others are thinking, 'There are so many things written on my label I'm ashamed of.' Yep, I get that too. But here's my suspicion: you've focused on your faults and mistakes and regrets for too many ages to count. It's time to start looking in another direction. Trust me, you're not going to be able to follow the sun by staring at the night. I'm going to suggest you turn your back on the darkness and walk toward the light."

Jake paused again to gauge the group. Some were checked out. There were always a few. But most were engaged, their eyes locked on his. He moved back and forth a little, ignoring the dull throb of pain in his legs.

"Still others are thinking, 'Me? No. Other people, sure. They don't see how powerful they are. I see what they are. Their talents. Gifts. But me? I barely make a ripple. There's next to nothing on my label.' But that proves my point. You see their glory, but not your own. And they see *your* glory, but not *their own*."

He paused to let the truth sink in. "It is the same with all of us. Me included."

Jake clicked to his next slide. An image of a woman standing on a precipice in silhouette with a vast mountain range behind her filled the screen.

"Finally, we have the people who know what's on their label, or maybe used to know, but they've forgotten, or they've gone into hiding. They won't let people see their strengths any longer, because something has frightened them, or a personal crisis has taken them out of the arena, or they're too ashamed of something they've done, or something has happened that has made them scared to show people who they really are."

Jake clicked to the next slide, a photo of a man emerging from a dark forest into bright sunshine. "It's time to step out of the shadows.

"The truth is, most of us are saying every single one of those things, I mentioned, but it's time to stop speaking lies about ourselves. It's time to stop!"

Jake smiled and joined the nervous laughter of those shocked by his shout.

"Yes?" He nodded and most of Jaclyn's team joined him.

"My new friends, it's time to come out of hiding. Time to discover what's on our labels."

The adrenaline that had never failed to kick in when Jake

spoke pulsed through him. They wouldn't all take hold, but the ones who did would never be the same.

"This isn't hype, this isn't motivational pabulum that will fade when you walk out that door at the end of the day. For the next six hours we're going to go through a comprehensive series of exercises that will help you discover in detail what is written on your label. And if you are able to actually believe what is written there, your life will change so immeasurably, you'll wonder how you lived in ignorance for so many years. Are you ready?"

Jake delivered his first session, then broke the audience into groups of five or six who all knew each other. When they settled, he said, "I want you to do a simple activity. You're going to go around your group and describe to each other what you see on each other's labels. I'll be wandering from group to group to see how you're doing. Don't make this hard. A few things for everyone, then on to the next person. Yes, it might feel strange and uncomfortable at first, but trust me, just go with it."

After offering them a few more guidelines, Jake wandered through the auditorium catching snippets from each group. Jaclyn's team grabbed the idea and sprinted with it. Nice. He reveled in the looks of hope and surprise on the faces in each group.

As he meandered around the conference room, his gaze kept returning to a woman who talked with her hands and leaned forward as she spoke to her group. Every few seconds she would touch the person on her right or left, and when she did the person's eyes brightened.

Jake ambled over until he was close enough to make out her words. She was heavy, probably on the upside of three hundred pounds, with piercing blue eyes that matched a sky-blue blouse, her face sun-kissed with the perfect amount of freckles. As she listened to each of the others in her group, she gave tiny nods of her head. There was an inquisitiveness in her eyes as if she was fascinated with their responses.

As he studied her, a middle-aged man from the neighboring group signaled him with a raised hand. Jake had a brief conversation with them about how to read a label when you didn't know a person well. After spending a few minutes with the cluster, he excused himself and moved toward another group wanting his input. But as he chatted with them, his intuition pinged and told him to talk to the woman in blue who had captivated him.

He returned slowly, wanting to time his interruption to the best moment. A few moments later, laughter. As it died, he leaned in.

"Excuse me." He tapped the lady lightly on the shoulder. "We're going to take a break in about five minutes and I'm wondering if I could talk to you for a few seconds before we do."

She stared at him with an expression he'd seen many times over the past nine years. Surprise. Nervousness. An *I can't believe the speaker wants to talk to me* look mixed with *Did I do something wrong?*

"Talk to me?" The woman pressed her hand against her sky-blue blouse just below her neck. "Right now?"

"If that's okay."

"Sure." She shifted in her chair. "I mean, yes, that's fine."

Jake led her to two empty seats well out of earshot of the rest of the groups and motioned toward the one on the left. "Can we sit?"

"Yes. Of course." She smoothed her pleated skirt and blinked.

Jake leaned forward, elbows on his knees, and clasped his hands. "Listen, I don't want this to be awkward and I don't mean to make you feel nervous, but I feel like I have to tell you something."

"Okay." She brushed back her hair and pressed her lips together tight.

"My name is Jake." He offered his hand. "What's yours?"

"Rachelle."

"It's good to meet you, Rachelle."

"You too." Her breaths came out in little puffs.

Jake started to speak, but before he could get the first word out, Rachelle blurted, "I'm talking too much in my group, aren't I? I need to give the others more time. And I kind of ended up taking over and I should have sat back more. I'm sorry about that. Really."

Jake shook his head and smiled. "I have to disagree. I think you're wrong. I don't think you're reading your label with any kind of accuracy. You don't talk too much. Not even close. And you haven't taken over."

He waved his hands toward the men and woman clustered in groups of five and six. "As you saw, I've spent a good deal of the past forty-five minutes going to each group, watching them, listening to them, helping them with questions if they needed it, offering suggestions, sitting in for a moment if they wanted me to. Encouraging them to speak. Lighting the match, to use a cliché."

Rachelle nodded. "Okay."

"I've done that with every group." Jake held up his forefinger. "All of them except one."

"Mine."

"Yes. Did you notice I haven't dropped in?"

"Yes."

"Why do you think I haven't engaged?"

"We're not made up of the important people in the company and you only have so much time."

Jake laughed and held his thumb and forefinger up to his eyes. "We need to buy you reading glasses for that label of yours."

"What?" Rachelle squished up her face and stared at him.

"The reason I've left you alone is because you've been leading beautifully. You've drawn out the people in your group like an artist. You've asked great questions and offered spot-on suggestions. You've done an excellent job of reading the labels in your group. It's been truly beautiful to watch."

Rachelle stared at him like he'd just told her that in a few seconds she was going to fly to the moon and back.

"And speaking of beauty, you are beautiful." Jake let the words hang in the air and watched Rachelle's eyes fill with tears.

"I'm so heavy." Rachelle let her head fall forward.

"That doesn't matter."

"It always matters." Rachelle's eyes dropped and she straightened her skirt though it didn't need straightening.

"And you're not just beautiful physically. Yes, you are beautiful on the outside, but the beauty you have on the inside spills out like a river and everyone around you gets swept up in it. Do you know that?"

Rachelle shook her head. "If only I could lose weight."

"Listen." Jake leaned forward and waited till she met his gaze. "That doesn't matter."

"I'm so heavy."

"It doesn't matter, beautiful Rachelle. It's time to come out of hiding."

"It does matter."

"Look at me." Jake waited till she lifted her face, eyes red. "It's time."

"I don't know how."

"Yes, you do. Not easy, I realize that. It can be brutal at times, but you can. I know. Time to come out of the shadows. To believe what's written on your label."

Jake clasped his hands in front of him. "If you want to lose weight, fine. But don't do it for anyone but you. Start to believe what is written on your label: Beautiful. Smart. A river of life to those around you. Natural leader. Friend. Your weight is no longer going to define who you are. Do you understand me?"

"You don't know me."

"You're right, I don't. Yet even in the few seconds I've seen you, the things I just described are so evident, anyone with eyes could see them."

Jake stood and Rachelle followed his lead. "I wish we could talk longer, but I do need to give you and your colleagues a break."

"Can I give you a hug?"

Jake grinned and craned his neck as if looking for security. "As long as we're not breaking any company rules."

Rachelle laughed and hugged Jake hard and he hugged back just as tightly.

"I have a friend who is a wonderful hugger." Rachelle wiped her eyes. "He says we should always give hugs that are fierce."

"I like that. Do you think he'd mind if I steal that idea?"

"I think he'd love it." Rachelle nodded as she stepped backward. "Thank you, Jake. You don't know how powerful this was."

"So good to meet you, Rachelle."

———∞———

At the end of the day Jake stood at the podium and clapped his hands. "Okay, friends. Time for a few minutes of Q and A, then I'll let you get back to your regularly scheduled lives. But my hope is they are never regularly scheduled again. I hope you choose to live lives of risk and boldness as you come to realize what is on your label."

He let his gaze sweep the room. There were some neutral faces, but most had bright eyes and expectant smiles. He'd made it back. A year and a half away—a little creaky in a few parts of his presentation—nothing anyone but he would notice. A few more sessions and he'd be back to firing on all cylinders.

After half a dozen insightful questions from the group, a man in the back row raised his hand.

"Yes." Jake pointed at him.

The man stood, his head cocked, his eyes narrowed.

"Tell me this, Palmer. What happens when all the gooshy feelings from one of your talks fade away, huh? What happens when your bottle isn't filled up with the things people expect you to pour out? The things they demand you pour out?"

Jake started to reply but the man interrupted.

"What happens when you go home one night and find out your wife doesn't think what's in the bottle is good enough anymore?

What happens when she reads the label and comes up with words that aren't the kind you'd want slapped on a Hallmark card?"

Jake's scarred legs went weak. The man was still talking, but Jake couldn't hear anything but Sienna's devastating announcement, which she dropped on him barely seven months after the attack: *I can't do it any longer. I really, truly thought I could, but I can't and I won't ever be able to pretend that your burns don't make me . . . I'm just not able . . . you know . . .*

"It's all candy and tulips for you, isn't it, Jake?" The man pointed at his own ring finger. "Used to have gold wrapped around this here finger. But my ex saw the dark places inside my bottle, and she didn't like 'em too much."

Jaclyn started to speak, but the man cut her off.

"No, Jackie, I'm going to finish. I'm not trying to hassle Jake. I really want to know."

He fixed his eyes on Jake and spoke once more, his voice now softer, the tone now tinged with sorrow. "What do you do when your whole life someone tells you what's on the label isn't enough? What if that scar follows you around your entire life?"

This isn't what I signed up for, Jake. I won't ever feel toward you the way I used to. I'm so sorry, but it's over.

The only sound in the room was the whir of air pouring through the heating ducts.

"You know what I mean, Jake?"

Jake gave a slow nod as his mind raced for an answer that he knew he'd never find.

I've filed for divorce. I know you'll say we can work it out, but we can't. So don't try. There's nothing you can do.

Every eye in the auditorium fixed on him. As heat rushed to his face, Jake shifted from trying to find an answer to trying to fight the panic threatening to take him to the floor. His legs wobbled and the corners of his vision grew darker.

"Jake?" Jaclyn appeared beside him and laid her hand lightly on his arm. "Are you okay?"

He blinked and stared at her for a few moments before years of experience navigating difficult questions kicked in. Jake fixed his eyes on the man and cleared his throat.

"Excellent question." He swept his eyes over the rest of the group. "The kind of change I'm talking about doesn't happen overnight. At times it will seem as if you can never erase what others have written on your label. But in time the ink will fade, replaced by the truth."

He paused and tried to think of a final, powerful thought to wrap things up, but all he could think about was how lame and cliché the words he'd just spoken were, and the panic started to seize him again.

Jaclyn saved him. "Thank you all for coming today, and let's thank Jake Palmer for sharing his life and his wisdom with us."

Jake barely heard the smattering of applause as he gave a half-hearted wave and a quarter-hearted smile. He'd never get the man's question out of his heart, because the exact same question had haunted Jake for the past year and a half.

Disquiet settled on him as he faked his way through the necessary good-byes, then rode the elevator back down and left the building. Everything he'd said during the past six hours was true. But it was also true that he'd shoved his own bottle into a locked closet at the back of his soul and conveniently misplaced the key. There was only one thing his label said these days. That he wasn't enough—not for his dad, not for his mom, not for Sienna, not for anyone—and he never would be again.

3

Jake handed his boarding pass to the woman at the kiosk. She scanned it, handed the pass back, and he trudged down the Jetway toward the 737 that would wing him from Chicago's O'Hare Airport back to Seattle.

He pressed his phone to his ear and said for the second time, "I'm not going this year. Drop it."

"Not an option. You gotta be there. Come on. Tenth anniversary."

"Forget it, Peter. You don't remember what happened last year?"

"That was your fault."

"Mine?"

"You didn't exactly engage."

Jake came to a stop on the ramp behind a woman with hair straight out of the late sixties. Groovy.

"No, it was your wife's fault," Jake said. "Can't go through it again this year. Last year sealed the deal. No more Jake Palmer at the annual summer gathering."

He was weary of the conversation. Weary of his business trip. Weary of his life.

"It won't be like that this time, I promise. Camille feels bad about what happened. Plus, it'll be good for you. Really. You've done the hermit routine long enough. Time to—"

"I'm boarding, Peter. I gotta go."

Jake hung up and stepped from the walkway onto the plane, taking his briefcase in one hand, carry-on in the other. He stared at the passengers in first class. He could afford to be there, but he'd never been able to rationalize the expense. One-fifty to three hundred percent more for a little extra room? Nah, it didn't compute.

His phone vibrated. Jake glanced down as he waited for the people ahead of him to grab a piece of that precious overhead cargo space. Peter. Again. He sent an automatic message saying he'd call back later, then stuck his phone in his pocket.

Peter Danner was a stellar friend and meant well, thought he was doing the right thing putting the full-court press on Jake to come this summer, but there was no way Jake would join the other five at the lake in three months. Last year had been brutal even without Camille rubbing the proverbial salt in his wounds. The tradition held too many memories of how life used to be, and he wasn't going to face them a second time.

The flight was full, one section packed with what looked like a girls' soccer team, the rest with the typical assortment of people from a cross section of life. He settled in next to the window in seat 11A, slid his briefcase under the seat in front of him, and stared out the window at the crewman loading luggage onto the plane.

A few minutes later Jake turned as an elderly gentleman with a full head of white hair and a well-worn brown leather jacket sat next to him. The man's face was tanned and ruddy, dotted with sun spots. The moment the man finished buckling his seat belt he inclined his head slightly and touched two fingers to his brow. "Hello."

"Hi."

The man stuck out his hand and shook Jake's with a strength that belied his age. Jake couldn't remember the last time he'd been greeted on a plane with a handshake, but something about the way the man did it felt right.

"Name is Leonard."

"Jake Palmer."

Leonard nodded and gave a quick smile as if he knew something Jake didn't. Jake tried not to stare at the gap where the man's two front teeth should have been. But for some reason it didn't look odd, as if this was the way a smile was supposed to be. He returned the smile with one of his own and hoped it didn't look phony. He wasn't in the mood for conversation, but after the usual pleasantries, Leonard pulled out what looked like a book on gardening and started to read.

Jake thankfully pulled out his e-reader and reviewed his notes to see if he could figure out what had gone wrong in Chicago. But even before he started he knew he wouldn't find the answer in his outline. The problem was buried somewhere much deeper.

By the time they flew over South Dakota an hour and a half later, Jake had skimmed through half a dozen articles on kayaking. Leonard apparently was done reading as well, because he closed his book and shoved it into the holder on the back of the seat in front of him. He did it with enough force to make the scarecrow-thin woman seated there rise up, twist, and glare at him with coal-black eyes. At first it seemed Leonard didn't notice, but as the woman continued to fling her scowl at him, he waved a hand as if to dismiss her, then focused on Jake.

"These planes? Way too small. Metal tube shooting through the sky like an elongated toaster with wings. Only the ninth time I've been on one in my life, and it'd make me plenty happy for this to be my last."

"I'm not a fan either." Jake knocked on the white wall of the plane to his left. "Can't wait till they invent teleportation so I can beam all over the country instantaneously."

"They've already done it." Leonard gave Jake that double-gap-toothed smile. "They have. I'm one hundred percent serious. Now it wasn't people or lab rats or even bugs, I'll give you that much. But way back in 2014 scientists took two qubits that were separated by a distance of three meters and watched and recorded the spin of one electron and saw that same spin reflected in the other qubit instantly. Instantly. No time passed. Teleportation. Proven."

"I have no idea what you're talking about." Jake grinned. "But it sounds dang cool."

"All I'm trying to tell ya is—think there've been break-throughs over the past hundred years? Ain't nothing compared to what's coming."

"You're into technology?"

"Nah, but I like to read. And I'm intrigued by things that prove we don't have next to nothin' figured out. See, I think there's way more to life than what our ears can hear or our eyes can see. We've barely scratched the surface of the surface of what's out there beyond our five senses. There's much more going on than we know."

A flight attendant passed by with a large bottle of water and Leonard flagged her down as if he were in a restaurant. After his plastic cup was filled, Leonard pointed at Jake and gave him a cryptic smile.

"What do you do, Jake?"

"I'm a speaker and a corporate trainer."

"Oh yeah?"

"I give talks to the public, I work with salespeople, CEOs, managers, individuals."

The cryptic smile again. "And what do you teach them?"

"How to help them see deeper into themselves. See that the things that hold them back are usually lies they believe are true. I help them see themselves as they truly are."

"For some that could be a rather disturbing vision."

Jake laughed and popped the last of his airline peanuts into his mouth. "Yeah, I could tell you some stories, wow. But I've found most people are well aware of their faults, their weak areas, those places where they've brought pain to themselves and those around them. And they dwell on those failings and continually beat themselves up with a stick so big they have no chance of seeing the other side; the areas where they bring light and hope and life to people. And even though others can see those qualities, the people themselves can't."

The smile on Leonard's face grew as he tapped the plane's armrest between him and Jake. "And because they are so focused on their own darkness, they miss the light and don't do all they could for themselves or those around them."

"Well said. I should hire you to write the copy on my website."

Leonard's face grew serious and he nodded as if it was a certainty that would happen. "When do you want me to start?"

"I was kidding." Jake laughed again. He liked this quirky guy.

"Don't worry, so was I." A knowing smile grew on his face. "I think you're doing people some good. You discover people's areas of light—that they can't see—point them out, then give them a plan on how to work from that perspective instead of the one where they're emotionally crippled. You take them through exercises to discover and define the things they could accomplish if they'd only see the truth about themselves and believe it."

Jake opened his mouth slightly and frowned as the old man's smile grew into a full-out grin.

"Do you realize you're quoting me almost word for word?"

"Yep, I do. I sure do, bucko."

Jake shook his head as the obvious explanation filled his mind.

"You've been to one of my seminars, haven't you?"

Leonard's eyes narrowed. "Like I said, I think you're doing people good. But don't you think your talks would be more powerful if you were living what you're preaching?"

Jake's face went hot. "What are you—"

"The owner of the company you just spoke at is a friend of mine. She told me you were coming." Leonard tapped his temple. "I read your book. I liked it. I happened to be in town visiting my daughter and decided since I was already here, I might as well hear you speak. So they let me sneak in a few minutes after you started and sit in the shadows in the back of the room. You didn't spot me, I'm guessing."

"No," Jake said.

"I felt for you during your, uh, stumble at the end of the day."
Jake didn't respond.

"Tough getting back in the saddle after a long layoff."

"Yeah, it can be."

"But we both know that it's more than the layoff, don't we?"
Leonard sighed. "Awhile back I watched your TED Talk after I
finished your book. The guy who gave that talk and the guy I
watched today are different people. Something happened to you."

Again, Jake didn't respond.

"You want to talk about it?"

"Nope."

"No worries," Leonard said. "You want to know what I think?"

"No."

"I think you can relate to the guy who heckled you more
than you'd ever want to let on." He pointed at Jake's ring finger. "I
think you used to have a gold band too."

Jake glared at him. "Interesting coincidence that we wound
up sitting next to each other."

"Yeah, quite a surprise." Leonard winked, settled back in his
seat, and continued at a volume that said he didn't care if anyone
else heard them. "So what's the scoop? Not married any longer?
Or do you take off the ring on trips so you can pick up women?"

Jake considered making a joke to deflect the question, but
chose not to. "Next week it'll be nine months since we signed the
papers."

"Pain in the butt, divorces," Leonard muttered. "I've had two."

"Then why the ring?" Jake pointed at Leonard's left hand.

"Yeah, well, the third time stuck."

Leonard blinked as if dust had landed in his eyes, but Jake didn't think it was dust. If Jake was guessing, Leonard wasn't the type of man to admit to tears even if they were streaming down his cheeks. Jake turned away to give Leonard a moment and stared out at the dusk stealing the last of the sun. A minute or two later, Leonard cleared his throat.

"Married to her for fourteen years. Till she decided to leave me for the world where there's no more pain. But I'll graduate from here someday, probably sooner than later. At that point maybe I'll see her again. She said I would. Not sure, but it's a thought, you know?"

"I'm sorry."

"Ah, what can you do? The moment we're born we have a death sentence hanging over us." Leonard leaned back in his seat and closed his eyes. "Okay, Jake. We're almost friends here. Tell your old pal Leonard what happened last year that makes you not want to go to the summer gathering this year."

"You listen to my phone calls too?"

"Couldn't be helped." Leonard grinned and a laugh sputtered out.

Jake joined Leonard and leaned his chair back, then scolded himself. "I always talk too loud when I'm on my cell phone."

"Most people do."

Jake closed his eyes and dumped his story on Leonard. "Every year for eight years, my wife and I and two other couples got together at a small lake in eastern Washington for a week of sun, water, great dinners, and deep conversation. Our best friends. We rented the same place, same dates in mid-July, and it was always one of the highlights of my year."

"But this year you don't want to go because it reminds you too much of your wife." Leonard waved his hand as if to wash away his words. "Sorry, I mean, ex-wife."

"Yeah."

"In other words, you didn't divorce her, she divorced you."

"That's right, detective. Thanks for that reminder of the facts."

"What happened? Why'd she leave?"

"That's a very long story."

"Got it," Leonard said. "You don't want to tell me."

"It's not that, it's—"

"Yeah it is. You don't know me." Leonard folded his hands and settled back in his seat.

"I'm going to plead the fifth, Leonard. At this point, the end of the why-stick is still a little too sharp, so it's pretty brutal to tell the story. Let's just say I loved her and did everything I knew how to do to show her that, but she ended up shattering my heart into so many pieces you'd need a microscope to spot any of them."

"Fair enough." Leonard reached into the satchel at his feet, pulled out a novel, and opened it toward the end, but he didn't read. "Is there any part of you that wants to go this summer?"

"Not much."

Leonard turned to his book, and the rumble of the engines had just started to lull Jake into the edges of sleep when he was hauled back to the conscious world by Leonard's tap on his arm.

"You asleep?"

"Almost. At least I was. Not so much now."

"Good." Leonard clasped Jake's arm and shook it. "Then open your eyes. I have an idea for you."

Jake blinked and gave his eyes a quick rub with his thumb and forefinger. "What? You've figured out a way to time travel with all your futuristic science stuff? I can go back and make that October night disappear?"

"What October night?"

"Doesn't matter. It's done. What's your idea?"

"It's a good one, and yes, maybe, in a way, it can help you go back." Leonard winked.

Jake squinted at Leonard. "Tell me."

The loudspeaker growled and the captain came on. "This is Captain Jeff Stucky from the flight deck, and if you could go ahead and make sure your seat belts are fastened we sure would appreciate it. Looks like we're going to hit a few miles of turbulence pretty quick up ahead here and we want to make certain you all stay safe."

Jake glanced at Leonard. He was smiling. It was obvious from the look on his new friend's face that he was one of those wackos who thought turbulence was nature's version of in-flight entertainment. Jake couldn't even start to relate. A friend once told him to think of turbulence like a raft on a river. Not so easy. Jake had run a few rapids in his kayak. The difference was rivers were on the ground, where the farthest you could drop if something went wrong was a few feet. A plane? Try six miles.

"We'll be looking for better air above or below us, so if you feel like we're climbing or dropping, don't worry, folks, it's all part of the normal routine."

The chop came thirty seconds later. Jake kept his eyes locked on the faint lights thirty-five thousand feet below. Somehow it helped to see something outside the plane that was stable. He yanked his seat belt tighter, as if that would do anything to make him more secure, and glanced at Leonard. The old man looked like he was getting ready for a siesta.

"You okay, Leonard?"

"You're not asking that question for me." A tiny smile broke out on Leonard's face as his head rocked on the back of his seat. "You're asking it for you."

"True." He took slow breaths.

"This is the perfect representation of your life right now, isn't it, Jake?"

The plane dropped what felt like a hundred feet. Jake tightened his grip on his armrest and quickened his breathing. "My life?"

"The turbulence came out of nowhere. Snuck up on ya." Leonard shifted in his seat, looking as comfortable as if he was at home in a ten-year-old recliner. "And now everything's out of control and you don't know how to stop it. Huh?"

Jake focused on the dim lights splattered across the darkness below and tried to ignore Leonard's words. But the man was right, and the truth hurt.

"Paths are right in front of us all the time, Jake. The right ones. Ones that can take us exactly where we need to go, but they're so hard to see, so hard to see. Most people are blind. But the water and path are there, take us where we need to be, oh can't you see, can't you see, even if they're sometimes too real to embrace."

"Huh?"

"From a poem I know. Seemed apropos for the moment."

"Okay."

Leonard shifted toward him, a playful look in his gray eyes. "You like these friends of yours?"

"Yeah."

"Do they understand you? Support you? Give you things to laugh at?"

"Most of them."

Leonard smiled and closed his eyes again. "It wouldn't be real unless at least one of your crew was a massive pain in the butt. One of the men or one of the women?"

Jake laughed in spite of the vise grip around his stomach, courtesy of the rough air. "You're on the far side of blunt, aren't you, Leonard?"

"I'm too old not to be. Cared what people thought till I reached fifty. When I hit sixty I started letting loose. Not all the way, but plenty. Now that I'm pushing hard on my mideighties, I don't have time for any subtle language that only muddles up the truth." He tapped his head. "What was I saying?"

"You asked if they were true friends to me. They are."

"Then be with them." He poked his chest. "At your age you think they'll live forever, but they won't. Neither will you. Who knows if this is the last year you'll gather together?"

Another question straight to the center of Jake's heart.

"Here's my idea." Leonard took a slow breath. "Don't go to the same lake. Go to a different one. Fresh start. Same friends, but none of the memories lurking about from being at the lake you've always been to. Could be a life changer. I know of a place. It's a lake with hope."

"Hope?" Jake frowned at Leonard, then turned back to the window. "Hope for what?"

As Jake uttered the words, the turbulence started to ease. By the time Leonard opened his eyes and pulled out a small tablet of paper from inside his coat pocket, the jolts from the plane were gone. Leonard scribbled on the pad, ripped off the sheet, and handed it to Jake.

"Here. This'll give you all the information you need if you feel like checking it out. Name of the lake and the website for the house I'm saying you should rent. It's secluded, off the beaten path, but still close enough to get groceries and most of the stuff you'd need for an entertaining week.

"The rent is cheap, the lake is usually glass, and the eagles are common. Has plenty of room for you and your friends. The nice thing is, most people don't find it, so it's peaceful. Only twelve houses on the entire lake and so spread out from each other you can't hear anything but the calls of the mallards as they lift off the lake in the early moments of dawn."

"Maybe you really should be writing my website copy."

Jake smiled, folded the paper, and shoved it in his front pocket. They touched down in Seattle fifty minutes later. When they reached the sign pointing toward baggage claim, Leonard offered his hand and Jake took it.

"I'm going to overstep my bounds here, Jake. But I'm too old to care any longer, so here goes." Leonard peered into Jake's eyes. "If I didn't know better, I'd say you're on the verge of doing something that'll make a lot of people in your life pretty dang sad. But then again, I could be wrong. So why don't you tell me I am so I can stop worrying about you."

Jake didn't pull away from Leonard's gaze, but he didn't answer either.

"Don't do it, Jake Palmer. Think hard about going this summer instead."

"All right. I will." He handed Leonard a business card. "Let's keep in touch."

"You mean that?"

Jake hesitated before saying, "Yeah, I mean it."

Leonard took the card, studied the front, then turned it over and read the printing on the back. "What is hidden will be revealed. What is hidden needs to be known." Leonard held up the card and waggled it. "You believe this?"

"I used to."

"I have a feeling in my gut you're going to get the chance to believe it again."

4

At nine o'clock the next morning, Jake paused at the door of his Kirkland office and stared at the black lettering on the glass. *Read Your Label, Inc.* His company, come back from the dead.

Peter had played a big part in convincing him to lease the new space and go back to work. Three months ago, Jake hired a new staff and started booking gigs again, but after his performance in Chicago, a voice on his shoulder was whispering it had been a mistake. That he should give it up and live off his product sales. His DVDs and online courses were still bringing in solid money every month. His latest book was selling well even two years after it came out. He didn't need to work again if he didn't want to.

A rapping on the other side of the glass lifted his eyes. Skyler, his executive assistant, stood inside. Smart, excellent intuition with clients, an affinity for exotic tea, very short blond hair, quick eyes, and a killer smile. She pulled the door open for him.

"How was Chicago?"

"Good trip. Good restaurants. Good client. My presentation wasn't the best, but I think a lot of them really connected with the ideas."

"So it was good?"

"Yeah." Jake chuckled as they walked down the hall and into his office together. He turned on his desktop computer.

"Do you prefer to hear about the major fires or the minor fires first?" Skyler cocked her head while she studied him, and while she didn't exactly bat her eyes, it looked like she was flirting with the idea.

"Let's hear about the ones you put out already."

"That would take soooo long." She settled into the burgundy chair.

"Majors then."

"None, I took care of them all."

"Minor?"

"Them too." She flashed her enchanting smile.

"Speaking of good—"

"Me?" She pointed at herself, then patted her shoulder. "Gosh, thanks, boss. I'm flattered."

Jake laughed and came out from behind his desk. "Is this the moment where you ask for a raise?"

"If you like."

"Give yourself a ten percent bump immediately."

Skyler cocked her head. "You're serious?"

"Yes." Jake returned to his desk and pulled up his e-mail. "You've earned it."

"Wow. Thank you so much."

"You're very welcome."

Skyler stood but didn't leave. "Um, should I wait till later in the day to tell you that your ex called and pushed me hard to get your cell phone number, or should I tell you now?"

A slice of pain shot through Jake's body. There was no need, no reason for them to speak. Ever. If possible he'd live the rest of his life never having another conversation with Sienna. He hated himself for wanting to have one with her right now.

"I think you should wait till Christmas."

"I'll make a note of it."

"What did you tell her?"

"I suggested she e-mail you."

"Perfect."

Skyler turned to leave. Jake started spinning through his e-mails.

"A little advice, Skyler."

"Okay."

"Don't get divorced."

"Uh, I didn't meet a guy and get married during the four days you were gone."

"Good move. Keep it that way."

"No guys, no marriage. Got it." She paused. "Unless they're difficult to resist, right?"

Jake looked up from his computer, realizing the conversation had taken an unexpected turn. She winked. "I just brewed a fresh pot of coffee. Want me to get you a cup?"

"I can grab it, but thanks."

Jake watched her leave, then stood and made his way into the kitchen. Three of the mugs next to the coffeemaker were adorned with quotes from his seminars, and he sighed as he looked at them.

Step Out of Your Bottle, It's Time to Read the Label.

Set Them Free. Read the Things They Cannot See.

Read It. Believe It. Live It.

A short time back, the sayings would have given him a shot of belief. In himself. Now the only shot they gave was to remind him he'd become a cliché—the guy who preached a message he didn't live himself.

Jake poured himself a cup of coffee with a miniscule splash of salted-caramel creamer, then ran his finger over the lettering on his mug. He just needed time.

Time, sure. Just like new uniforms were all the Mariners needed to make it to the World Series.

The click of heels on the kitchen floor spun Jake around. Skyler. She strolled across the kitchen and leaned back against the counter, her hands resting on the black quartz countertop. She glanced furtively out toward the hallway and said, "Would it be all right if I asked you a completely inappropriate, potentially embarrassing question?"

Jake's heart rate quickened. Had she found out about his accident? Anyone who did some serious Internet searching could finds shreds of information about it, but his pleas for privacy had been mostly successful in keeping his name out of the story. And why would she search in the first place?

"Sure." He gave a halfhearted smile. "Embarrass me."

"We seem to work well together." She paused and folded her arms and looked at him from under her eyelashes. "It's caused me to be curious as to how we might work together outside of the office. If you know what I mean."

"You're asking me out."

"I'm just thinking a drink sometime might be nice. Nice and

casual." A hint of red crept into her face. "I mean it'd be nice. But also casual."

"Yeah, I get it."

Jake stared into her brown eyes and the hint of a smile that moved over her face. She was curious? So was he. After she'd worked in the office for less than a week he'd imagined what it would be like to get to know her on a more personal level. Yes, a drink would be wonderful. He sucked in a quick breath and gritted his teeth against the emotion spinning through his heart.

"Sorry, Skyler." Jake stared at his mug as nervous laughter sputtered out of his mouth. "That's not something that's going to happen."

Jake took a sip and left the kitchen without waiting for her to respond. But in the hallway, he turned back.

"It's just that—"

"It's fine. You don't have to explain." Skyler's voice was monotone. She wouldn't look at him. "I shouldn't have asked. Not professional. I get it."

"I like you. I think you're outstanding and in a different life I would have already asked you out. It's just that . . . dating anyone right now isn't something I can do."

She glanced at him, then away. "Your divorce is still too fresh."

He lied. "Yeah. That's it."

"I understand."

"It's not about—"

"Really. It's okay."

Jake sighed. Skyler wiped down a clean counter. He returned to his office. The problem wasn't having the resolve to turn down anyone who asked him to grab coffee or lunch. That was easy. Necessary. A nonnegotiable of his life now. The problem was the incessant droning of the voice inside that longed for companionship. Why couldn't he shut that part of himself down? Not good for man to be alone? Bingo. The gift of singleness had not been dropped in his lap the day after his divorce was final. Immovable object? Meet irresistible force.

5

A light rain started as Jake slogged from his Jeep to the front door of his home in north Bothell. As he reached for the doorknob, his phone vibrated and he glanced at the caller ID. Peter.

Jake answered and said, "Yes, I'm thinking about it."

"Stop thinking, Clark, and tell me you're coming."

Jake sighed, opened his door, and stepped into his entryway. "Is this the ten millionth or twenty millionth time I've told you to stop calling me Clark?"

"You didn't actually tell me just now." Peter's booming laugh plowed through the phone. "Say those two simple words. You can do it, I know you can. *I'm. Going.*"

"May. Be." Jake set his briefcase down and flicked on a light.

"Nice progress, Clark! In four days you've moved from *not going* to *maybe.*"

"Yeah."

"Listen, Jake. I know you've lost a lot in the past year and a half. Don't lose us too."

"I'll let you know soon, one way or the other."

Jake hung up and the silence of his house struck him like a

hammer as it did every night. He should start leaving music on, but that's what Sienna did before she left; it would only remind him of how alone he was.

He flicked on a few more lights, set his briefcase on the kitchen counter, and went to his bedroom to get into gym shorts and a T-shirt. Jake did a fast weight workout for his upper body in the guest bedroom he'd converted into an exercise room. After a quick shower, he dried off and tried to avoid looking in the mirror but failed. From the top of his head to three inches above his belly button, he was still Sienna's Adonis. But everything below that point more closely resembled Dante's *Inferno*.

He couldn't even see his belly button unless he looked hard. What the doctors called skin grafts were mixtures of violent reds, dark pinks, and tiny charred swirls still black as night nineteen months later. A tapestry of grotesque blotches—browns, reds, splashes of albino white—wrapped his legs, his ankles, and his feet like a lava flow of real-life horror.

Jake ripped his gaze away, breathing more heavily than at any time during his short workout. He eased back into his bedroom, dressed, then ambled toward the kitchen to get dinner. But he found himself stepping into the darkness of his den.

He flicked on the light. On his bookshelf was a photo of him and Peter atop Mount Rainier. But he was drawn to the framed photos that lined the wall to the right of the door. Five pictures taken each fall at the finish of an Ironman triathlon.

Jake glared at the photos, ticked off at them, yet still not able to take them down and donate them to the local garbage heap. His gaze settled on the picture on top: his first Ironman. Boise,

Idaho. The only goal in that race was to finish. He'd grown a beard that summer as he trained and didn't shave it off till he finished the race. Jake shook his head as he recalled the ugly thatch of black hair surrounding his mouth. But such triumph had shined in his eyes, and his arms were stretched over his head as if he could reach the heavens.

He'd never come close to winning in his age groups, thirty to thirty-four, and then thirty-five to thirty-nine, but that had never been the point. The goal was always to better his previous year's time. The goal was to push his body beyond what it thought it could do. The goal was to force his body into submission so it would be in a condition to allow him to conquer any mountain, figurative or literal. The discipline gave his life meaning, and it was one area where the only person he had to be good enough for was himself.

But now there would never be two more photos to complete the set. He'd promised himself seven Ironmans, but he wouldn't be keeping that vow. Nor the ones he made about climbing Kilimanjaro. Or riding across America on a bike. Or a thousand other dreams he'd told himself would come true. He was lucky he could walk, the doctors had said.

Jake continued to stare at the framed photos, his breathing steady, his heart rate low, but a fire was building inside. He rose slowly and approached the pictures. When he reached them, the volcano inside erupted. With four sharp blows of his fist, he smashed the glass of each frame, then ripped them from the wall.

As if he were someone else, Jake slumped into the chair in front of his desk and watched himself grab the hem of his sweats down by his right ankle and pull the fabric up over his calf. He stared at one of the darkest globs of charred flesh anywhere on the lower half of his body. At one time that spot had boasted an M-Dot tattoo, the mark of someone who belonged to the exclusive club of those who had completed an Ironman. Now it was buried in a mass of scar tissue forever.

Jake let the pant leg fall. He rose and slammed the door of his den as he walked out toward the kitchen. Another night of a silence that screamed too loudly in his ear was the only thing on the menu.

After his emotions settled, he flipped on the stove and warmed up spaghetti from four nights ago, then sat down on his couch to take part in the same exciting activity he engaged in most evenings. A movie. Then a few pages of a novel. Then an hour or so working on his stupid model train set in the garage. Exciting times.

After his meal was warmed up, he turned on his TV. An old Sean Connery movie, *Just Cause*, filled the screen. The one where the best James Bond ever was a Harvard professor lured back into the courtroom after twenty-five years to take the case of a young black man condemned to death for the murder of a child.

On-screen, Connery was saying, "Just give me a sign," to Ed Harris as he searched for the clue that would solve the crime. Jake put on his best Sean Connery accent and held his arms out wide.

"Jush give me a shine. Am I shawpost to go on the trip? Jush give me a shine!"

Should have made him laugh. It didn't, but he told himself the effort was noted by someone somewhere in the vastness of the universe. By God? Possible. But unlikely. God had abandoned him that night at the gas station. He hadn't even let the punks who had ruined Jake's life get caught. *All things work together for good? Yeah, right. Sure they do.*

Jake finished the movie, decided not to read or work on the model, and by ten fifteen his head was on his pillow. Sleep had started to take him when his cell phone vibrated. He opened his eyes a crack, picked up his phone, and opened the text.

> Hey Jake. It's Leonard. We met on the plane. Just thinking about you. Hoping you decided to spend the week with your friends. I don't think you'll regret it.

Jake shook his head and smiled. Half of him thought he'd never hear from the old guy again. Leonard thought he should go, huh? Funny. It felt like more than a thought. For some strange reason it felt like a command. When he'd asked for a sign he didn't expect an answer. But what was the point in asking for one if he didn't follow through when it arrived?

Plus, Leonard had nailed him during the flight. The old man was right. Jake was on the verge of an extremely poor decision—to go down the same path his mom had taken when Jake was just a kid. He told himself the thoughts weren't too serious, but he admitted that too much flirting with the idea could easily become deadly serious. And he'd vowed never to give his dad the ammunition to tell everyone, "I told you so," after Jake was gone. But even that resolve weakened after the disastrous Chicago trip.

A week with his friends would at least put the UFC match going on in his brain on hold. And if he got nuts and decided it was time to close the final chapter, at least he'd have the chance to say good-bye to them. He snatched his phone off the end table next to the couch and dialed Peter. He picked up on the first ring.

"Give me the answer I want to hear."

"I don't want to go, Peter." Jake rubbed his eyes.

"Yeah, got that part. But I'm not asking if you want to go. I'm asking if you'll be there. Simple question, simple answer."

"Yeah, I'll be there." The words felt like taffy being pulled out of his mouth. "And I won't be a downer for anyone. I'll fake it if necessary."

"Yes! I promise, you won't have to fake it. It'll be good for—"

"But I'm only going on one condition." Jake sat up and stared out his window at a half-full moon. Or a half-empty moon. All in the perspective.

"What?"

"Change of scenery. We go to a different lake this year. That'll give me a chance to have a good time."

"What? A different lake? What are you talking about?" A sigh of exasperation came through the phone. "You gotta be kidding. What kind of a tenth-year anniversary trip would we have if we go to a different spot?"

"I just told you what kind of trip it will be. One I can try to enjoy. It's the people that make the trip, not the place."

"It's the people *and* the place," Peter said. "That's where all the great memories are."

"Exactly. That's where *all* the memories are. I'm not going to jump into a shower of heart-shredding scenes from my past like I did last year. That was a bloodbath."

"Can't you just ignore them?"

"Sure. No problem. I'll be like an alcoholic getting a shot of whiskey offered to him every five seconds. Easy to ignore. You're right. Let's not switch."

Peter blew out a long breath. "The rest of them aren't going to like it."

"I get that. If going back to the Okanagan Valley is that important to them, go there. I'll stay home and everyone will be happy."

"All right, I'll convince Camille, but you get to tell Susie and Andrew."

"You really don't want to give me a reason to change my mind."

"Fine. I'll tell 'em."

Jake pushed off his covers and made his way to the window, continuing to stare at the moon. Half full. Peter was right. Even though it would be tough dealing with the memories, being around Peter, Susie, and Andrew would be good for him. Camille? He'd put up with her. Small price to pay.

"Next question." The sound of Peter chewing floated through the phone. "If we're not going to Okanagan, where are we going to go?"

"I met a guy on a plane."

"Oh yeah, this sounds promising."

"It's a good story, I'll tell you sometime. He told me about this lake in Oregon. I checked it out. It's about halfway down the state, far enough inland to have guaranteed warm weather, but close enough to the coast that if we wanted to drive out there we could make it in about two hours."

"Hey, Clark?"

"Yeah?"

"All pressure and joking aside, I really think you need this trip."

"Yeah, okay."

"And more than that, I think this trip is going to be a life changer for you."

Jake considered staying silent, but if he couldn't confess how he felt to Peter, who could he tell?

"It needs to be, so I agree."

"You do?" Peter's voice went up. "What do you mean it needs to be?"

"I'll tell you if I'm right once the trip is over. See you, Peter."

6

Jake didn't want this journey. Didn't need it. Now that the trip had arrived, he regretted committing.

As he zipped down I-5 toward Oregon on a warm July morning, he checked the weather for the area surrounding this Willow Lake, where the five of them would be staying for ten days of riotous fun. Yeah, right.

His phone said nine out of the ten days would be full-on sunshine. Wonderful. How exciting. Jake tossed his cell onto his passenger seat and bumped his fist into his forehead. He didn't need sun while they were there. He needed rain. Every day. Wouldn't have to put on shorts that way. But that was another fantasy that wouldn't be coming true.

Come on. He needed to shake off the Mr. Gloom act and believe good things were coming. Wasn't that the other thing he'd promised Peter? He would act happy. Besides, he didn't need to hide from his friends—they didn't care about his scars.

Six hours later he exited the freeway and found himself coasting along a winding, leafy road heading west. Forty-five minutes after that he took Mullins Road heading southwest, and twenty-three miles later he reached the turnoff to Willow Lake. He took a left, and when he came to a Y in the road, the only indication he was getting close was a signpost that said Willow Haven, Population 165.

He slowed and turned onto an asphalt road that looked like it had barely survived a meteor shower. Jake glanced at his temperature gauge. Seventy-nine. He turned off the AC and rolled down his windows. The air felt good, and he stuck his hand out and let the wind rush through his fingers. The road led him through a dense cluster of pine trees, which cleared after a quarter mile. A flock of quail launched themselves into the air in front of his Jeep and the scent of wildflowers filtered through his window. Maybe it was just his imagination, or the power of suggestion, but a peace he didn't expect landed on him hard.

Three minutes later he saw a small sign on a huge willow tree that said Exerevnitis Lodge. This was it. He turned into the driveway and followed it for fifty yards till it stopped in front of a two-story cedar house full of windows and surrounded by juniper bushes and walnut trees. A large sign hung over the front door: "Life. Love. Passion. May You Find All Three Here." Tough not to like the place with a greeting like that.

Jake put his Jeep in park, shut off the engine, and closed his eyes. Scattered memories from the past nine years flitted through his mind. Times on the other lake, long dinners full of laughter and tears, and stories that drew the six of them together in a way few groups of friends ever experience.

Peter said it would be the same. How was that possible? Two couples and him, flying solo for the second year in a row. How could he watch the others doing the things couples do—the laughter, the conversations, the knowing looks and inside jokes—and not be reminded every second of what he'd lost? Not be taunted by the truth that he'd never again have someone to share life with? Every moment of the coming week would be tainted. Every conversation overshadowed by the past.

No. He wouldn't let it happen. This was a new day.

A loud rap on the window next to his head yanked Jake out of his contemplation, and he bolted up in his seat and cracked his knees on the steering wheel.

"Wow!" Pain shot through his legs and he gritted his teeth. He rubbed his knees. It would take a while to get the blood circulating again. He turned to see Peter's tall, lanky frame leaning down, his nose almost touching the window, a big grin on his face. Jake grimaced and pulled his keys out of the ignition. He opened his door and gingerly got out as Peter stepped back.

"What were you doing in there? Meditating?" Peter rubbed his light brown hair. "Get out and come see this place."

Jake stepped out of his Jeep, rubbed his knees again, and glared at his friend. "You trying to give me a heart attack?"

Peter laughed and grabbed Jake in a bear hug. "Good to see you, Clark."

"I thought we were done with that."

"You'll always be Clark to me."

"Let it go. I have."

"No you haven't. Not deep down." Peter threw his arm around Jake's shoulder and pulled him toward the cabin's front door.

"Where's Camille?"

"We got here an hour ago, settled in. She went for a run."

Jake tried to keep a scowl from reaching his face, but apparently he didn't succeed.

"Don't worry, she'll be good. She promised."

"That would be greatly appreciated."

"She's your friend too, Jake."

Jake clomped up the six wooden stairs to the front porch and admired the woodwork on the front door. It was teak. He glanced to his right and left at the wraparound deck.

"You want to come inside or take a look at the lake first?" Peter pointed in opposite directions, both arms outstretched. "It's pretty sweet. You can go either way."

"Lake first."

They walked to the right and followed the deck toward the lake. The deck planks looked like Cherrywood. Beautiful. Jake reached the corner of the house, and as the walkway opened up to a massive deck, the lake came into view. Crystal water spread out to his right and left like liquid glass. Perfection, not even the hint of a ripple. It mirrored the three or four clouds in the otherwise unmarred sky.

Jake guessed the lake was somewhere around a half mile across. Length? Probably three or four miles. It looked like the house sat somewhere in the middle of the lake. Green rolling hills rose from the other side, and the only hint of civilization was a house Jake could just make out that sat on the edge of the water directly across from them. He looked to the right. Apparently there was a boat launch at that end of the lake, but from this distance he couldn't tell.

Their rental home sat forty or fifty feet above the surface of the lake and had sweeping views in both directions. A well-groomed path led halfway down to the water. The rest of the way was serviced by thirty or forty narrow wooden stairs that led down to a storage shed and a sizable dock.

Two kayaks, the larger of the two a fire-engine red, the other a muted orange, hung on a large Maplewood storage shed. A dark green canoe rested upside down on the dock. Jake would definitely be making use of the boats.

"Impressive," Jake said as a smile crawled onto his face.

"Check out the grill." Peter grinned and pointed behind Jake.

Jake wandered over to a huge grill that sat in the far back corner of the deck. The corner closest to the lake housed a ten-person hot tub. Six wooden Atlantic steamer chairs formed a semicircle in the middle of the deck. He spotted a large, sunken fire pit in the far northwest corner of the lawn. A chill shot through him. Wouldn't be a place he'd hang out, but if it got cold enough at night the others might enjoy it.

"This place should work."

"You chose wisely, Jake."

"Thanks."

He glanced at the french doors at the back of the house, then continued around the other side of the cabin, walked through the first door he came to, and found himself in the kitchen. Not as large as their usual summer home, but certainly gourmet. Peter would have fun in here.

The living room boasted cathedral ceilings and expansive windows facing the lake, and a large river rock fireplace took up the far wall. The home was furnished with rustic log furniture and soft leather couches. The dining room table was made of myrtlewood. Stunning. Jake ran his hand over its surface and imagined the conversations he'd be having around this table over the next ten days.

To the right of the fireplace were shelves packed with books, some well-worn, some with spines that spoke of never being opened. Above the books was a painting Jake thought strange at first, but as he studied the picture, his aversion turned to intrigue. The painting was of an ancient, winding stone staircase that rose out of a thick green wood into even thicker clouds swirling with blues, reds, and muted golds. As the staircase climbed into the clouds, the clouds grew brighter till the stairs vanished into the light.

"Weird, huh?" Peter said as he joined Jake.

"It kind of makes me think of Jacob's ladder."

"Yeah, it should. It's like a portal."

"A what?"

"Portal. Camille's kind of into the idea, so she loved it when she spotted this picture. She's shown me others like it. They're portals or tunnels, or whatever you want to call them, into the heavenly realm. Just like Jacob's ladder. Supposedly they're all over the world, but especially in Ireland."

"Okay." Jake tapped his head.

"I know, it's wacky, but she likes the idea."

Peter strolled over to the living room's coffee table and picked up a brochure. "Hey, did you see this?"

"What?"

Peter held up a trifold brochure. The headline on the front implored, "Take a Thrill Ride on Mountains of Sand!"

"We can rent ATVs and head out on the dunes. We gotta go. All of us. Only two hours from here. Listen to this part: 'The Oregon Dunes National Recreation Area is over 300,000 acres of untamed and exhilarating dunes available for exploration year-round.'"

"Yeah, maybe."

"Maybe? No way it's maybe, baby, we're going."

They wandered back onto the deck through the french doors and stood with hands resting on the railing overlooking the glassy water.

"I gotta tell ya once more, you did good. This place is a find. Can't believe it wasn't already booked." Peter grinned at Jake and slapped him on the back. "Listen, I think I just heard Camille come back, so I'm going to get my bags unpacked before she can ask why I haven't done it already. You want me to grab your things and bring them up to your room?"

"Nah, I'll get 'em later."

"I'm just saying, you don't have to be a hero. I'm here, I can get them for you. Your car's open, right?"

"I'm good, Pete. Really."

Peter clasped him on the shoulder. "Embrace the week, Clark."

"Yeah, baby. All the way. You got it." Jake grinned.

Peter pointed at him and said, "Don't mock me."

"Never."

Jake eased into one of the deck chairs as Peter meandered off. A slight breeze ruffled the surface of the lake, and Jake watched a mama duck and her babies skirt the shoreline. Most of him still

56

didn't want to be here, but enough of him did. Even with the challenge of facing what he'd now lost, this was a chance for him to stop living the lie for a few days.

A knock on the front door floated through the french doors out onto the deck. The knock was immediately followed by the sound of the door opening. Right after that a woman called out, "We're here!"

Jake rose from his chair and smiled. The voice belonged to one of his favorite people in the world.

7

Jake shuffled toward the front door, where Susie and Andrew Hawthorne stood embracing Peter. Words spilled out of Susie like a fountain, and her laughter lit up the room.

Susie, his sister in every way except by blood. Jake stopped halfway across the living room and waited for her to spot him. When she did she threw her hands in the air, pranced over, and grabbed him in a bear hug.

"Yes! Finally. I've been dying to see you."

"Hey, Sooz."

Susie hugged Jake longer than normal. Jake hadn't seen her since his divorce was finalized right after last year's gathering and hadn't talked to her since this past May. He knew the fierce hug was her way of saying how much she was hurting for him. When they finally pulled apart, she took him by the shoulders.

"How are you?"

"Great. Really. Doing great." He grinned and pointed at her pink top and faded designer jeans. "Nice duds as always."

"Thanks." She released Jake's shoulders and her face grew serious. "Now, how are you really?"

"Like I said, I'm good."

"This is me, remember? Now, how are you?" Susie wasn't smiling. She pulled off her pink newsboy hat and shook out her thick blond hair that somehow always managed to look good.

"I just told you." He laughed. "How many times are you going to ask me that?"

"Till you tell me the truth." Susie poked Jake's chest right over his heart. "How's it going with this?"

He offered a tiny smile. "Still broken, but slowly healing up."

"No contact?"

Jake glanced around the room and lowered his voice. "I'm not sure the other guests on the show would be interested in the subject, so I'm thinking we talk about it in, say, a decade or two."

"Fine. Not now. At least not in detail. We'll save that for later. But for the moment, I do require an immediate answer, thanks."

Jake shuffled over to the far corner of the family room and Susie followed. He stared at the sun doing a tango with the surface of the water and sighed. "She's dating someone. It's serious. I'm guessing she'll have a ring by the time I set up my Christmas tree. There might already be one on her finger."

"Oh, Jake. I'm sorry. How long have they been dating?"

"Six months, but it's good."

"How is that good?"

"I've finally given up my fantasy that'd she'd have a heart transplant and become the woman I thought I was married to for seven years." He turned and glanced into Susie's sympathetic eyes. "I'm over it."

"Does that mean you're ready to date again?"

"Not funny, sis. You know that's never going to happen. Not with the way I am."

"The right woman won't care." She took both his arms and squeezed.

"I had the right woman and she did care. You should've seen the way she looked at me—pity and disgust. Mostly disgust. Maybe all disgust."

"She couldn't see what was right in front of her," Susie growled.

"That's the problem. She did see it. All the time. She couldn't even touch me."

"Come here." Susie grabbed his arm and pulled him across the living room and out onto the deck. "Wow, nice view."

Jake grinned. "Yeah, I think we might survive here for the next ten days."

Five sprinkler heads along the back of the lawn popped up and sent their fine spray out over the dark grass.

When they reached the railing, Susie peered at him. "What are you staring at?"

"After all this time, I still can't stand the sight of them."

Susie glanced out over the lawn in the direction Jake was looking. "Can't stand what?"

"Sprinklers." Jake shrugged. "I know, I'm nuts for letting it bug me."

"Sprinklers? What are you talking about?"

Jake tried to laugh.

"You want to tell me?"

"Nah." Jake waved her off. "Not a big deal."

"Let me rephrase that." Susie jammed her hands into her hips and put on a mock fierce face. "You're going to tell me."

"All right." This time, he did laugh. "But the short version only. It's stupid to even think about it, but the summer I turned thirteen my dad had me put a sprinkler system into our lawn. Part of my Be-a-Palmer-Man education." Jake clacked his teeth together. "I got an F."

"What happened?"

"I can't believe I never told you about this. I put the whole thing in, but my lines weren't straight on six of the sprinklers." Jake lowered his voice and imitated his dad. "'Jaker, that's not quite going to make it, is it? No sir, nohow. That isn't the way a Palmer puts in a sprinkler system.' I told him it was close enough. Not the best choice of words, as you can imagine. You knew my dad."

Susie's face went stark. "Yeah."

"So I told him I'd dig up that section and do it again. But he decided that wasn't good enough. He thought it would be a good lesson for me to dig up the whole thing, even the parts that were done right, and redo the entire system. The whole thing."

"You're kidding."

"Got a C-plus the second time around."

"No."

"Oh yeah, but on my fourth try I got a B-plus and my dad only redid a quarter of it the next weekend." Jake slumped forward, his elbows on the deck railing. "So when I see sprinklers, it doesn't give me the warmest of fuzzies."

"Wow."

He cocked his head. "What was it you wanted to say to me?"

"It can wait."

"No, tell me." Jake straightened up. "Seriously, I'm fine. Just a little trip down the part of memory lane that has a few potholes in it. I'm good."

Susie sighed, rested her hip against the railing, and stared intently into his eyes. "Do you remember what happened when my family moved into the house next door to yours the summer after third grade?"

"We became best friends."

"And what happened after we decided we would be friends forever? Do you remember where you took me?"

"No."

"You took me into the field across the street from our houses and up into that tree fort of yours that should have been condemned—I can't believe our parents let us hang out in that thing, but given the kind of parents we had, it probably shouldn't surprise me."

Susie leaned her elbows on the railing and gazed out over the lake. "You told me something as we sat on those half-rotted boards that I'll never forget. Maybe because it seemed so secret at the time, or maybe it was because it was pretty mature for a kid to say, but it's always stuck with me."

"Yeah?" Jake had no idea what she was going to say. "And you think I need to hear it again now."

"I *know* you need to hear it again now."

Susie narrowed her eyes in that way that said he'd better listen, and more than listen, take whatever she was about to say to heart.

"Okay."

"Little ten-year-old Jake Palmer stares at me sitting in that tree house and says, 'I don't think we're really ourselves until who we are on the inside is the same as who we are on the outside.'"

"I said that?"

"Yes." Susie poked him in the chest again. "It's time to start acting like it."

"I'm trying."

"Good. Oh, oh!" Susie shook his arms. "I forgot to tell you, I wrote a song for you. You're going to love it. Andrew even helped me with the lyrics."

"Can't wait." Jake folded his arms and grinned. Just being with Susie lifted his spirits.

"Yeah, it'll make you cry, but that's good for the soul."

"No doubt." He strolled with Susie toward the barbecue. "How's the summer concert series going?"

"The audiences haven't been huge, but it's been sooooo fun. I'm doing the classic get-someone-from-the-audience-to-get-up-and-dance, and for the most part it's been a show highlight."

"Most part?"

Susie laughed. "So I get this guy up there who's so nervous—"

"Why'd you pick someone who would be nervous?"

"I didn't pick him, my team did. And they claim the guy begged to get up there."

"Bad?"

"Couldn't dance. At all. I don't mean he was terrible. He literally could not take a step without stumbling or falling over. And you know how I get when I'm nervous for someone."

"You didn't."

"Yes! Couldn't stop laughing. Loudly!" Susie groaned. "Felt sooooo bad. But I ended up taking him and his daughters out to dinner afterward, gave them a bunch of CDs, so it worked out in the end."

"He must have felt like an idiot." Jake smiled.

"Yeah, Jake, maybe he did." Susie paused till he looked directly at her. Serious face again. "But at least he had the courage to step into his fear."

"That wasn't subtle."

"Time for you to get up onstage and dance again, Jake."

8

After promising Susie they'd talk more about her music and his stage fright, Jake strolled into the kitchen and glanced at the counter, full of bowls of pasta. Peter stood at the stove stirring a fattening-looking cream sauce. Another of Peter's masterpiece meals looked to be well on its way to completion.

"Looks like you're whipping up a simple concoction for our first dinner."

"Chicken Alfredo with artichoke hearts, pine nuts, mushrooms, and of course, garlic." Peter pointed to his right. "Kalamata olive bread, olive oil and balsamic vinegar for dipping, roasted tomatoes with basil, and tiramisu for dessert. Nothing special."

"You are going to let me do one night of hot dogs and hamburgers, aren't you?"

"Sure. Absolutely." Peter turned and winked. "As long as I don't have to eat them."

Jake snatched a spoon out of the silverware drawer to dip in the sauce for a quick taste.

"Don't even think about it. There's just the right amount for everyone."

Jake frowned at the almost overflowing pot of Alfredo sauce. "I think you've got more than enough. Or are you planning on a few surprise dinner guests?"

"What?" Peter kept his gaze buried in the stove.

"You're cooking for five, not eight. Right?"

"Leftovers. Heat 'em, serve 'em."

"'Leftovers are beneath those with a cultivated palate.'" Jake whacked Peter on the arm. "I'm quoting you when I say that."

"Better to have too much than too little." Peter opened a cabinet over the kitchen counter and rummaged through it, found what he wanted, and sprinkled the spice into the pot.

"You want to tell me what's going on?" Jake cleared his throat loudly. "You think I'm stupid?"

Before Peter could answer, his wife sashayed into the kitchen. Great. The moment Jake had been waiting for.

"Hey, honey." Peter glanced up. "Good run?"

"I can't believe this is it." Camille blew out her obvious disgust. "How are we all going to fit in this place for a week?"

"The cabin is plenty big."

"I mean this." Camille waved her arms around the kitchen.

"It's fine." Peter sighed. "It's only a little smaller than—"

"A little?" Camille spun in a tight circle and waved her hands. "Try half the size. Maybe less. We're supposed to cook here?"

"We will cook in here."

"I can't cook in here."

"Since you haven't cooked a meal once in the nine years we've been gathering together, I wouldn't worry about it."

"I make the lunches." Camille jammed her hands into her

hips. "Same thing as cooking. Still have to maneuver around a kitchen the size of an outhouse. I'm not saying it won't work, I'm just saying it's going to be a pain in the butt."

"You'll survive." Peter slapped a plastic grin on his face.

"What are you cooking, dear?" Camille sidled up next to Peter and scowled at the pans on the stove.

"Pasta. Alfredo sauce. What's it look like?"

"I told you to save that dish for Monday night."

Peter ignored the comment and Camille jabbed her elbow into Peter's ribs.

"Ouch!"

"Well?"

"I know you said that, dear." Peter looked up again and glared at her and pointed at his ear. "These work."

"But you didn't save it. Or you ignored me when I told you the order of the meals. We talked about this in detail. Hello?"

Peter and Camille both pulled out their dagger eyes. Jake was easing backward out toward the living room when Camille shifted her gaze away from Peter, fixed her eyes on Jake, and pranced over to him.

"Jake! So good to see you. You look wonderful." She reached up and gave him a quick hug.

"Good to be seen. How are you, Camille?"

She raised her arms and flexed her biceps. They were taut and tan. "Not bad for a thirty-six-year-old, huh? Not bad for a twenty-six-year-old."

Jake gave a weak smile and nodded.

"Did Peter tell you I'm going to do a triathlon this fall?"

Right on cue. Expected. Camille had brought up the one hobby Jake loved more than any other, the one he would never do again. Laryngitis would look so good on her.

"He didn't mention it."

Camille smacked Peter on the back. "Well I am. I've been training all spring and summer, and there's no way I'm not going to break my personal record this time."

"That's a good goal. I hope you make it." Jake started to move toward the living room again, but Camille blocked him.

"Should be hard, but really fun."

"Yeah, should be awesome."

"And how can I not be great in a place like this?" She swept her hand toward the kitchen window, which looked out over the deck and lake. "Plus we're all together again for ten days of fun in the sun. I love it."

"I hear you."

Camille leaned toward Jake and lowered her voice. "I hope it's not going to be awkward between you and me this week. I'm your friend too, you know."

"I know, and it's fine."

"Good. I told Peter that's how you'd feel." She patted him on his upper arm.

Yeah, that's exactly how Jake felt. He glanced at Peter, who had turned away from them and was rustling through a bag of groceries on the kitchen table.

"I hope we have a chance to catch up a bit while we're here. We haven't talked much since last summer." Camille's mouth smiled at him, but there wasn't any smile in her eyes.

"Hope so." Jake nodded and motioned toward the stove. "I'm going to get out of here and let you two figure out your menu for the rest of the week."

He pushed past Camille, through the family room, and out onto the deck, asking himself for the five hundredth time why Peter had married her in the first place. Jake stood at the railing of the deck and stared out over the lake. He'd die for Peter and maybe he was. In a way, being around Camille was like a slow death.

A few minutes later, Peter came up beside him and handed him a drink. They stood in silence as a breeze brought the scent of pine swirling around them.

"I'm sorry about that. Sometimes Camille isn't the most sensitive person on the planet."

"Her performance in there isn't giving me a lot of hope for the coming week."

"I'll talk to her, but she's had a hard year. It's not about you, it's about her trying to figure out where she fits in now that our kids are hitting the midteens and starting to get their own lives."

"I get it. I do. I'm just saying it doesn't exactly make me want to slice open my chest and bare my soul this week."

"You're going to have to do it someday. You ever want to find yourself in another relationship, you gotta let yourself be known."

"I don't want to be in another relationship."

"Yeah you do."

"No. I don't."

"I know a woman who would be perfect for you."

Jake clamped his mouth tight to keep from spewing his drink across the deck. "You're kidding, right?"

"Okay, I might have missed a couple of times, but I've become more discerning."

After Jake and Sienna's divorce was final, Peter decided his new calling in life was to be Jake's matchmaker. Every three weeks like a clock hitting midnight, he'd set Jake up on blind dates. No, that wasn't accurate. They weren't blind dates because Jake hadn't agreed to any of them. They weren't even dates. They were frontal assaults sprung on Jake without warning.

9

"H ello."

  Jake had looked up from his laptop on a Friday afternoon in February to find a midthirties woman with short black hair standing over his table at the coffee shop. She had bright eyes behind brown glasses, and a stack of three books under her arm.

"Yes?"

"Are you Jacob Palmer?"

"Jake. Yeah."

"I'm Irene Barring. It's good to meet you." She sat in the chair across from him and set her books on the table.

"Who?"

"Peter's friend."

"Peter's friend?"

"Am I at the wrong table?" Irene glanced around the coffee shop.

"Unfortunately not."

"Excuse me?" Irene cocked her head and frowned.

"No, no, I don't mean it like that. I just mean Peter didn't tell me. I thought I was meeting him here, not you. So this is a bit of a shock."

"Nice." Irene grabbed the edges of her books and pressed her lips together. "Not the way I wanted to break on through to the other side."

"The Doors."

"You know Jim Morrison's work?" She leaned forward, eyes growing wider.

"Only because my roommate for two years after college was way into classic rock. I couldn't get him to stop talking about it."

"Then you may not know that Morrison was a prophet. He has more to say to us than anyone other than Sri Ramana Maharshi."

"Jim Morrison? A prophet?"

"Yes."

"What about Elvis?"

"That's good. Very good. Very funny." Irene smiled and pointed at him. "Peter said you had a great sense of humor. But I'm serious. Morrison was not a singer, not a rock star, he was a poet who was thrust into a world he didn't want to be in. If we forget the music and look at the days before The Doors, and then immerse ourselves with the verse he created, we find a man so consumed by his spirituality, his entire being reflected truths we still are just barely starting to grasp today."

She reached over and picked up Jake's cup of coffee and took a sip.

He cocked his head and stared. "Would you like some of my coffee?"

She laughed. "I had to see if we're compatible."

"Are we?"

"Yes." She grinned. "So far anyway. I'll let you know when we pass the next signpost."

"You're talking about the man who suggested we crawl into our minds and play a game where we go insane, where we forget the people around us, where we forget the world, where we let go so we can break through."

"Yes!" She took his hands. "Maybe I should meet your old roommate. It's rare to find someone who knows Morrison's work like that. I am truly impressed."

"He's married. My old roommate." Jake shut his laptop, picked up his coffee, and stood. "I'm sorry, but I have to go. It's good to meet you, Irene."

"Are you a spiritual man, Jake?"

"I believe in God and in his Son and in the Spirit of God. So I'm thinking that pretty much disqualifies me from ever worshiping in the halls of the Lizard King." Jake backed away from the table and waved good-bye.

The second time Peter dropped one of his setups, Jake could have sworn he was on a reality-TV prank show and the woman was a paid professional actor. Jake was sitting at Third Place Books at the end of Lake Washington with no greater ambition than to read his book and sip an overpriced cup of java.

"Hey, Jake, what are you doing here?"

Jake blinked and glanced up at Peter. A woman stood next to him, a shy smile on her face. Pretty, reddish-blond hair at shoulder length, average figure, height maybe five-five or -six, and an engaging smile.

"Having coffee. Reading. You?"

He opened his palm toward the woman. "We were headed back to the office after a sales call and decided to grab a quick cup of coffee to debrief on the meeting."

"Instead of debriefing in your office?" Jake tried to use his heat vision to drill a hole in Peter's head, but unfortunately it got stuck in his imagination.

"So many distractions there."

"But this is five miles from your office."

"So?"

"This is a bookstore. An out-of-the-way bookstore. There's three coffee shops between here and there. And you know I hang out here."

Peter turned to the woman. "I am so sorry. What am I thinking? I gotta introduce you two. Jake, this is Maggie Welker. Maggie, this is my best friend, Jake Palmer."

"Hi, Maggie. It's good to meet you."

"You too. Peter has told me all about you."

Nice smile, but there was an overeagerness in her eyes that screamed DANGER.

"Oh?"

"Yes. Oodles and oodles and lots of gobs."

Maggie should have stopped right there, or Jake should have advised her to stop, but it didn't happen. They sat down and Peter pushed Maggie's crazy button.

"Why don't you tell Jake a little about yourself?"

"Okay, okay, if you really want to hear a little bit about me. But after that, I want to hear about you." She scrunched up her face, smiled, and poked the air in front of him. "I love flowers, I do, and if that's wrong, well, piddle on you, they're beautiful and they brighten everything up, and they smell so gooooooooood." She clutched her arms across her chest. "Do you love flowers, Jake? I betcha do, I know you do, or Peter wouldn't have ever introduced us in the first place."

"Well—"

"What's your favorite kind? I mean your over-the-moon-and-back-again favorite flower. I bet it's the same as mine, betcha it is!" She wiggled in her seat.

"I don't really have a—"

"Oh, come on. Sure you do. You might not think about it all the time, I understand, men and women are different and we don't always think about the same things, but if you dig deep, deep, deep, there's an answer there, I promise you." She paused and poked him lightly in the arm with a forefinger whose nail was bright yellow. "And I want to hear it."

Jake stared at the woman's expectant eyes and tried not to laugh. She nodded and he realized she wouldn't stop till he gave her an answer.

"Sunflowers?"

"Ooooooooooo! Are you serious? You can't be serious, but I know you are! Sunflowers are mine too!" Maggie bounced in her seat and glanced back and forth between Jake and Peter. "Yes, yes, yes! Can you believe that? Can you? Can you?"

"No, I can't."

She turned to Peter and punched him in the arm. "Stick me with a pin if you don't think that's the most wonderful dollop of sugar you've ever tasted!" She laughed again. "But not too hard with that pin. Ha!"

Jake endured another ten minutes before he excused himself, leaving the woman with a look on her face that seemed to say, "Aren't you going to ask for my hand in blessed matrimony first?"

"Peter, I'll call you tonight."

When he reached Peter that evening, Jake muttered, "I'm going to kill you."

"She gets nervous meeting men."

"I'm going to maim you first."

"She's not usually like that. Really. That was weird. I've never seen her like that. If you give her a chance—"

"You let her sell for you? You let her represent your company?"

"Probably not for long. I didn't hire her. But—"

"Please tell me that was a joke, setting me up with her. You really thought I'd like her?"

"Like I said, she got nervous. I didn't expect that and it was over the top, but—"

"She was a wacko. Like all the rest."

"Not the one that you met last month. She was cool. You guys truly connected, didn't you? Tell me I was wrong with her. And what about the one four months back? Are you telling me you didn't like her either?"

It was true. Both of those women were interesting and Jake had liked them. But it didn't matter what he thought of them, or even what they thought of him.

"It makes not the slightest difference if any of them are great, not great, weird, not weird, or somewhere in between, I'm not going to date ever again. You know this. You know why."

"You gotta get over that."

"Until you've lived it, don't judge it. You can't imagine."

"I'm just trying to help. Get you to have some fun. Get back on the dating circuit."

"Not going to happen."

"Ever?"

"*Ding!* I think he's got it, folks. Ever. Next time you're tempted to go Jake stalking with a woman in tow, repeat this phrase: 'Jake is never going to date again. King Arthur will return to Britain before Jake gets into a relationship, so I'm not going to try to set him up ever again.' Got it?"

"Got it."

"You promise you'll never do this to me again, right?"

"I swear."

Deep down, Jake appreciated Peter's persistence. God said it wasn't good for man to be alone. Didn't Jake know it. But unless God had a major renovation plan for his body, he'd be alone for the rest of his life.

A few weeks later Jake went to Peter's office to pick him up for a Mariners game. While sitting in the lobby waiting, Jake spied a kayaking magazine, picked it up, and quickly became engrossed in an article about two men and one woman who had shot the Clarks Fork of the Yellowstone River in less than twelve hours. An incredible accomplishment.

"Excuse me."

The voice sliced through his study of the article, and Jake

dropped the magazine to find a striking dark-haired woman in a dark blue and gray skirt gazing down on him, trying not to laugh.

"Yes?" Jake blinked and caught the look in her eyes. "That's not the first time you tried to get my attention, is it?"

"No." She smiled. Playful green eyes. In an earlier life he would have allowed himself to be attracted to her.

"I think it was my third attempt to get your attention. Maybe the fourth." She pointed at the magazine. "You must have found an interesting article."

"Yeah, I did." Jake opened the magazine and pointed to the article. "How to be stupid crazy in a tiny little boat and have the time of your life doing it."

"You've done this?" She pointed to a photo Jake had been studying a moment ago.

"A few times, but not on rivers like that one. I'm not that stupid and not that crazy. But I will admit a big part of me wishes I could do it."

"It's such an invigorating sport." She smiled. Nice smile. Very nice. "You're a kayaker?"

"About five years now. You?"

"Going on fourteen months." The woman pulled one leg behind the other and Jake couldn't help but notice the curve of her calves. Lyrical.

"You like it?" Jake asked.

"I love it." She sat on the edge of the leather chair on the other side of the glass coffee table. "But I feel like I'm still getting started, nothing too tough yet."

"Have you been anywhere interesting?" Jake glanced at her,

then looked back at the magazine. If he stared at her eyes too long, he might never find his way out of them.

"I did the Rogue River in Oregon with some friends last summer."

"That's such a great trip. Stunning beauty, nice smooth stretches, and some really fun white water."

Jake studied the woman. No wedding ring. She wasn't flirting. Yet she wasn't going away. There had to be a reason . . . wait. Right. Duh. She'd interrupted him for something more than small talk. Before he could voice his realization, she pointed at the magazine for the second time.

"That's my magazine."

"Whoops." Jake tilted his head back and a laugh puffed out. "I saw it lying on the chair over there and assumed it belonged to the office."

"No, I should have taken it with me. I dropped it there, went back to my office to get something, and—"

"Here." Jake reached over the coffee table to hand it to her.

"Would you like to keep it?"

"No, but thanks."

The woman smiled and took the magazine. "You're a friend of Peter's?"

"Yeah, Jake Palmer." Jake stood and offered his hand.

She took it. "Ari Conwell."

"Pleasure. You work for Peter?"

"For nine months now."

"You've been able to stand him for that long? I'm impressed."

Ari smiled. "He's told me a lot about you, Jake Palmer."

"Oh?"

"He says life rarely gives people friends like you."

"Yeah, sorry you had to hear that. Peter is getting mushy in his old age."

Before Ari could respond, Peter strode out of his office and clapped his hands. "Clark, sorry to keep you waiting. Be right there. Just need to grab something out of the conference room."

As Peter rushed by them, Ari frowned. "I thought you said your name was Jake."

"It is." Jake started to explain, then stopped himself. "It's a long story."

"Nice to meet you, Jake. Clark." She smiled and reached for his hand.

"You too." He gave her fingers a quick squeeze and let go. "But no Clark. Just Jake."

"Okay."

Again the smile. Intoxicating, but what he saw behind the smile was even deadlier. Time to move.

"Take care, Ari." Jake motioned down the hall with his thumb. "I'm going to use the restroom."

But before he could step away, Peter marched up to them. "Ari, Jake. Jake, Ari. But I'm sure you already introduced yourselves."

"Yeah." Jake focused on Peter. "Ready?"

They'd walked out without Jake repeating his good-bye to Ari. He'd almost turned as they reached the front door of Peter's office, but he didn't give in to the temptation.

"Jake? You with me?"

Peter's voice brought Jake back to the present. He blinked at his friend, who was now standing at the corner of the deck overlooking the lush lawn.

"Yeah, I'm with you."

Peter pointed at a spot on the slope below. "I'm thinking that would be a good spot for our Cowboy Golf tourney later this week."

"Sure. Perfect."

"I need to get back in, keep working on this meal. Camille told me she could watch things for a few minutes, but, uh . . ." Peter pointed at him on the way back to the kitchen. "And get ready, I have a fun surprise for everyone coming just before we chow."

Jake tried to believe the surprise would be a good one. But at the moment, he didn't have enough faith.

10

A ndrew stood with his thick arms outstretched at forty-five degrees, hands braced on the door frame of Jake's room, his rugged, six-two body filling the opening.

"What's Peter's surprise?"

"No idea," Jake said.

Andrew glanced around the small room and then at the twin bed Jake sat on. "Nice bed. Nice décor. Looks like a girl's room."

"Probably was, but this is the room the single guy gets. But hey"—Jake pointed at a long bookshelf to his right—"pretty decent collection of kids' books. Takes me back."

"That's good?"

"One of the best escapes from my dad."

"Yeah, that's right." Andrew pointed at the book in Jake's hand. "What's that one?"

"*The Silver Chair.* C. S. Lewis."

"I've heard of it. A King Arthur story, right?"

"No. You know The Chronicles of Narnia? You've heard of *The Lion, the Witch and the Wardrobe*, right?"

"Sure."

"That's the first one of seven—in the original order anyway. *The Silver Chair* is the fourth book in the series. Far and away my favorite. Probably read it five times before I turned twelve."

"That's the one about the girls who become queens."

"Actually it's about a prince named Rilian, who is the only heir to the throne of Narnia, and his father is dying. Rilian vanished ten years earlier and the kingdom's greatest champions have disappeared or been killed trying to find him. Because of this, even though his heart is broken, the elderly king forbids anyone else from searching for Prince Rilian. So the great lion Aslan sends two children from our world to find and rescue him. They eventually find him deep in the earth. He's been enchanted by a witch, who turns out to be a serpent, but in the end they set him free from his enchantment. The end."

"Rilian forgot who he was."

"Yeah."

"Sounds like a good one. Really good."

They stared at each other, Andrew's eyes telling Jake something so clear, he didn't want to admit it.

"Listen, J, I'm never going to be as eloquent as my better three-quarters, but let me just say I care about what you're going through just as much as Susie does. You're going to make it out the other side of this tunnel. Find out who you are again."

Andrew lumbered over to the bed, plopped down next to Jake, threw his arm around Jake's neck, and yanked him close. "And you know I'm here for you no matter what. Yeah?"

A shout came from downstairs. Sounded like Camille. "Dinner! Now!"

Andrew shook his head and grinned. "I think we better roll."

"No doubt."

———— ✾ ————

Three minutes later they all sat around the myrtlewood table now filled with Peter's culinary wizardry. Before they began to dine, Susie gave her glass a quick rap with her fork and they turned their attention to her. "I'd like to propose a toast to our tenth year of being together."

"Hear, hear," Peter said.

But before Susie could begin, a knock on the front door echoed through the room. Jake turned to Peter and frowned, but his friend was already on his feet, loping toward the entry. He glanced around the table. Susie gave him a nervous look. Andrew had a sudden interest in studying his food. Camille gave him a Cheshire-cat smile and Jake's stomach clenched. Peter's surprise was a person? This would not be good.

Jake twisted in his seat toward the front door, but his vision was blocked by the fireplace.

"You made it." Peter's voice was soft but Jake still heard the smile wrapped around his greeting.

A softer voice, female, said, "So sorry I'm late. Got a little lost after I found the town."

"I'm just glad you chose to come."

"Didn't think I was going to."

"But you did. A wise decision. You're going to have a great time. I promise."

Then silence. Knowing Peter, he was giving this new arrival a quick hug.

Their voices grew softer and he couldn't make out the words. Jake stared at Susie, who sat at the end of the table and had a view of the front door. She glanced at him with a mix of compassion and expectation in her eyes, and Jake knew he was going to administer a slow death to Peter as soon as he had the chance.

His ol' buddy Pete had grabbed the brass ring of romance and melted it down into a yellow, misshapen glob. This was beyond awkward setups and chance meetings. It was a betrayal and without question would ruin the week.

"Ready?" Peter's voice filled the room.

"Sure."

"Good. Here we go, you're about to be onstage." Peter laughed and their footsteps echoed on the maple hardwood floors.

A second later, Jake's heart rate spiked. It was her. Ari. The woman he'd met in Peter's office. Same long dark hair, trim figure, those eyes that without question hid a great deal behind them, and skin that had seen more of the sun since he'd met her back in May. He looked away and ignored the feelings that tried to surface.

"Friends," Peter said, "I'd like to introduce you to a buddy of Camille's and mine, Ari Conwell. As a result of significant arm-twisting and constant nagging, not to mention the fact that she works for me, she's agreed to join us for part of the week. That way when we play games that require pairs, the teams will be even. That's the entire reason Ari is here. Nothing more."

Ari grinned and lifted her hands in mock surrender.

"Don't worry. I warned her that we like to go deeper than most folks with our conversations and she's okay with that." Peter glanced at Ari. "Mostly okay. I told her she could plead the fifth at any time during the week. But no more than once of course."

Jake again glanced at the faces of his friends. None of them looked surprised at seeing this party crasher. Not a big shocker.

"I'll get to intros in a second, but first a bit about Ari. I met her eleven months ago when she started working at my company and she almost immediately became part of the group that gathers at our home every Wednesday night. She's lived in the Northwest most of her years and now spends her days helping me negotiate contracts." Peter rubbed his hands together and glanced at Ari. "Now, let me tell you a few snippets about these ragamuffins around the table."

He pointed at the head of the table. "That's Susie Hawthorne. Susie was born in Minnesota but moved to the San Fran Bay area with her family in third grade, and she's been there ever since. She's an indie singer-songwriter with a solid career going, and she's still crazy about the Minnesota Vikings even though she hasn't lived there for, uh, a number of years, and they're one of only two teams to go to the Super Bowl four times and never win. No, we can't figure out why she still loves them either.

"Next to her is her husband, Andrew. He's into high tech and systems, one of those people who actually understands security and computers and is smarter than I could ever be even with three lifetimes of brains. Plus he has the most amazing collection of Hot Wheels cars you'll ever see in your life.

"They have three sons and one daughter, and they've been

known to start making out in the middle of dinner, card games, or on the water out in the boat with all of us there. You've been warned."

"We do not!" Peter ducked as Susie tossed a roll at his head.

"Camille you know, which brings us to the legendary Jake Palmer, who you met briefly in my office in May. He's been my best friend in the world and universe and beyond since our first day of college together and is generally regarded as one of the best corporate trainers on the planet. At least that's what he tells me, but I've never really believed him and you shouldn't either."

Jake tried to smile but he was certain it came across as more of a grimace. Ari gave him a little wave and a tiny smile that threatened to drag those asinine feelings up out of his gut. "Okay." Peter clapped his hands. "Let's grab you a plate and a chair and a glass."

A few minutes later, Ari sat next to Susie, directly across the table from Jake. At least Peter wasn't sadistic enough to seat Ari beside him, but directly across from him was almost as bad.

Peter nodded at Susie. "Now how 'bout that toast?"

Susie stood and glanced at each of them before she began.

"To old friends, and new friends we're soon to grow close to." She tipped her glass to Ari. "Ten years of friendship is a long time. Most friendships come and go. But not ours, no, not ours. Isn't there a little voice deep inside that says we'll still be toasting our little group in another ten years? In another twenty? I'm certainly hearing that voice. So here's to a week of love and laughter and adventure and celebrating life, going deep and seizing the unquenchable future. And remember, it's not a true toast unless you look in everyone's eyes before you drink and hold their gaze for at least a second. To us!"

They all raised their glasses and clinked them together. When Jake's glass met Ari's he did look at her, but for much less than a second. He couldn't even be certain their eyes met. Welcome to the next ten days.

The first half of the meal consisted of Jake making controlled and polite conversation while focusing most of his energy on not looking at Ari and trying to catch Peter's eye so he could scorch his friend with his gaze. But Peter didn't glance his direction once.

Between the meal and dessert, Andrew raised his glass and said, "One more toast before we get our sugar fix. Today marks the fifth anniversary of the release of Susie's first album. Which would not be in existence but for Mr. Palmer. To you, Jake."

"Indeed!" Susie said as she and Peter and Camille joined Andrew in the toast.

"What happened?" Ari asked.

Susie pointed at Jake, who motioned with his hand to indicate less is more.

"Through his training he met the head of a small record label. Jake convinced her to listen to my music, then he and Andrew talked me off the ledge every time I thought I wasn't going to make it, and Jake even spent three weeks with us as I was making my first record. Without his support and belief in me, it never would have happened."

"You're embarrassing me, Sooz."

"Good. For a second there I didn't think it was working."

"Ahhhh, yes, it is." Jake covered his eyes with his hand and sighed.

"By the way, Jake didn't limit his efforts to Susie and Andrew," Peter said as he looked at Ari.

"Oh really?"

Peter raised his glass again and looked at Jake. "Do you want me to tell them what you did for me and my business? Or what you did for Camille and me for our honeymoon? I think Ari might be interested."

"No, bud. I think you've already done quite enough this evening."

11

After consuming a piece of Peter's homemade tiramisu, Jake wandered out onto the deck, spread out his arms, and set his palms on the dark-stained railing. A camp robber launched itself off a tree to his left and landed on the railing on the far side of the deck. It stared at Jake as if wanting to give him a message. Eventually it flew off, leaving Jake in peace to watch dusk steal over the lake. The sun still hung high enough over the mountains to the west to light up the lake with the richest colors of the day. Photographer's dream.

Leonard was right. A gorgeous spot to retreat. Relax. Find restoration. Unless of course you were stuck for more than a week with a woman like Camille and another woman like Ari who would prevent any of the three Rs from happening.

As if on cue, a bald eagle swooped by him not more than fifty feet from the deck. He watched the great bird till it soared out of sight. Symbol of freedom. A reminder that he'd never be free to soar again till this life ended. Was he bitter toward God? Yeah. Should he be? Probably not. God wasn't the one who made him pull off the freeway on that cold October night a year and a half ago. Still, why did he allow the incident to happen? Nothing good had come of it.

No justice. No lesson. No hope for the future ever getting better than it was right now. Only loss. Trust God? Not easy these days.

"Hey."

Jake spun. Susie. She danced toward him doing her disco moves, which always made him smile. "You okay?" Susie peered at him with that look that forbade him to tweak the truth. But sarcasm? That was never off-limits.

"Yeah, fantastic. Wow, it's like I'm a kid at Disneyland. So glad I let Peter talk me into coming this week."

"Me too. I'm getting tired of checking my mailbox for the wedding invitation."

"That's not funny."

"I'm sorry, Jake. I just want you to be happy. And you have to admit, there are two types of guys. The ones who need to be married. And the type that *really* need to be married." She drummed her fingers on the railing. "Which camp do you think you fall into?"

"Did you know he was inviting Ari?" Jake leaned on the railing with his elbow and stared at Susie. She shifted her gaze to the lake and Jake had his answer. "Why didn't you tell me?"

"He made Andrew and me promise not to."

"Do you realize this is the only time I ever get to truly be myself? Where I can swim without wondering if people are gawking at me? Where I can talk about the incident without people getting a sudden fascination with the coffee swirling around their cup?"

"I know. That's what I told him, but he has this matchmaker complex when it comes to you."

"How can one man be so lucky?" Jake pushed himself up from the railing. "Have you seen him?"

"Peter?"

"Yeah."

"Camille said he was going down to the water before cards."

"I looked. There's no one on the dock."

"Haven't you been down there yet? There's a little path off to the right that takes you to a small clearing in the trees. You can't see it from up here."

"Thanks, Sooz."

"It's still going to be a good week. I feel it."

"Hmm."

Jake eased down the forty steps toward the dock, resting every now and then, and finally stepped onto the path Susie had mentioned. Poplar trees on either side formed a kind of tunnel that ran along the edge of the lake. Jake wound down the path and after twenty-five yards saw an opening in the trees. It led to four chairs made out of thick wood stained to a dark brown, arranged around a cold fire pit. A grove of birch trees surrounded the chairs in a half circle overlooking the water.

Peter sat in the chair on the far side like a stone, his hands wrapped around his camera, the only movement his forefinger as he snapped pictures of a burnished sun balancing on the horizon. A breeze ambled in from the left, just enough to ruffle the trees outlined against the darkening sky. The noise of laughter floated down from the cabin. The lake was glass.

Jake slid into the chair next to Peter and joined his friend in watching the trees at the far end of the lake poke their tops into the bottom of the sun. Without speaking and without looking his direction, Peter set his camera on the armrest of his chair and picked up two glasses. He handed one to Jake, then settled back in his chair and took a drink. They sat in silence for another few moments before Jake broke it.

"Do you prefer to die by the sword, or shall I poison your coffee at some point during the week?"

"Do you like her?" A slight smile crept onto Peter's face, his gaze still straight ahead. "I think you do."

"Definitely poison. It will be slower and more painful."

Another smile from Peter. This time his teeth showed.

Jake shook his head. "Leftovers, huh?"

"You'd never have let me invite her if I'd told you about it ahead of time." Peter shifted in his chair and turned to Jake. Jake stared straight ahead.

"You think?"

"So you admit it. I was right."

"Right about what?"

"Finding someone you'd be interested in."

Jake's gaze shifted to the dead black coals inside the circle of rocks that formed the small fire pit. Once upon a time, the remnants of those branches and logs had been green and growing.

"This was supposed to be a time for the five of us to be together. Where I could be myself. Where I don't have to hide."

"You know, you could always step out of the shadows and stop hiding from everyone that you don't already know." Peter shifted in his chair and rapped the wood of his armrest.

"Yeah, and I could go sled across the North Pole in a bathing suit."

"My idea would be a lot more freeing. And a lot warmer."

"Freeing?" Jake smacked his stomach with both hands. "Try living in this body for a day, then talk to me about how showing it to a complete stranger will set me free. It's going to be a fun ten days."

"Didn't you hear me when I introduced her to everyone? She's not staying the whole time."

"Really."

"Probably not. I could only get her to commit to three days."

"I wish she'd taken the three-minute option."

"That wasn't on the menu."

"You swore you were never going to do this to me again."

"I did?" Peter pretended to recoil from the look on Jake's face. "Oh, that's right. I guess I did."

"Again, why'd you do it?"

"God told me to."

Peter kept a straight face but Jake didn't believe it for a second. "Yeah, right."

"Maybe he didn't, but I know he would have if I'd asked."

"Why, Peter?"

"Do I really need to tell you?"

"Uh, yeah, I think you do."

Peter cocked his head and rubbed his chin as if needing to contemplate his answer. "It's time to stop feeling sorry for yourself. The fruit is ripe. The water has come to a boil. The wine has aged long enough and must now be sampled."

"Is it possible for you to come up with an analogy that doesn't involve food?"

"No."

"I'm leaving tomorrow. I hope you and Ari and everyone else have a great time."

"No you're not."

"I'm not?"

"No."

Jake rose, smiled, and tossed a stick into the water. "Take lots of pictures for me."

12

At six the next morning, as Jake reached the front door and pulled it open a crack, a voice from the breakfast table jolted him. He spun to find Susie at the table sipping something steaming out of a dark red mug.

"Wow." Jake sucked in a quick breath and popped himself in the chest. "Thanks for jump-starting my heart."

"You're welcome." She rose from the table and glided over to him, pink slippers moving like ice skates over the hardwood floor, and pointed at her cup, then the kitchen. "I'll get you a cup of coffee. You can join me at the table and we'll talk."

"No thanks."

"It's Black Fedora," she said in a singsong voice. "Your favorite coffee in the world."

"Tempting, but I need to finish packing my car."

"Peter told me last night that you were thinking of leaving. I told him no way. I guess I'm wrong. I guess it's true."

"Yeah, it is." Jake rubbed his dark hair.

"Wow. Okay." Susie nodded and drilled him with her eyes. "You and I only get a chance to see each other in person a few times a year and you're leaving after less than a day? Nice move. And it looks like I wasn't even going to get a good-bye. Thanks, I love you too."

"It's not that." Jake shut the front door.

"Then what is it?"

"I just need to go."

Susie tapped the right side of her face next to her eye. "I saw this coming, but I didn't think it would happen so fast."

"Saw what coming?"

"That you already like her."

Heat rushed into Jake's face. "Shut up, sis."

"I have to admit, she is kind of perfect." Susie tilted her head and scratched her chin in mock concentration. "And now that I think about it, there's a high likelihood she likes you back."

"What part of 'shut up' didn't I communicate properly?"

"I saw the look on your face when Peter introduced her to all of us. I watched you during dinner last night." Susie leaned against the front door. "I've been right there for every romance you've gone through since your first one in sixth grade. You don't think I can see the signs by now? You don't think I know your type? I know you, Jacob."

"Not as well as you think you do."

"I saw hers too."

"Her what?"

"Don't be stupid." Susie took his arm and led him across the living room toward the kitchen. "Let's get you some java, then have a little conversation."

"If you know what's going on inside me, then you also know why I have to get out of here."

They reached the kitchen and Susie handed Jake a mug, poured him a cup of coffee, then pointed to the french doors. "Lemme get my shoes on and let's go for a little walk."

On their way out she grabbed a folder off the kitchen table. They made their way onto the deck, then around the side of the cabin and up the long driveway. They wandered up the dirt road that meandered farther up the lake to the right. They walked a hundred yards in silence before Susie spoke.

"I have a wild thought, crazy, no logic to it whatsoever, but give it a listen, okay?"

"Sure."

"I've been sensing something about you every time I thought about this week and the five of us being together. I even had a dream about it, which I'm not going to tell you about yet, but I think this week is about something deeper than a girl, or you avoiding this girl."

"You had a dream."

"Yes." Susie picked up a large stick that lay on the side of the road and swung it like a light saber. "But that comes later. Right now I want to tell you about what I think the deeper thing is, and I want you to keep an open mind."

"I'm a human sieve."

"Good." Susie chuckled, then stopped and glanced up and down the empty road. "And promise not to think I'm crazy."

"That part is going to be a challenge. I've thought you were crazy since we were both eight. One of the things I like best." Jake grinned.

"I'm serious. This is important."

"Okay, bring it on. Tell me. Make me think you've lost it out here in the wilds of the Oregon backcountry."

"I found out about something last night that confirmed my dream. I think you're here with me this week because you're the one, the only one, who can help me find this something. It's a place. And it's a place you might want to find as well."

"That doesn't sound insane." Jake narrowed his eyes. "Yet."

"Here comes the crazy part." She looked at Jake, eyes blinking, her hands rubbing up and down on her shorts.

"Ready, Coach." Jake held up both hands like he was about to catch a football.

"I think you're supposed to help me find something at the end of this lake."

"Oh yeah? What's that?"

Susie poked the stick in his direction. "This is the part where you don't laugh and ask if I'm crazy."

"No laughing, unless it's out there as far, far away as Star Wars or—"

"It's farther. Way."

"Wow. Okay, no laughing." Jake suppressed a smile. "What's at the end of the lake?"

"A lost corridor." Susie lifted the stick.

"A what?"

"A lost corridor. A trail, a kind of tunnel or something. A path that takes you from one place to another."

"I know what a path is. But I've never heard of one getting lost."

"Listen." Susie's eyes grew intense. "Supposedly, if you can find it, and get through it to the other side, you'll find whatever you want most in the world. It will be given to you."

"Where did you come up with this fairy tale?"

"I didn't. I discovered it."

"How? Where? Before I buy a ticket for Loco Land, I'd like to know who built the park."

"I have to give all the credit to the piano man."

"Andrew?"

"He's plunking around on the keys last night when you went down to the water to mope—"

"Hey!"

Susie winked at him and continued. "He opens up the piano bench to see if there's any music and finds this."

She opened the folder she'd been carrying and handed him three yellowed pieces of handwritten sheet music with lyrics scrawled in a dark pencil. Jake looked for the name of the song-writer, but all he found was the name *Emily* printed in small, neat letters at the bottom of the first page.

"May I?" Susie said after a few moments. She extended her hand and Jake handed the pages back to her.

"It's a song about a lost corridor at the end of this lake that can fix the problems of anyone who finds it. At least that's my inter-pretation. Listen."

Susie held the music in front of her and began to sing.

Paths are right in front us, if we have eyes to see,
Drawing us and healing us, where we need to be.
Blinded eyes and hardened hearts keep us from the race,

Water and path will take us there, if only we'd embrace.
Oh can't you see? Oh can't you see now?
Willow Lake, oh draw me now, to the tunnel at the end,
Grant to me my deepest wish, you promised this to send.

"I know, I know, not great lyrics, but still, pretty intriguing idea." Susie shoved the paper back into the folder and frowned. "What's wrong?"

Jake stared at her, guessing his face had turned a shade lighter. The words of the song were almost the exact same words Leonard had spoken to him on the plane.

Paths are right in front of us all the time, Jake. The right ones. Ones that can take us exactly where we need to go, but they're so hard to see, so hard to see. Most people are blind. But the water and path are there, take us where we need to be, oh can't you see, can't you see, even if they're sometimes too real to embrace.

"What's wrong, Jake? You look pale."

"That doesn't surprise me."

"Are you going to tell me?"

"It's nothing."

"Uh-uh. You're not going to skip past this." Susie huffed out a laugh. "You look like you saw Yoda."

"No, just a bit of a shock. The guy that told me about this place, the cabin I mean, he said something just like the lyrics to that song."

"See! That means you have to help." Susie waved her light saber stick again. "We will use the ways of the forrrrrrrce to find the corridor, Luke."

"You're serious? You want to go looking for a mystical corridor?"

"Yes."

"You're not into that whole portal thing like Camille is, are you?"

"Come on, Jake!" Susie whacked him on the shoulder. "I'm not saying it's real, I'm just saying these kinds of legends often come from something true, then grow out of proportion over time. All I want to do is see what's there. It might be something extremely cool, and I've wanted to do a concept album forever. This could be my inspiration."

"The land where dreams come true . . . sounds like a kids' show."

"It's not dreams come true. I think it's more about fixing what's broken."

"It's a great story, but you don't need me to help you look for this thing. Get Andrew to go with you."

"I already did. He's not into exploring."

"What about Camille?"

"Yeah, right. If I told her, she'd devote every waking moment to looking for it, plus I'm not into her taking over my little adventure."

"I think Peter would love this."

"You think Camille is going to let Peter gallivant off with me for half a day without him telling her exactly what he's doing? Besides, she's got every minute of his day planned out, right down to the allowable minutes for showers."

"She's not that bad."

Susie quirked an eyebrow.

"Yeah, she is."

They both laughed.

THE LONG JOURNEY TO JAKE PALMER

"What about the new girl, what's her name?"

"Nice try, Jake. Do I have to bring up the truth of what we already discussed regarding your feelings?"

"No."

"I'm not going to ask Ari. I want to go with you." Susie clasped her hands together. "Will you come with me? Just for a few hours. It'll be like when we were kids."

"I can't, and you know why."

"No. I don't."

"I see that look in your eye, Sooz. That crazy look that says there's a part of you deep down that believes it's more than a legend. That it could be true. Maybe it's only one percent of you, but it's there." Jake rubbed both hands over his face. "And given my mental state, do you really think it would be good for me to dwell on the idea that there was something out there that could heal me? A comic-book version of hope isn't the best entertainment choice for me."

"All I'm trying to do is—"

"You don't have to try to save me. You don't have to do anything. I'm fine. I'm making it. I'll climb out of this hole."

"I'm not asking you to do it for you, I'm asking you to do it for me. I can already hear the songs in my mind. But I need the source material. Even if we don't find anything, just searching for this place will help."

"Do you remember the time in fifth grade when you spun that story about my turtle? And I called you on it because you're so bad at lying?"

Susie sighed.

"You haven't gotten any better in the past twenty-nine years."

"You're right. Sorry. It's just that . . ." Susie tossed the stick into the woods and turned to keep her disappointment from him. But even if he hadn't caught the look on her face, her body language was shouting the message. "You're my brother. I can't help it."

She started back down the road to the cabin.

"Sooz?"

"Yeah?"

"Give me a few to think about it, okay? Tell you what. Instead of leaving now, I'll head to the grocery store as soon as it opens, pick up a few munchables and some Gatorade for the way home, then come back and give you an answer."

"Just grab a few things from here."

"You think Camille would stand for that?"

"No."

Jake caught up to her and put an arm around her shoulder. "Thanks for looking out for me."

Susie squeezed his waist and smiled.

"But either way, I'm not staying. After we *maybe* go searching for never-never land, I'm leaving. And that maybe is like a ten-percent chance maybe."

"Jerk."

Jake laughed and yanked Susie in close, then rubbed his knuckles on her head. "I love you too, sis."

13

Jake arrived at the grocery store and fought a strange feeling he shouldn't go inside. It wasn't fear that swirled around him, but some other emotion he couldn't define. As if stepping through the door of Willow Lake Fresh Foods would send him on a quest he wouldn't ever return from. Right. He snorted a chuckle and reached for the door. His only quest was to get away from the lake and go home.

A sign just inside the store boasted of fresh crab and salmon straight from the coast. If he were staying he might have picked up some of each. The scent of cinnamon rolls seconds out of the oven filled his nostrils, and the sound of Hall and Oates pumping through ancient overhead speakers filled his ears. The potato chip section offered little variety, but the bananas and pears seemed fresh and he couldn't resist snagging a few old-fashioned donuts. A large Gatorade and he was set. Plenty of food to hold him over for the seven-hour drive back to Bothell.

He headed to the front of the store pushing a cart that screeched every few seconds. The front wheel seemed determined to cut loose and head for the grocery store heaven in the sky. At the register, Jake was surprised to see a kid in his teens saunter up to the end of the checkout stand. Must be bored. Jake's items would barely fill one bag. Plus he didn't expect a town this small to have extended help.

"Okay if I put cher stuff in paper?"

"Yeah, that works fine."

"Where are you staying?"

"How do you know I'm visiting?"

The kid winked under his thick mane of blond hair. "Small town. Everyone knows everyone but I don't know you."

"Right." Jake smiled. "I'm staying, or was staying, out on Willow Lake. Some friends and I rented a house."

"Cool. I like it." The kid cocked his head and gave a cryptic smile. "Got a little Indiana Jones in you, huh?"

"What?"

"He was the guy in that old movie *Raiders of the Lost Ark*." The kid pointed at him and winked again. "Great flick. You should see it."

"I've seen the film. Why do you say I'm like him?"

"I'm guessing you bumped into someone from around here and they told you about the corridor and now you've come to search for it. Right?"

"The what?" A shiver slalomed down his spine. Susie's magical corridor was appearing out of nowhere right here in the local grocery store.

"The corridor. You know. The corridor. The path. The ancient mystery everyone tries to solve."

Jake studied the checker, but given the expression on his face, the kid might have been describing the weather. Jake had the sensation of being looked at, so he glanced to his right and left. There. To the left, fifteen paces away, an older woman slid a tray of maple bars into a brass-colored display case. Had she been staring at him? He waited, but she appeared consumed with her work.

"Can you tell me a little more about this, um, corridor?"

The bag boy shoved Jake's food and drink into an oversized paper bag. "It's just our local legend. Like the Trees of Mystery down there in northern California, where they say you can experience the 'supernatural magic of the redwoods' or the Oregon Vortex and the House of Mystery with its supposed force field that reverses gravity."

"And?"

"That's it." The kid handed Jake his bag and grinned. "All made up, but still kinda fun, you know?"

"No, I don't." Jake didn't move. "You still haven't told me anything about this corridor."

"Oh. Right. Sorry," the kid said. "It was probably started by my grandfather's grandfather, the story, you know? My G-pa is the only one who still talks about it, and everyone is pretty tired of it. He's the only one who believes it's really real, you know? He says I'll find it someday, that I'll need to find it someday and I will if I keep looking, but I'm not going to waste my time on it, but it's still fun to pretend, you know?"

Jake stared at the checker, who shrugged. "But what's the legend?"

"Yeah, right. Geez, what's wrong with me?" The kid grinned. Big toothy smile. "There's this hidden corridor at the end of the lake that can't be found. But if you ever do find it, on the other side of it there's this place where you'll get the thing you want most in the world, get everything fixed that's screwed up in your life, you know?"

"Did a woman in her midthirties, pretty, short blond hair, come in here yesterday and put you up to this? Give you twenty bucks, tell you what I looked like, and say that if I came in you should tell me about the corridor?"

"What? No. The story's been around for a long time, man."

"You're sure?"

"I've lived here my whole life." The kid motioned around the store with his arms. "Pretty sure, you know?"

"No, I don't know." The kid apparently wasn't able to speak one sentence without saying *you know*, but it didn't bother Jake. It gave the kid a certain appeal. "What do you think is at the end of the corridor?"

"I'm not exactly a spiritual person, but you know . . . the legend says it's heaven, or Nirvana, Shangri-la, whatever you want to call it . . . that's the idea."

"How did the legend get started?"

"G-pa says it's been going ever since people came here in the 1800s."

"But no one other than your grandfather knows much about it? You don't know anyone who's searched for it?"

"A couple of my friends and I have gone out there a few times over the years to look for it, but that was back in seventh, eighth grade. There's nothing really there, but it was fun exploring and pretending it was real, you know?"

"Why'd you stop searching?"

"Like I said, it's a joke. A bedtime story for little kids." The kid stared at Jake like he was an idiot. "I Googled 'Peter Parker New York' when I was that age and found out there's a bunch of him living there. At the time I thought that proved Spider-Man was real. But I don't anymore. You think I'm still twelve?"

"Is your grandpa still alive?"

"Yep, he lives on the lake. But I wouldn't go dropping in. He doesn't like strangers."

"Thanks, I'll keep that in mind."

As he made his way to his Jeep, Jake tried to shrug off the coincidence of hearing about the corridor right after talking to Susie about it. He still wasn't convinced he hadn't been set up. He set the groceries in his cargo hold, shut the tailgate, and was just about to open his door when a voice stopped him.

"Stay away from the corridor, young man."

It was the maple-bar woman, gray hair tucked up in a bun, with more than half of it spilling out in a tangled mess. She stood ten feet away, legs shoulder-width apart, arms drawn tight across her chest.

"Excuse me?"

"I've lived here a long time. Born and raised here. Same with my mom. Same with her mom." She stared at Jake with a mix of compassion and crazy, then nodded and started to turn as if she'd explained everything.

"Why should I stay away?"

"Your new punk kid friend in the store didn't tell you about the ones who went off searching for it and never returned, did he? Didn't tell you about the ones who did return, but couldn't ever remember their name after that till the day they died. Didn't mention the ones that claimed they'd found it, but wouldn't say any more than that and spent the rest of their days searching for it again, barely eating, barely sleeping till they wasted away to nothing."

"Who are you?"

She pawed her hand at him. "Doesn't matter. I'm just trying to help. Take my advice or leave it, I don't care which you do, just couldn't let you go off and get yourself all disappeared or messed up in the noggin without saying my piece."

"Who are you?" Jake repeated. "Tell me more about the corridor."

"Bah!" The woman shuffled away so fast Jake might not have caught her even if he believed she'd tell him anything more.

As he stared at her retreating form, two thoughts struck Jake at once. First, if there had been any chance he could convince himself to turn Susie down, the chance was gone now. He wouldn't be leaving the lake today. And second, he didn't need to ask why he'd felt hesitation just before he'd stepped into the store. Stupid, asinine, unquenchable hope had shoved its ugly head out of the bottom of his soul. It was going to take a Herculean effort to shove it back underground where it belonged.

14

A re we going?"

Susie stood on the porch, hands on hips, toe tapping on the wood under her foot, a rare expression of frustration on her face. Jake eased out of his Jeep and stood next to it studying her. Some kind of fire had been lit under her, and the only way to put it out would be to do a little exploring together.

"Yes."

He ambled toward her as she leaped off the porch and galloped toward him. Susie grabbed his arms and shook them. "I knew it, I knew you'd come through for me. This is going to be so good, Jake, I promise."

As they walked back to the house, Andrew strolled through the open front door. "Well?"

"He's going." She pointed at Andrew. "Didn't I tell you, sweetie?"

Andrew laughed. "How'd she convince you to go?"

"Apparently Susie isn't the only one that's convinced we're sitting on top of an ancient local mystery."

"Really."

Jake smiled and shook his head. "At the grocery store I ran

into a kid who told me about this lost corridor at the end of this lake. Says no one can find it, but if you ever did, it would lead to a place where whatever you wanted most in the world would be handed to you, just like yours and Susie's song says. And this kid's grandpa apparently says it's not a legend, that it's real."

He chose not to mention the old woman.

"Are you serious?" Susie yanked down on Jake's T-shirt. "See? See?"

"Two hours." Jake held up two fingers. "Two. Then I'm done. Headed home."

"All you could get was two hours out of him?" Andrew laughed and kissed Susie on top of the head. "You think that's going to give you enough time to find the corridor, get to the other side, and convince Bigfoot to come back to the cabin with you?"

Susie punched Andrew and glared at Jake as the two men broke into laughter.

The next morning—which felt like seconds after Jake had closed his eyes the night before—Susie was there beside his bed, her face hovering in the darkness two feet above his.

"Let's go."

"The idea wasn't great yesterday afternoon. It holds even less appeal now."

"You know I'm not going to let you drop this, right?"

Jake pulled his pillow over the top of his head and spoke into it. "I suppose."

"Wha'd you say?" Susie yanked the pillow off his face.

"I said, 'I have to get on warm clothes.'" He slapped his palm over his eyes. "Because it's so early! How 'bout you let me go back to sleep."

"You promised. Two hours, you said. You'd give me two hours."

"Was I delirious? What time is it?"

"Early."

"How early?"

"The song this Emily wrote says the corridor is open early in the morning, 'when the dew is still full on the green, and first slice of sun has not yet been.' So we have to go now." She punched him in the stomach. "So get outta bed."

"No problem, be ready in an hour. Two at the most."

"Plus, you know Camille will go semiballistic if we're not back in time for breakfast."

"Really good point."

Ten minutes later, he and Susie tiptoed across the kitchen, out the back doors, and onto the deck. Dawn had just started overtaking the night sky, and gray was splashed all over the water's surface. The only movements were fish jumping to snag a fly for breakfast.

They pulled down the two kayaks from the storage shed wall, set them in the water, and slipped into them. Jake and Susie talked little on the way to the end of the lake. Susie was probably lost in the creation of a song even as they made their way across the water. Jake? His mental gymnastics were more painful.

He knew Susie didn't believe for a second there was such a thing as a lost corridor with a pot of gold at the other end. But as she often said, "I haven't quite figured out everything in the universe and there might be one or two things left that will surprise me." It was that part of her that hoped for a straight-from-God, legitimate miracle for him. And he loved her for it.

But while she held on to a sliver of hope, Jake was awakening to a great deal more. Not the man inside. That part was locked down behind a steel door and concrete-reinforced resolve to crush any kind of belief in a magical land. But the little boy inside was not so easily dismissed and right now would not be quiet. A place where you could get what you wanted most in the world? Just thinking about the possibility shredded his eight-year-old heart.

A corridor that could restore him to the way he was before the incident? A fantasy for books and movies. Not real life. Not even for little-boy imaginations that would take the idea and resurrect it in dreams during the night and gut-wrenching longings during the day. But Jake couldn't shut up that insistent little kid down deep inside. He never should have let Susie talk him into this.

"Hey." Susie slapped her paddle on the lake and sent a tiny curtain of water into his face. "Wake up. You look like you just found out Santa Claus left a rock in your stocking."

"He did."

"Have you ever allowed yourself to consider that you're looking in the wrong stocking?"

"What's that supposed to mean?"

"I'm just saying that maybe you need to trust that everything going on with you right now is orchestrated. There's a plan behind it. Yeah? Possible?"

"Let's just get to not finding this place so we can get back."

"I love your enthusiasm."

"Sorry." Jake gritted his teeth. "It's just . . . just that . . ."

"Just that if this corridor 'castle in the sky' is somehow on the ground, then your life could return to normal and you'd get Sienna back."

"I don't want her back. Yeah, of course I'd like my life back, and that would mean her, too, but I can't let myself even consider the possibility. Don't you get that, Sooz?"

Susie ran her fingers through her blond tresses. "No, I don't. Because I'm not in your shoes. But I don't believe in coincidences, and I do believe every one of our circumstances is filled with a power we can't even start to comprehend, so I won't be ready to dismiss the impossible until I die. And I don't think you should either."

Jake dug his paddle into the water and pulled ahead of Susie. She was right—of course she was right—about believing in the impossible. But she was also right about not being in his shoes. And at the moment they were squeezing tight enough to cut off his circulation.

Neither spoke again till they reached the end of the lake forty minutes later. The area seemed almost separate from the rest of the lake. The water narrowed to form a deep cove one hundred yards across. The sounds behind them faded into silence, and the birdcalls that had accompanied them until now stopped. A dense wall of cattails ran the entire length of the cove and extended to the west at least two hundred feet. Behind the cattails a grove of alder trees formed what looked like an impenetrable fortress. No wonder no one ever found this supposed corridor; you'd have to search for weeks just to plow through the cattails, then the thick bank of trees.

"Where do we even start?" Jake scanned the cattails in front of them.

"In the dead center."

"Why?"

"That's where they always put magical, lost corridors. No one thinks the entrance would be in the dead center. That's too obvious. So they always search on the sides where it would be harder to find, but we're smarter than that. We know what they're doing."

"Trying to use reverse psychology on us."

Susie nodded with a knowing look and with a swift stroke propelled herself forward.

"Did you get this from *Finding Legendary Corridors for Dummies?*"

"Yep." Susie reached the edge of the cattails. "And the book says our entrance is going to be right here."

But there was nothing. They spread out. Susie went right, Jake left. Took their time. Poked into the cattails with their paddles, searching for something, anything out of the ordinary. But an hour and twenty minutes later they'd reached the opposite ends of the cove with nothing to encourage their quest.

"Ready?" Jake jerked his head back toward the other end of the lake as Susie approached from the south side.

"I suppose. You?"

"Yeah, I didn't expect to find anything." A lie. There was that infinitesimal part inside that believed. But now that sliver of his soul had to go dark.

"I'm sorry, Jake."

"You ever buy a lottery ticket?" Jake pulled his baseball hat down lower on his head.

"Once or twice."

"Did you think you were going to win?"

"No, not really."

"But it was fun to pretend you might, yeah?"

Susie gave him a sad smile. "But the stakes for you are a lot higher. And pretending isn't fun."

"It was fun being with you." Jake dug into the water and spun his kayak in the direction of the cabin. "When we're old and dying we'll look back on this day with fondness."

"But not till then."

The last of Jake's hope seeped into the lake. "Nah, not till then."

A few moments later a blue heron behind Jake cried, and he turned to look at the bird. It was the first call they'd heard since they'd entered the cove nearly two hours earlier. The bird stared at him for less than a second, with a strange look of intelligence in its eyes, then turned and took to the air, flying low, right toward the center of the cattails. The instant it passed over the reeds, a flash of light reflected off the water directly in front of them, and then onto the cattails, as if someone had a mirror and reflected the sun off the surface of the lake. He stared at the spot, but the flash didn't come again. He glanced to the east at the rising sun. Just a trick of the light. At least that's what he told himself. But the little kid inside started whispering again, saying the flash of light was much more than a trick.

And because of that annoying little boy, Jake knew he wouldn't be going home for at least a few more days.

15

That night after everyone had filled their plates, Peter rose from his spot at the end of the dinner table and rapped his water glass with his fork. "It is time, my friends."

He glanced at Camille and motioned at the paper and pens in front of her. She handed a notepad to each of them along with a pen.

"Time for what, you ask? No, none of you are asking, since you have already guessed we have arrived at the moment to start our annual Summer Session Questions. But for those of us new to the gathering"—he glanced at Ari—"let me give a quick explanation."

Peter picked up the piece of paper sitting on his plate, held it in front of his chest, and pointed at the large type at the top. "As you can see, Ari, there are seven questions at the top of the paper. We'll all jot a few notes next to the questions as we eat. Then, over the rest of dinner, we'll tell each other our answers. It's an incredibly powerful way to get to know each other better, to dream with each other, and to encourage each other, to catch up on the year that was, and the year to come.

"You can answer in a sentence, a word, a paragraph, or in a

five-hundred-page dissertation, although one year Susie took that idea literally, which I suggest you don't. But—"

"I did not!" Susie laughed and threw her pen at Peter, who blocked it with his arm and joined her laughter with his own.

"Yeah, you did." Andrew smiled and pulled Susie toward him for an extended kiss. "It's one of the ten thousand reasons I love you."

"Get a room." Peter laughed, then turned back to Ari. "As I was saying, answer each question however you want to. The only two rules are: you can't stand on the Fifth Amendment, and you have to tell the truth, the whole truth, and nothing but the truth, so help your neck, because if you don't we'll wring the truth out of you anyway."

Susie jabbed her finger at Peter as she looked at Ari. "That part is true."

Ari nodded, then pointed at the polished wood stick next to Peter. It was stained with a clear finish and looked like a wand. "What is that?"

"Ah, yes! The baton." Peter lifted the stick and twirled it in his fingers. "The person who is in the midst of answering their questions holds the baton. When they are finished they hand the baton to the person they'd like to have answer next. There is of course a rule that goes along with the baton, namely that you can't refuse the baton when it's handed to you."

Jake picked up his sheet and stared at the questions even though he knew them by heart.

- What are you proudest of over the past twelve months?

- What do you regret the most over the past year?
- What has been the most painful?
- Who did you meet this past year that you'd like to get to know better?
- What happened that you felt the best about?
- What are you most looking forward to in the twelve months to come?
- How can we help you get there?

Perfect. He was so excited to talk about the torturous journey his life had been for the past year and nine months in front of a woman he barely knew. Even better was the chance to say those things in front of Camille. Sure, Peter would make Camille vow not to take his words back to Sienna, but that didn't matter. This wasn't a safe place. Not anymore.

"Jake, you with us?"

Jake looked up at Peter. "What?"

"You with us? Andrew just asked you to pass the baked potatoes. Twice."

"Yeah, I'm here. Just thinking about the questions." Jake glanced to his right and left for the potatoes, but they weren't there. He looked at Andrew, who had them in his hands.

"When you didn't answer I jumped in." Susie patted him on the arm and whispered, "You'll make it through the questions, don't worry."

Jake groaned inwardly. Not worry? Right. After everyone filled their plates with potatoes, salmon, and asparagus, Peter rapped his glass again.

"Okay. We'll get to the questions in a minute, but first, to give you a little more time to think about your answers, Camille is going to lay out the plan for the rest of the week."

Camille shifted forward in her chair and waited till all eyes were on her. She clapped her hands once and started in. "We have ATVs on the dunes tomorrow. Play days on the water on Tuesday and Thursday. Wednesday will be spent relaxing."

Jake tuned Camille out. Same routine as always. Wednesday night would be their annual poker tournament, and so on throughout the week.

He caught Susie's eye roll and returned it with one of his own. As he glanced at the end of the table, he caught Ari staring at him, one corner of her mouth turned up in a smile. She winked at him, which brought heat to Jake's face. He picked up the last piece of french bread and immersed himself in applying a thick layer of butter.

Yeah, it would be nice if their ten days together weren't planned out like they were at seventh-grade church camp, but he had to give Camille a little credit. Her ideas were always fun.

"Well done yet again, dear." Peter leaned back with his hands behind his head. "Anyone have any objections?"

No one did. At least out loud. Jake would have voted for a day where everyone took time for themselves.

"Excellent. All right, we'll give everyone a moment to make a few notes and then we'll begin."

Peter turned to Jake a few minutes later and handed him the baton. "Jake? Would you do the honor of starting us off?"

"You should choose someone else to get the party started. I

think my answers would put everyone to sleep," Jake said with a weak laugh.

"I think your answers will fascinate," Camille said, her eyebrows raised. "Besides, you can't refuse the baton. I think you made up that rule ten years back, Jake."

Jake grimaced and picked up the questions. "Well, okay then." He cleared his throat and began.

"Proudest moment of the past twelve months: deciding to come here this week. Biggest regret: hibernating so successfully in my self-pity cave. What's been the most painful: finding out that Darth Vader is Luke's father. Who I met that I'd like to get to know better: I had no cave visitors other than you guys, so no one. What happened that I felt best about: still thinking about that one, honest answer. Really. What I'm looking forward to in the next twelve months: See previous answer. How can you help me get there . . ." Jake stopped staring at the questions, set them down, and glanced at everyone but Ari.

"I know I haven't been the most responsive friend for a while now. Or the most positive. But I appreciate the effort you've made. More than you know. So I guess you can help me by continuing to be exactly who you are. You all bring me life." He pushed back from the table and stood. "Excuse me. I need to grab some fresh air."

Jake eased around the table and out onto the deck. Awkward. Embarrassing. Far too revealing. He should have left Willow Haven as soon as he and Susie got back from the end of the lake that morning.

The moon was cresting the hills to the right, and the lake had vanquished even the hint of a breeze. To his left, stars muted by the moon's light hovered just above the horizon. Had to still be in the midseventies. Perfect evening sandwiched between his overtoasted-bread life.

He turned and glanced back into the cabin. Muted laughter floated through the french doors, and a sizable portion of it came from Ari. Only two days of knowing these people and already she was part of the family. There was an ease to the woman mixed with a vulnerability that pulled at him like a two-ton magnet. Why couldn't Peter have asked a woman like the flower lady to come this week? Jake would have taken off his linen drawstring pants within the first day, faced the repulsion, and gotten on with life. But this? He shook his head and pressed his first three fingers hard into his forehead.

Peter glanced his direction, then pointed. Could they see him? Probably not. The darkness outside against the lights inside would prevent it. But Jake knew what would come next. Peter would soon come out, or ask Susie to go get him. Not tonight, folks. Tomorrow he'd be fine, but for the moment he needed to be alone.

Jake took the stairs down to the water, each step soft to keep the stairs from creaking. When he was halfway down he heard the french doors open and the sound of Peter's and Susie's voices above him. He stepped off the stairs and squatted in front of a large juniper.

"Where is he? He came out here."

"Give him some space, Peter."

"Did he go down to the lake?" His voice stopped. "Hard to see."

The deck creaked and Jake pictured Peter leaning on the railing, scanning the stairs and the dock in the dim light.

"Come on, Peter. This wasn't the week Jake expected."

"It's good for him."

"Isn't that for him to decide?"

"We're here for only ten days. It's time to engage."

"It's only day two. He needs a little time away from the madding crowd."

"He's been basically alone for a year."

"You know what I mean."

"He's had enough time away from people. Besides, we're his closest friends. If he's not going to be open with us, who will he be?"

"Not all of us are his closest friends."

"You mean Ari."

"And Camille."

"She won't tell Sienna anything Jake says."

"It doesn't matter what's true, it only matters what Jake believes. And right now he believes that there's a high probability that whatever is said in Vegas won't stay in Vegas."

"If he'd just relax about Ari, he'd be—"

"Come on back inside, champ. Give your pal some downtime."

The conversation faded amid the sound of Peter's and Susie's footsteps on the deck and the opening of the french doors as they went back inside. He appreciated Susie's defense even though Peter would ignore her words. He eased down the rest of the stairs, then took the little path that led to the area where he'd sat with Peter the night before. He settled into the far chair and focused on the undulation of the moonlight on the water.

The most maddening thing about Peter's words was that they

were right. He did need to engage. His only friends couldn't be ones he saw just once a year. He saw Peter, yes. But not Susie or Andrew. Yes, technology made it possible to see them via video, but it wasn't the same as being physically together, and it was so easy to let weeks and months slip by with no contact. But he wasn't ready to rip off the deepest layers of his heart and have people shower him with sympathy. He didn't want sympathy; he wanted real connection.

The creaking of the stairs lifted him from his ruminations, and Jake braced himself for Peter's arrival. He squinted into the tunnel of trees and brush, but it was too dark to make out the form of his friend. Then again, it might be Susie. Her, he wouldn't mind. As long as it wasn't Camille. But of course it wasn't any of them.

"Hi, Jake. Can I join you?"

Jake lurched forward and knocked his drink onto the ground.

"I'm so sorry." Ari stepped under the branches at the edge of the clearing and into the half circle of trees.

"No worries." He picked up the now empty glass and set it on the armrest of his chair. "I'd had enough anyway."

Ari set the tips of her fingers on the back of the chair farthest from Jake and repeated her question. "Are you okay with me joining you for a few minutes?"

No. It wasn't okay. Not even for a few seconds.

"Yeah, sure. Sit down." Jake squinted at the path back to the stairs and asked a question he already knew the answer to. "You came alone?"

"Uh-huh."

Ari eased onto the chair and perched on the edge as if ready to leave in an instant if necessary. But the relaxed tone of her voice said she would stay as long as was needed. She stared out toward the water for so long, Jake almost broke the silence. But then she sighed and turned to him.

"I figured we might be wise to have a conversation. Don't worry, it will be brief. I can tell you're not really up for getting to know me, and that's fine. But I thought I'd see if we can get rid of the rather large pink elephant crowding the house and deck up there, and the dock down here."

"Me?" Jake poked a finger into his chest. "Ari, I promise you, I don't remember saying I didn't want to get to know you. The aliens must have taken over my body again. I hate it when they do that."

She gave a polite smile. "You didn't have to use words."

"Can we just say I'm Switzerland on this one?"

"Sure." She turned back to staring out over the water and again the silence lingered.

"What's your plan for shooting the elephant?" Jake asked.

Ari laughed and it seeped into Jake's soul. An intoxicating sound.

"I don't want to shoot it, just usher it out the door."

"Okay."

"By the way, I didn't know either." She scooted even closer to the edge of her chair, folded her hands, and offered a little smile. "From the way Peter described it, I thought it would be a few of his friends and me."

"He lied to you?"

"No, he simply said that his best friends gathered every

summer and he wanted me to come because there would be an odd number this year." Ari pushed her dark hair back over her ear. "I told him no at least five times. Felt like I'd be crashing a private party."

"But Peter can be persuasive when he wants to be."

"Even when he doesn't want to be."

Jake laughed. "Quite true."

"So I was as surprised to see you as you were to see me."

"That helps."

"How long has he been setting you up?" Ari said.

"Too long. Going on a year now." Jake shook his hands, fingers curved like he wanted to throttle Peter. "How 'bout you? Does he do the same thing to you?"

"Set me up on blind dates?" Ari shook her head and her hair swished back and forth like water. "Not till this weekend." A look of dread spilled onto her face. "I'm not saying this is a date. You and me. I'm just saying, Peter . . . I mean, it seems like he's trying to . . ."

"I get it. I know what you mean." Jake smiled. "We could do something cruel and mean and embarrassing to Peter to get back at him."

"Really, really cruel."

They both laughed and the awkward tension between them seeped into the ground.

Jake glanced at her, then back to the lake. "Do you mind me asking, are you divorced?"

"Yes, I mind."

They both smiled.

"Widowed." Ari's voice grew soft. "Three years now."

"I'm sorry."

"I knew it when I married him." Ari stood and ambled to the edge of the bank and faced the lake.

"Knew what?"

"Tony had a heart condition. He told me after our fourth date that he had a sixty-forty chance of living past his midthirties. But I was already falling in like with him, and love soon followed. I ignored the odds and believed and prayed he'd be one of the sixty percent. But it turned out he was destined to join those in the forty-percent club."

"No kids?"

Ari shook her head. "We wanted to play for a few years first. A few turned into four, turned into six, and by the time we were ready for children his heart problems flared up."

"I'm sorry."

"What about you? Any kids?"

"We had . . ." Here it was. The perfect chance to tell her what had happened to him and let the rain fall where it may. But the words turned to sand in his mouth, and instead Jake couched the truth in an explanation that told her nothing. "We, uh, were just about to start trying when we had a turn of events that stopped the process. A year later my ex-wife filed for divorce."

"I see." She turned and focused on him.

Of course she would be too kind to press him on the lame answer, but her eyes didn't follow protocol. They seemed to bore into him as if a light had been switched on inside and was searching for the truth. She finally turned away and changed the subject. But the new topic wasn't much easier to discuss.

"Why does Peter call you Clark?"

Jake sighed and shook his head.

"You don't like it?"

"I used to."

Jake spun the base of his glass slowly and watched it give little bumps as it moved over the rough wood. At one time the bottle had moved so smoothly, but these days every turn was a struggle.

He sighed again and said, "Peter gave me the name years ago. We were doing an exercise from one of my workshops. Reading each other's labels. I told him he was Aragorn from Lord of the Rings and he told me I was Superman. After that he started calling me Clark, for Clark Kent."

"Are you Superman?"

"Was Superman. Past tense. I'm not him anymore. Never will be again."

In his peripheral vision he saw Ari lean in slightly, her gaze fixed on his face. He finally turned to her and she didn't have to voice the question in her eyes. He knew what it was. Might as well answer the question.

"Peter called me Superman because I was in good shape back then. Because it seemed like I could do anything. Because I'm a few notches smarter than most people. Because a few gals said I was handsome and kind of looked like him if you squint from a mile away and it's dark."

"And you're not any of those things anymore."

"No, not these days."

"I don't know about all of those things, but on one point I

don't believe it's a matter of debate. You are handsome. And you do look like him."

A jolt of desire shot through him—to be considered handsome again, to be desired by a woman. But he couldn't go there. Wouldn't.

Ari leaned closer and the scent of her perfume caught him. "What happened to Superman?"

"That's a conversation for another day." Jake stood and gave a smile he hoped hid the pain. "But thanks for making the effort to come down. Good chatting with you, Ari."

As he walked away, she said she'd look forward to that conversation, but he knew another day would never come. He'd already said too much and chided himself for letting his heart open to her even the sliver that it had. Dangerous. And stupid.

16

That night, Jake lay in bed replaying his conversation with Ari, and then the one with Susie, and then the scenes from their failed search at the end of the lake. The truth? He didn't believe. The idea that there was a magical corridor at the end of the lake that would lead you to what you wanted most was a nice setup for a kid's story, not adult reality.

Sure, C. S. Lewis could send people through a wardrobe or through a wall at the top of a school, but this was real life. He should let it go, enjoy another day or two as much as he could with Ari hanging around, then head home and try to convince himself to get back to helping people who still had lives worth living.

Sleep came easy that night, but two hours later, Jake bolted upright gasping for air, his chest heaving, the dream of being on fire still as vivid in his mind as when he'd been asleep. His pillow was drenched with sweat, as were the sheets under his back and arms. But the sheets were dry from his midsection down. Always dry from his midsection down. His skin grafts would never sweat.

There was no point in trying to go back to sleep. A few hours from now? Yes. Once the adrenaline coursing through his veins subsided, he'd be able to sleep again. But not now. He rose from the bed, pulled clean sheets and a pillowcase from the hall closet, and replaced the damp ones. As he did, a thought flashed through his mind like lightning. He knew what he had to do when dawn arrived.

———∞∞∞———

Jake woke three hours later with the same sensation he'd had in the middle of the night. The idea hadn't faded, only grown stronger, and was impossible to shake. He had to return to the end of the waters. Search for the corridor. Find it. Press on through to the other side. He tried to convince himself the flash of light he'd seen with Susie was a trick of his imagination. His mind was in full agreement with that assessment. But that irritating voice deep in his soul continued to implore him to believe.

He eased out of bed and dressed in minutes. Swimsuit, black compression top. He took his linen pants to leave on the dock for when he returned. He'd be back long before Ari would be up, but just in case, he'd be ready. The sun hadn't yet kissed the top of the mountains to his right as he moved onto the deck overlooking the lake, but by the time he reached the water with his kayak, the lake would be sprinkled with a dazzling display of diamonds from the early morning rays.

As he paddled toward the end of the lake, a peace fell on him. He didn't rush and didn't hold back. The rhythm of his strokes stayed in concert with the beating of his heart, and the anxiety he'd awakened with disappeared into the dark waters under his kayak. He'd be to the west end of the lake in less than forty minutes at this pace. Plenty of time to find the corridor, see what was on the other side, and get back before the rest of the world woke up.

Find a magical corridor. Right. Jake laughed at himself. Stellar plan. Might as well cure cancer and figure out world hunger while he was at it.

When he reached the end, he stopped forty yards from the cattails and closed his eyes. Had to see it in his mind. Jake pulled up the memory of where he'd seen the shimmer yesterday, locked in on it, and opened his eyes. There. To his right. That was the area. No doubt. He paddled toward it slowly, eyes fixed on the spot where the light had flashed, but now there was nothing.

After forty-five minutes of staring at the spot, pushing his kayak into every inch right and left of the area, searching twenty yards in each direction, there was still nothing. Jake smacked his paddle on the water and shouted at himself. "Idiot."

He'd let himself start to believe, let hope slither through that crack in his soul, and now he'd pay for it, because it wasn't a crack any longer. He'd ripped his heart wide open and let himself imagine what it'd be like to be whole again, to be with a woman again, to be with Ari.

As the echo of his cry vanished into the early morning air, a sound to his right caught his attention. Fifty yards away to the northeast sat a small battered rowboat. A man sat like a statue with his back to Jake, a fishing pole draped over the side of the boat. No one else was on the lake, and yet here, at the spot where Jake was searching, sat a man in a rowboat.

Jake paddled toward the boat with soft strokes and when he was twenty yards away called out, "Good morning."

The man turned and something seemed familiar about him. But the baseball cap shoved down over his head and sunglasses kept Jake from making any kind of connection about who the man might be.

"Yeah, I suppose it is."

Same thing with the voice. Vaguely familiar. Then the man smiled. His two front teeth were missing.

"Leonard? You've got to be kidding me."

"Good to see you, Jake Palmer." Leonard glanced at the sun now fully above the ridgeline of the mountains to the east. "Early to be up."

"Getting up early gives me time to be alone."

Leonard nodded and bobbed his forefinger at Jake as if he knew exactly what Jake meant.

"What are you doing on this lake, Leonard?"

"It's home." A sly grin appeared on his face.

"You live here?"

"Forty years come November."

Realization hit Jake like an ice bucket shower and he almost laughed. Of course. "Let me take a wild guess about your life. You have a grandson who works at the grocery store in town."

Leonard nodded, winked, and jerked his thumb toward the north side of the lake. "My place sits about midlake on that side. Right across from where you're staying. Before that, I lived on fifteen acres four miles north of here next to the stream that fills this lake. A lot easier to take care of half an acre than fifteen."

"The house directly across from the one we rented. That's how you knew so much about the rental."

"Yep."

"Why didn't you tell me you lived here?"

"Did you ask?"

"No, but when you suggested we rent here, I'm kind of surprised you didn't let me know you live on the lake."

"A lot of surprises around here, you'll probably be finding. I suppose part of me hopes you do."

"Like?"

Leonard reeled in his line and set his pole in the bottom of his rowboat before speaking again. "Any luck finding the corridor?"

Jake's heart rate spiked. He wasn't ready to tell Leonard what he was doing. Susie and Peter knowing was bad enough. "Corridor?"

"Really, Jake? You're here at the end of the lake just hanging out while every sane person is still asleep? It doesn't look like you're fishing. I might be old, but I'm not stupid." Leonard didn't smile. "Do I look stupid to you?"

"No, but—"

"Then don't ask me stupid questions. We'll get along better."

Jake studied the man in front of him. Leonard wasn't kidding. The old man gave two quick pulls with his oars and a heron shrieked, gave two hard flaps of its wings, and streaked off over the water. Leonard let his rowboat drift up next to Jake's kayak, and he took hold of the kayak's curved edge with a gnarled hand.

"You gonna answer my question or sit there like a water-soaked log taking up valuable lake space?"

Jake repressed a smile. "No. Haven't had any luck."

"How'd you get suckered in?"

"To believing the corridor is real enough to waste my time coming out here?"

Leonard responded with an almost imperceptible nod and a look that said the question was mildly stupid.

"I don't believe. But that doesn't mean I can't do some exploring in case I'm wrong."

"That's your problem."

"What's my problem?"

"There you go, asking stupid questions again."

Jake studied the man's eyes, now fixed on his, narrowed, a challenge in them.

"If I believe there's a corridor, there's a much greater chance there will be one. If I don't believe, I'll never find it."

"I kinda suspected you weren't as stupid as you've been sounding." Leonard nodded as if confirming his assessment. "Who was the gal you came out here with yesterday morning?"

"You were spying on us?"

"Spying? Nah. Not at all. I was here. You came by."

"Why didn't you reveal—?"

"You ask a lot of questions, you know that?"

"Are you going to answer them?"

Leonard pushed off of Jake's kayak, dipped his oars in the water, and pulled away.

"Do you believe, Leonard?"

"On this day, the story is about you, not me." Another strong pull and Leonard's boat moved farther away. "But be careful, Jake, if you ever do overcome your lack of faith, you might not like what it brings you."

"I thought the corridor is supposed to give you what you want, what you need. It's supposed to fix things."

"That's what the legend says. But when legends become reality, they don't always end up being what you expected them to be." Leonard pointed at Jake. "What you want and what you need are often two different items, young Jake."

"I met an elderly lady at the grocery store. She said to stay away. That the corridor makes people go crazy. Or makes them disappear."

Leonard stared at Jake for more than ten seconds before saying, "Sounds like you should give that serious consideration before continuing your pursuit."

With that, Leonard rowed off, his face like stone. Jake wanted to paddle after the old man, pepper him with more questions, but something told him this wasn't the time, and even if he did get a few more bits of information, it wouldn't help. Whatever was real or not real about the corridor, Jake was starting to believe the truth was less about the head and more about the heart.

17

At nine the next morning, Peter strode into the living room wearing dark blue swim trunks, a gray tank top, and a big grin. He jangled the key to the boat they'd rented for the week and bobbed his head and body like a six-foot-five slinky.

"The water is calling our names and everything on the menu is available. Wakeboarding, skiing, tubing, knee boards—they're all lined up like little soldiers ready to take orders, but they won't wait forever and neither will I. So let's lock and load. Who's with me?"

Susie laughed. "Gotta love Peter's mixed metaphors."

"I'm in!" Camille shot her arm up, rose to her feet, and did a jig.

"There's two, it's me and you, baby." Peter pointed at Susie. "Sooz, you don't wanna lose. Right?"

"No, don't want to lose." Susie grinned, then pointed at Andrew. "But this big lug suggested we go on a quick stroll up the road a ways and"—Susie affected her best Godfather voice—"'it's an offer I can't refuse.' But by the time you get the boat in the water and take someone for a run, we'll be down there and ready to roll."

Andrew grabbed Susie and pulled her close. "I love this woman. Have I ever told you guys that?"

Peter gave an exaggerated shake of his hand and pointed at Susie and Andrew. "Okay, Susie. You get second run. Andrew, you're number three. Right? Am I right or am I right?"

"Yeah! You're right, Pete." She gave her own hand the same rapid shake and wiggled her finger as she pointed it at him.

"You're mocking me, Susie."

"Yes, of course I am. 'Cause I love you, Peter."

Camille put her hands on her hips and nodded at Ari. "You want to come, Ari?"

Ari shrugged. "Sure."

Peter flashed two thumbs up. "Great. You'll love it as long as you don't let Jake drive the boat. You've heard of the *Titanic*, right?"

Jake rolled his eyes. Peter grinned and tossed the keys at him. Jake caught them with one hand.

"Did I say I was going?"

"You didn't have to. I know you're in." Peter grabbed the air with both hands like he had hold of a wheel. "Faster than a speeding hydro? Stronger than a double-thick ski rope? Able to leap over struggling wakeboarders with a single bound?"

"That's funny. I'm busting."

"All joking aside, Clark, there's no one here better at driving the boat, and I'm not going out there by myself with two women. They'd be tempted to toss my body to the sharks and never look back."

"No problem." Jake stood and jerked his thumb toward his room. "Let me go change and I'll meet you down there."

By the time they launched the boat, Susie and Andrew had finished their walk and all six were gathered in the boat and on the dock. Peter stood at the back of the boat checking the ski rope for knots and called out their next moves.

"Okay, here's the order. Ari goes first." He looked at her. "House rule. Since you've never been to one of our annual get-togethers, you have the honorary position of being first to cut up the glass."

"I don't need to—"

"Oh, I get it. A rule breaker. In the office you follow protocol, but out here you think it's the Wild West, huh? Wow, life on the lake gets craaaazy."

"No, Peter, I wouldn't want anyone to think I'm a rebel." She laughed and glanced at Jake.

"Excellent." Peter turned to Susie and Andrew. "Then like we talked about: Susie, then Andrew, then Camille, then me. If anyone wants to go again, we'll repeat the cycle. We all good with that?"

As Ari slipped into a life jacket, then wrestled her feet into the boots of a red and gold wakeboard as she sat on the back of the boat, Jake clambered into the ski boat and adjusted the rearview mirror. His attempt to ignore how perfect Ari looked with her hair pulled back and the sun dancing on her tanned skin failed miserably. He had to knock it off. He wasn't going there. Forget it.

"Jake? Hello?"

Peter was staring at him. "What?"

"You doing a Walter Mitty on me again? This is like the third time since we got here."

"No, just . . ."

"Then let's go. Ari is starting to freeze."

Jake jerked his head back and found Ari bobbing in the water. He started the boat, adjusted the mirror once more, and called back to Ari. "When you're ready, just tell me to—"

"Hit it!" Ari grinned and Jake didn't hesitate.

He pushed down halfway on the throttle as he looked in the boat's rearview mirror. Ari struggled for a few seconds but finally popped out of the water and smoothly shifted her board straight ahead, but her weight was too far forward and she went over the front of the board. Jake shoved the throttle all the way down and turned the wheel hard to the right. The boat whipped around till it faced Ari.

"You okay?"

"Stupid move." She grabbed the rope as it trailed by her. "Ready when you are."

She again popped out of the water after fighting for a bit and again went down seconds later, this time because she was leaning too far back.

Jake wheeled around a second time and when he reached her said, "Do you want to be done?"

Ari pressed her lips together so hard they turned white. She gazed up at him and shook her head, eyes like coal.

"Can I give you a thought? Just a quick reminder?"

Again she didn't speak, but did give a quick nod.

"You don't want the board vertical coming out of the water. You'll end up pulling against the whole lake that way. Keep it at a forty-five-degree angle. That means the edge of the board will be underwater as you come up, but that's okay. And don't try to stand up, let the boat pull you up."

Ari nodded again as she stared at the water right in front of her.

Jake shifted the boat into drive and eased forward slowly till the ski rope went taut. Then he pulled the throttle back into neutral and glanced in the mirror. "Ready?"

"Hit it!"

This time Ari went from being immersed in the water to riding on top of it in three seconds.

"Weight back, weight back . . . ," Jake muttered to himself and Ari complied.

She leaned to the right and the board sliced over the wake out onto the smooth water. She let go with one hand and brushed her dark hair off her face. The fierce frown she'd worn for the past five minutes slowly turned into a soft smile and Jake flashed a thumbs-up. For the next ten minutes she sailed back and forth across the wake. No tricks, nothing spectacular, but her cuts were smooth and it was obvious the blood of a natural athlete flowed through her veins. A few minutes later she let go of the rope. Her momentum slowed and she sank into the water.

"Nice run, Ari." Peter leaned over the edge of the boat and gave her a thumbs-up after they spun around to pick her up.

Jake cut the motor and said, "More than nice. I wish someone had been taking pictures. A couple of your cuts were beautiful."

Ari smiled as she pulled her feet out of the wakeboard and pushed it toward the boat. Peter snagged it out of the water and lifted the board into the boat.

"My turn," Camille announced.

She slipped on a yellow life jacket and then a pair of red

waterskiing gloves. By the time Ari clambered back into the boat, Camille had both feet in the board and had laced up the boots.

Peter glanced at Camille, turned to Jake, and whispered, "Did I miss something, or was the plan to go back to the dock for Susie?"

"You didn't miss anything." Jake stared at the smooth water in front of the boat.

"Camille?"

"Yes, sweetie?"

"Susie has the next run. Then you."

"Look at where we are, Peter." Camille threw up her hands. "We're in the middle of the lake. It would take at least five minutes to get back there."

"Two."

"Five, two, whatever. I'm just thinking it makes sense for me to go on the way back. I promise you, Susie will not care."

Peter wore the plastered smile Jake had grown to hate. Once again, Camille was going to do what Camille was going to do. Ten seconds later she bobbed in the lake gripping and regripping the handle of the rope.

Jake started the boat, eased forward, and called out over his shoulder, "Ready?"

"I've been ready. What are you waiting for? Hit it!"

Jake gripped the throttle of the boat harder than necessary and pushed it down. The engine surged and Camille popped out of the water. She cut hard to the right and shot over the wake onto the glassy surface of the lake. After a regrip of the handle, she cut back over the wake and launched herself three feet into the air and made a perfect landing on the other side.

"Wooooooooooo! I've still got it!" Camille thrust one arm into the air and grinned.

For the next ten minutes Camille continued to jump the wake, shift from one foot forward to the other foot forward with little effort, and congratulate herself on each move. The performance was impressive. As they approached the area where they'd started the run, Camille let go of the rope, slowed, and finally sank into the water, both arms thrust above her head.

Jake cranked the boat to the left and circled back to pick her up.

"That was a sweet run. Thanks, Jake. Great driving."

"No problem."

Camille freed herself from the board, swam back to the boat, and climbed aboard. She unbuckled her life jacket, still breathing hard as she stood dripping water onto the floor of the boat. She looked down at Ari and said, "Not bad, huh?"

Ari nodded.

"But you were good too." Camille held out her fist and Ari bumped it with her own but turned her gaze away immediately.

Peter took Camille's life jacket and tossed it toward the front of the boat. "Hey, Jake, let's go grab Susie."

"I'm so sorry that took longer than I thought it would." Camille tapped her head and laughed. "Stupid me, I should have realized I'd stay up for a while."

Jake stared at Camille wishing the woman would work on her acting skills. She wasn't sorry at all. Her behavior would be much easier to take if he could at least doubt what she was doing. He started the boat and turned to Ari.

"You really looked good out there. How long has it been since you've been up on a board?"

"A few summers back."

"Do you wakeboard a lot?"

"I've been a couple of times."

"How many?"

"I don't know, three or four." Ari bit her lip and studied the blue carpet on the floor of the boat. "Something like that."

"Which is it, three or four?"

"Three."

"Three? You've gotta be kidding me. Only three?" Jake frowned and locked his eyes on Camille. "Once you got up, Ari, you looked like you've been on a board for years."

Ari nodded but didn't respond.

"I'd say that's some amazing natural talent, wouldn't you, Camille? I think we can say that Ari has got it, and is getting more of it, don't cha think?"

Camille tilted her head to the side in disgust, and Jake let it drop.

A few minutes into their run back to the dock, Ari looked at Jake and said, "Peter didn't mention you taking a run."

"Nah." Jake forced out a smile. "I'm the designated driver today."

"I see."

Jake ignored Ari's penetrating gaze. For the next two and a half hours he drove without looking at her once. At least not head-on. His peripheral vision wasn't as cooperative.

Finally, he and Peter dropped everyone off at the dock, and Jake turned the boat in the direction of the boat launch at the east end of the lake. Peter waited only a few seconds before asking the question Jake had expected all day.

"You want to take a run, Clark?"

"I'm good."

"Ari's going to be up at the house, I doubt she's going to bring out the binoculars and watch you."

"I said I'm good."

"A quick run. Down at the other end of the lake. West end. We'll stay there, take you on a lightning-fast run, okay?"

Jake stared at Peter. "Just between us. We don't tell anyone about it."

"Done." Peter motioned for Jake to step aside and took the wheel. "You get ready, I'll get us there. We'll be back to the boat launch before anyone suspects anything."

"Good."

"You want to tell me why you don't want anyone to know if you go for a ski?"

"Because someone will say how cool it was that I went, then ask if my legs feel okay, and then Ari will have a whole lot of questions that I'd rather not answer."

"Got it."

Peter threw the throttle down. Four minutes later they reached the end of the lake. Two minutes after that Jake was in the water telling himself what a stupid, glorious idea this was.

"Hit it!"

Jake bit down hard on his lower lip and ignored the pain that shot through his legs like a blade. By the time his ski was on plane, both his legs were on fire. Horrible thought but the perfect analogy. He focused on the unbroken water to his right, leaned in, and a second later his ski was skimming over the surface of the lake. He drew a full breath into his lungs and cut back as hard as he could toward the wake. Three quick bumps and he was on the other side getting ready to carve another turn and throw up another wall of water.

Exhilaration surged through him and masked the pain for a moment, and then another, as he pushed into one turn after the other. He was back. If only for a few minutes, he had returned to the rush of pushing his body to its limit and feeling the joy of streaking across the water at fifty miles an hour. After three more turns the pain in his legs won and he dropped the rope. As he watched Peter slow and circle back toward him, sorrow and joy battled in his heart. The rush of being himself again fought the knowledge that he could only live in his former glory for fleeting moments in time.

Peter floated up next to him and gazed down, concern etched into his face.

"You okay?"

"The spirit is willing and my flesh will be forever weak."

"Glad you went?"

Jake nodded, paddled to the back of the boat, and hoisted himself aboard. His breaths came in gasps and he sat on the swim deck for two minutes before turning and climbing aboard.

Peter tossed him a towel. "You looked good out there. Like the old days."

"Ten turns not even a quarter as low as I used to go isn't good. It's pathetic."

"But you skied."

"Yeah, I did." Jake couldn't stop himself from smiling. "Thanks for pushing me. I'll pay for it for the next two days, but it was worth it."

As Jake toweled off, his gaze swept over the reeds and rushes and cattails at the end of the lake. A lost corridor. One that would fix everything that was wrong. It was a fantasy too tantalizing for him to continue to contemplate. If only.

Then it happened. A quick flash of light between the reeds, so fast he wondered if he'd imagined it. Then again. Once more and it didn't come again. But each time, something jolted deep in Jake's soul, and his heart started pounding faster than when he'd been out ripping up the lake.

"What are you looking at?"

Jake sucked in a quick breath, his eyes fixed on the spot he'd seen a shimmer.

"Jake?"

"Yeah." He turned and blinked at Peter.

"You sure you're okay, Clark? You're doing the ghost look. And you're about ten shades lighter than normal. What? Are you in pain? What?"

"Nothing." Jake put the towel over his head and rubbed his hair dry. "Probably just the shock of getting back up after so long. My heart loves it, not so much my legs."

"What did you see?"

"Nothing."

"You don't have to hide it from me, Jake."

"Hide what?" Jake took the towel off his head.

"The corridor. Susie told me."

"It's a pipe dream."

"Maybe it is. Maybe it isn't. What did you see? Just now," Peter said.

"Just the light reflected off the water, playing on the reeds. That's it."

"Let's look for it together. Get up early tomorrow before any-one else is awake and find it this time."

No point in mentioning he'd already searched a second time on his own. "No. If God wanted me to find it, I would have the first time."

"Maybe you have to work for it. Maybe it's not going to come easy."

"Maybe you're wrong."

"Was I right about the skiing?"

"You were wrong about inviting Ari."

"The week isn't over yet, pal."

18

After dinner that night, Jake escaped to the fire-pit alcove down at the lake. When he arrived at the chairs that looked out on the water, he spotted an old tin can half-hidden behind a clump of grass and plucked it off the ground. He set it eight or nine feet in front of his chair, picked up a handful of tiny pebbles, and slumped into the chair. First toss a miss. Same the second. Third hit the side of the can. Fourth? A complete miss. Fifth, the tiny stone hit the back of the can and dropped in.

A moment after Jake sank his third stone, the rustle of leaves and branches lifted his head. He squinted into the fading light to see who was coming to shatter his solitude. Ari. Not again. Wasn't there anyone else this woman could talk to?

"It looks like we both like the same spot."

"Apparently." Jake tossed another stone toward the can. Didn't come close.

"Nice throw."

Jake nodded and plastered a thin smile on his face.

"You don't have to worry. I'm only here because the couples are getting couplely. I'm not interested in a relationship."

Jake puffed out a laugh. "Stop reading my mind, it's disturbing."

"No, not a mind reader." Ari smiled and sat on the arm of the chair next to him. "Just somewhat astute at reading the extremely obvious. How could anyone miss it, the expressions that fly off your face every moment I'm around you? The way you often find something you have to do when I walk into the room?"

He scrunched up his face. "That bad?"

"Worse."

"I thought my Switzerland impression was YouTube-worthy. Viral potential, you know?"

"Not quite. It's more like the North Pole." She smiled. "I'm not taking it personally. Should I?"

"Nope. Not for a second. I'm just in the same spot it sounds like you are. Not really interested in getting involved with anyone right now. That's all."

"I won't take much of your time."

"Good."

Ari laughed and Jake joined her. Did she know he was only half-kidding, that half of him wanted her to leave immediately and the other half wished she'd stay forever?

"I just wanted to tell you a couple of things," Ari said. "First, I've decided I'm going to stay at least a few more days. Maybe the whole time."

"Oh?"

"I can tell you're excited."

Jake's face heated up. "No, I'm just . . . it's just that—"

"It's okay, Jake. I get it. Like I said, I know it's not personal. The other thing is, I simply wanted to say thanks for today out on the water. You made it easier to handle."

"It wasn't anything." Jake leaned forward and picked up another handful of pebbles. "Camille and I aren't the best of friends, so when she starts doing her 'I'm better than you so let me put you in your place' thing, it doesn't take much to get me going."

Ari held out her hand palm up, and Jake stared at it. Five seconds. Ten. She didn't move, and he finally spilled half his tiny stones into her palm.

"Thank you." She tossed her first rock and it pinged off the side of the can. The second one went in. So did the third. "Do you mind me asking why you're not friends? I thought all of you were lifelong buddies."

Jake sighed. Did he really want to get into this with a complete stranger? Yes. No. He looked into Ari's inviting eyes, found himself slipping into them, and yanked himself back out.

"No. We're not." Jake turned back to tossing pebbles at the can.

"Okay." Ari stood and started to shuffle away.

"Camille was, is, one of my ex's best friends. I never thought Peter should marry her in the first place, but he did. When the four of us started hanging out, she and my ex-wife took to each other immediately."

"Which makes having her here extremely awkward."

"Yes." Jake motioned toward the chair and Ari returned to it. "And last year when we were here, she defended Sienna's decision to divorce me, said some things to me that would even shock people on those smutty relationship TV shows. That did nothing to make me feel more chummy toward her."

"I see."

"You want to sit?"

Ari sat again on the arm of the chair. She watched Jake toss his pebbles at the can and occasionally threw one of her own. She was better, but he didn't care. The part of him that liked having her there was winning.

"I know Camille," Ari said in a voice so soft Jake almost missed it.

"What?" He frowned at her.

"Not like you think I mean. Not the Camille up there at the house, the Camille I lived with growing up."

"Sister?"

"Mom." Ari shifted on the armrest and stared at the ground in front of the chair. "My mom always had to win. Everything. I've been competing with her my whole life, so when Camille got out there on that board today, a lot of the old feelings came back."

"I see."

"You know how girls are supposed to subconsciously marry their dads?"

"Yeah, I've heard that."

"I did the opposite." Ari flipped her hand over. "I married my mom."

"Oh?"

"I loved Tony, but he had to win. In everything. I was a decent golfer in high school. I played on the team for three years and even came in second my senior year in district championships. When Tony and I got married we started playing together and I beat him easily, but soon after that he became obsessed with the game till he could beat me."

"And he gloated."

"No. It would almost have been better if he had. He pretended that wasn't what he was doing. Said he only played so we'd have a sport to do together. Of course when I suggested we learn how to cross-country ski together, he had no interest."

"Wasn't something he could get better at than you. No winner and loser."

"Exactly." Another toss at the can, another swish. "At dinner parties he always had to top a story I told with one of his own that was more entertaining."

"He was always onstage."

"Yeah." Ari tossed another stone at the can. Again dead center. Nothing but net. "There's an old quote about Teddy Roosevelt from his daughter Alice that goes, 'He wants to be the corpse at every funeral and the bride at every wedding.' That was Tony."

"And your mom."

"Yes." Ari gave a sad smile. "What about you? Who did you marry?"

It was the question he'd known the answer to the moment Sienna left him. Deeper down, the answer had been there from the early days of their dating. Too deep to stop him from promising to make her happy. Jake stared at Ari. Should he tell her? The truth he'd never spoken out loud?

Ari gave her head a slight tilt. "Please don't tell me if you'd rather not."

Jake rubbed his eyes. "She was beautiful and always into looking good."

His mind flashed back to a moment with Sienna six months before his legs were destroyed. They'd been scanning through photos on Jake's laptop to find a series of shots to enlarge and put on their kitchen wall. When a photo of them in the Bahamas during their fourth year of marriage flashed on-screen, Sienna pointed at it and said, "That one for sure."

The two of them stood up to their ankles in azure-colored water. Sienna wore a black bikini and Jake had on his navy blue swimsuit.

"I love that shot." She snuggled closer to him on the couch. "It's perfect."

"For the kitchen? Isn't that a little weird to have a shot with us in our bathing suits up in the kitchen? How 'bout we put this one in your project room or the master bathroom?"

"No, it needs to go in the kitchen. I love that shot. It's not a poster, you silly, it's just four by six. Small. No one will even notice it."

"Why that one?"

"You know why."

"You want people to notice it."

"Fine. I admit it." Sienna smiled. "I was the ugly duckling—"

"Who turned into a princess and—"

"Married the prince." Sienna waved her finger over the shot. "You and me. Royalty. I just want people to see us for who we are."

"I'm not a prince," Jake said. "Talk about the ugly duckling. I was the ugly frog."

"Maybe." Sienna laughed.

"Maybe? You've seen pictures of my bulbous form and my pimpled face. Maybe?"

"That's the point! That was then, this is now. Someone kissed you and you turned into the perfect prince. Handsome, smart, athletic . . ."

"Are you trying to say you love me?"

"Maybe I am." She giggled and kissed him. "Look at you. You're Adonis. Tan. Six-pack. Muscles. Gorgeous face."

"I don't work out to look like Adonis and the only reason I'm tan is because—"

"But it is a nice side benefit." She kissed him again, this time on his abs. "Let's never grow old, okay?"

"Might have a tough time keeping that from happening."

"Doesn't mean we can't try."

Jake rubbed his face again and glanced at Ari. "I stopped being enough for her. I couldn't be what she needed any longer."

Ari's only response was to toss another stone at the can. Dead center yet again. Jake motioned toward her chair.

"Listen, if you're going to force me to keep talking to you, you might as well get comfortable."

"I'd never force you to do anything." She stood, smiled, and strode away.

Jake rose and called after her, "I was kidding."

She waved without turning around and kept going. He watched her till she turned at the end of the path, stepped onto the stairs leading up to the house, and disappeared. Jake sank back into his chair and considered whacking himself on the head. Idiot. Embarrassment turned his face hot. But the stronger emotion vying for attention was one he refused to acknowledge. He couldn't think of anything he wanted more at the moment than for her to turn around and come back.

19

The next morning, with the sun just high enough to toss some of her light in Jake's direction, he sat in his kayak at the end of the lake and saw a shimmer from the corner of his eye. He whipped his head toward the spot, but before he could fix his eyes, the light vanished. He stared at the reeds where he'd seen the flash, willing it to return, but nothing came. But it wasn't his imagination. Maybe it was nothing more than the edge of the morning sun reflecting off the green stems of the cattails, but he refused to believe that. He knew what he'd just seen: the entrance to the corridor.

Without taking his eyes off the spot where he'd seen the shimmer, Jake grabbed the tiny anchor between his legs and dropped it into the water. The splash wet his arms, and the chill strengthened his resolve.

He grabbed the sides of his kayak and pushed himself up, then dragged his legs back, lifted them over the side, and slipped into the water without a sound. With slow, smooth strokes he swam toward the place between the reeds where he'd seen the flash.

A sensation stirred deep inside. God's voice, speaking so softly Jake couldn't decide if it was real. It had been so long.

Believe, Jacob.

"I believe. Help my unbelief."

Immediately the shimmer came again. Stronger this time. Longer. Jake kept his eyes fixed on the spot, and it shimmered a third time seconds later. Then again, flickering on and off like a lamppost that was coming to life. A few moments later the shimmer morphed fully into a razor-thin light, just enough brighter than its surroundings to illuminate a tiny opening far back in the cattails.

Another three strokes and Jake reached the cattails. He tried to stand but the water was still too deep and he went under. Panic surged through his body and screamed that when he surfaced the light would be gone. He sputtered to the surface, sucked in a mouthful of air, and searched for the light. Still there. Relief buoyed him.

He grabbed the cattails and pulled himself forward, then repeated the action and tried to stand again. This time his feet sank into the soft bottom of the lake, shallow enough for him to rest his legs, the surface of the water just below his chin. Deep breath. Push on. As he made his way forward, Jake watched the light grow wider, then narrow, then widen again. It . . . what? Pulsed? Was that the right word? No, it was more like someone was opening and shutting a curtain on the light.

By the time he reached the reeds where the light seemed to come from, the brilliance had faded into nothing, but it didn't matter. He saw the path, hidden by the cattails unless you were standing right in front of it. And he was.

It almost felt wrong to part the plants, but Jake dismissed the thought. He hadn't found the corridor as much as been invited in, and he wouldn't let any negative thoughts keep him from finishing this journey.

After ten paces, the ground turned from damp, to dry, to covered in a fine green moss softer than any carpet Jake had ever walked on. The cattails were almost gone now. The ones that remained were small and scattered. After a few more steps, the last of them transitioned into poplar trees with leaves that kissed his arms with an otherworldly coolness and seemed to inject hope and strength into his whole body.

As he eased forward, the leaves, the branches, even the dirt at his feet grew brighter. No, that wasn't the right word. Not brighter. The colors were different. More intense, as if the path were a photo and the color saturation had been amped up. Jake had no doubt he was still on this earth, but there was a feeling of holiness about this path as if heaven had infused it with a life he'd rarely seen, let alone touched.

He stopped for a moment and marveled at the trees. They formed a tunnel around him, giving him just enough space to walk through—maybe three inches of room on each side. As he looked back, he realized the trees were closing behind him as he passed, as if he'd been given an exclusive invitation into this Eden. The sounds of the birds on the lake faded and the quiet of the corridor was almost overwhelming. Anticipation rose in Jake till he thought he might explode.

The sensation of every molecule in the trees growing more vibrant intensified. He reached out for the green leaf next to him. His skin tingled, and the green seemed to soak into his fingers and feed a hunger he hadn't known existed till that moment.

Was he imagining the changes? Maybe. Maybe his anticipation had somehow created the sensations he was now feeling. It didn't matter. Whether it was truly happening or only in his head, at the moment all he wanted was more.

Jake looked down at his scarred legs. They should have tired by now from the swim and the push through the wall of cattails. But they felt okay. More than okay. He flexed his right leg and it felt stronger than when he'd slipped into the water.

He tilted his head back and pulled in a deep breath. The air was almost too thick to breathe, but as he pulled it into his lungs, Jake felt lighter. Stronger. Superman. He continued forward, the corridor now curving slightly to the left.

A few minutes later it straightened out again and twenty, maybe thirty yards ahead he spotted a thick screen of willow vines covering the end of the tunnel of trees. Jake stopped ten feet from the vines. He'd made it. Found it. More accurately, the corridor had found him. Nothing stood between him and his destination but a curtain of green. Laughter spilled out of him. He had no doubt what was beyond the veil. Only a few more steps and he would be in paradise.

He pulled in one more breath of that thick air, cleaner and more crisp than the air from the most glorious summer morning he'd ever known. Then he closed his eyes, thanked God, pushed the boughs aside, and stepped through.

As his eyes feasted on the field in front of him, the hope that he'd tried to kill shouted the truth about this world within a world. Here was a glimpse of the earth before the fall. More than a glimpse. This is how it was when life exploded out of every blade of grass. The world before it was broken and subjected to futility.

A rabbit streaked across the grass just in front of his feet and Jake wanted to laugh. A rabbit? It was faster than it should have been. Bigger. Of course it would be.

For a few minutes he wandered through the grass, spinning in slow circles, taking in the splendor of the meadow, the trees, the waterfall at a distance. When he reached the edge of a pond two hundred yards from the corridor, he stopped and watched the water flowing toward the lake.

No, he couldn't make the night he was burned vanish as if it didn't exist. It happened. No, he wasn't going to get Sienna back. But he could be restored to what he was before. Get his body fixed. Get back to who he was before. That was his core desire, and God had brought him here to bring it to pass. A line from the book of Matthew surfaced in his mind. *I have come to save that which was lost.*

The sense of power that swirled around Jake was palpable. He let it soak into him and fill him with images of how strong he would be again once the healing of his body came. He knew his legs and stomach and lower back would start to change at any moment. He had no doubt. Eyes closed, Jake turned his face toward the rising sun.

A minute later, maybe less, a tingling started in his right foot, then his left. It slowly worked its way up over his ankles, then into his calves. *Yes. It comes.* Restoration. Freedom to be himself again. His heart slammed against his chest and his breathing quickened. The tingling sensation moved faster, up over his knees, then his quads, hamstrings, faster still, till everything from the soles of his feet to his belt line radiated with a power he'd never known. After he couldn't hold them closed any longer, Jake opened his eyes and looked down. He cried out, but not in celebration. His legs hadn't changed, and as Jake stared at them, the healing sensation he'd felt turned to a dull ache.

Jake staggered forward and pain shot up his right leg. But it was nothing compared to the pain ripping through his soul. A hurricane of confusion battered his mind as he stared at the red distorted flesh holding him up. A second later they couldn't even do that. He slumped to the ground, all the strength in his legs sucked out.

Where was the healing? What had just happened? Why the tingling sensation and the feeling of strength shooting into his legs and stomach if they weren't going to be healed? The absurdity of the situation struck Jake like a fist to his jaw. There was no one here to explain anything to him. No guide, no instruction manual. No Leonard to try to pull answers out of. The only thing he had was an expectation he would be healed. And that was based on what? Nothing more than fragments of a legend and the cryptic musings of an old man.

Maybe this was just the first stage, to test his belief. Maybe the true healing was still to come. But Jake knew that was a fantasy. There was no healing coming. As he looked around the meadow, he realized the colors he'd thought were so brilliant were simply that way because of the early morning sun. Now they looked muted. The trees? The pond, the grasses? Beautiful. And ordinary.

Jake dug his fingers into the thick, wild grass. "Why, God?"

He bowed his head as the anger simmering deep inside fought to break out. He'd believed. How could he have found the corridor if he hadn't? How could he have gotten through if he hadn't believed? He'd made it. But there was no restoration here. No granting of his greatest desire. Nothing but a beautiful oasis that mocked his deepest need. Unbidden, tears welled in his eyes, and he didn't fight the grief of loss.

An image of Sienna, disgust and loathing on her face, formed in his mind so clearly it sucked the breath out of him. For the first time, he didn't fight that look or try to rip it from his memory. Jake embraced it, let the pain flood his mind and body and soul and heart.

His tears turned to heaving sobs that racked his body, and still more tears came. After an age had come and gone, he opened his eyes and let his gaze sweep over the field. It made no sense. But maybe this was it. Maybe Susie was right, and the legend had grown out of this beautiful place that was nothing more than a hidden oasis.

But the sliver of hope inside Jake had been unleashed, and it wasn't going back underground. Not yet. There had to be answers. Jake would find them. And he would start with Leonard.

20

As he clambered back into his kayak, Jake glanced around for Leonard, but the old man wasn't at the end of the lake. No matter. Jake would find him soon enough. The wind sliding in from the northwest whipped up a sizable chop on the water but Jake pushed through it, toward Leonard's house, ignoring the burn in his arms. It'd been too long since he'd had a decent upper-body workout, and this would make up for lost time. He reached the small cove in front of Leonard's house in thirty-five minutes and peered at the property.

The house was small with a battered deck out front. A weeping willow tree just off the corner of the deck to the right held the remnants of a kid's tree house. In front of the house was a carport. An old blue truck sat under the covering along with a small red scooter with a basket on the back.

A brown garage stood ten yards from the house. A midsized trawler that was probably once a brilliant white sat next to the garage. Probably designed for ocean fishing, given the build and the two motors hanging off the back. Leonard was tinkering with one of them.

Jake slid his kayak up to the small wooden dock in front of Leonard's property and tied it off on a dinged-up cleat. He climbed onto the dock and clumped across it. Leonard didn't give any indication he'd seen Jake as he crunched across the gravel driveway that led up to the garage.

"Hey, Leonard."

Leonard slipped a socket wrench over the boat's drain plug and gave it eight fast turns. "There. She's ready." He spun and stared at Jake. "You liking it here? Forgot to ask that yesterday."

"Yes."

"Good." He stuck his fists on his hips as a smile touched the side of his mouth. "Glad you took my advice."

"Me too."

"Same with your friends?"

"Yes."

"Good. Good. Nice to hear that."

Jake eased up closer to Leonard as the man rose and wiped off his hands on a purple shop rag. "I want to ask you about the corridor."

"You like fresh food?" Leonard pointed over Jake's shoulder and to the right.

"Can I ask you a few questions about it?"

Leonard cocked his head and squinted at Jake. "How 'bout I give you a tour of my garden."

"Sure."

Leonard's took up at least twenty-five square yards. As they strolled through it, Leonard pointed out his corn, chickpeas, zucchini, and cabbage. When they came to the northeast corner of the garden, Leonard bent down and squinted at Jake.

"You and your friends like cantaloupe?"

"Definitely."

Leonard reached down, pawed at the leaves, and plucked the largest of the cantaloupes from the vine and handed it to Jake. "Best-tasting cantaloupe you'll ever sink your teeth into. Guaranteed. So much better than that cataloged store-bought crud."

"Thank you."

"When you finish that one, come back for another. More here than I can ever eat."

They wandered through the rest of the garden, and Jake smiled at the lushness of what the old man had grown. When they reached the southwest corner, Jake frowned at the plant in front of them.

"You're growing pot?"

"Stupid question. What does it look like to you?" Leonard flicked his hand as if to dismiss the query. "Unless you've never seen the plant before. And I doubt that's the case."

"I just didn't take you for a pothead."

Leonard kicked the dirt in front of him and it landed on Jake's feet. "I'm not growing it for me, ya twit." Leonard pointed up the hill to his left. "The guy up there planted a crop. It failed—doesn't know the first thing about growing a garden. So I told him I'd grow it for him."

"And share in the profits."

Leonard gave him a disgusted look. "No. I wouldn't take a dime off that skunkweed. Makes people dumb. Poison for the lungs and the brain."

"Then why would you grow it for him?"

Leonard stared at Jake like he'd just stated that the sky was green. "I do it because he's my neighbor and he needed help."

"I see."

"No you don't, but doesn't matter." Leonard turned and strolled back toward his house.

"I want to ask you a few questions about the corridor. You said—"

Leonard didn't stop, didn't turn, but spoke plenty loud enough for Jake to hear. "You think I'm deaf? Heard you the first time you asked. Enjoy the cantaloupe."

"I found it."

Leonard continued walking away. "Yep. I know you did. I saw it on your face when you first got here."

"Then why won't you talk to me about it?"

"Congratulations, Jake." Leonard didn't turn.

"More than found it. I got through, Leonard. I made it to the other side."

Leonard whipped his frame around faster than Jake thought possible. As he lumbered toward Jake, the light in the old man's eyes grew in intensity.

"When?" As Leonard squinted at Jake, his countenance shifted from surprise to suspicion. "Don't lie to me, boy."

"You've been there, haven't you? On the other side."

Leonard stared toward the end of the lake. "You're a genius. You figured out the most obvious fact since man discovered water is wet. Discussion over."

Leonard trudged back up the hill toward his house.

"What?" Jake called after him. "Are you kidding? You give me clues, cryptic hints about how to find the corridor, then when I do, when I get to the meadow, you try to bury the subject? Why?"

The old man disappeared into his garage and Jake followed. He found Leonard standing in front of his workbench, fiddling with a broken pair of pliers, his breathing uneven. Jake stood halfway back, watching Leonard, waiting for the right moment to speak again. It was apparent the man could answer at least a few of Jake's questions, but even more obvious was that whatever answers his new friend held, they wouldn't be unearthed easily.

"You still here?" Leonard stayed facing the workbench, light from a small window casting him in silhouette.

"Yes."

"You gonna give me a speech about not leaving till you get some answers?"

"Only if it's necessary."

Five seconds later the pliers clunked onto the workbench. Leonard turned and strode past Jake without looking at him. Jake followed Leonard onto his deck, and they both settled into chairs that faced the lake.

"Start." Leonard gripped the armrests of his chair hard enough to turn his fingers white. "Tell me what happened."

Whatever Leonard's relationship with the corridor was, the mix of emotions was clearly love-hate. Likely a heavier dose of the latter.

"What are you waiting for?" Leonard barked. "I see it all over your face. You want to tell me."

"Okay, let's start by you telling me what you see on my face.

The letdown because there's nothing on the other side? There's no healing. No getting things fixed. Nothing on the other side but a field and pond and grasses and trees."

"Something like that."

"You said I'd find my deepest longing."

"Probably. Sounds like something I'd say."

"It's just a field."

"You already said that."

"So why the charade? Why string me along?"

"So you didn't get it." Leonard spoke the comment more to himself than to Jake.

"What I want most?"

Leonard wagged his finger.

"Right." Jake jerked his head to the side in exasperation. "Stupid question. Yeah, sure. It was great. Got exactly what I wanted. All my dreams came true and I'm going to Disneyland. Want to see my legs? My stomach?"

Leonard just stared at him, his mouth open, that gap-toothed grin mocking Jake.

"I need answers."

"Yeah?" Leonard kicked at a leaf on his deck. "And you think I can give them to you? Where'd you get a cockamamie idea like that?"

"It has to be more than a pretty little meadow."

"Why do you say that?"

"As I stood there next to the pond, I felt healing coming. I didn't imagine it. I didn't create it. It was real."

"From what you just said, it doesn't seem like it was real."

Leonard waved his finger at Jake's legs. "Seems to me that's exactly what happened. You imagined. All of it."

"I didn't imagine a corridor that didn't exist the day before. I didn't dream of it opening up with a flashing light showing me the way."

Leonard squinted into the sun. "The lake and sun create tricks that fool the eyes, young Jake. And the imagination of desiring minds takes over from there."

"Why are you playing games with me, Leonard? Why not tell me what you know?" Jake blew a hard breath through his teeth. "There's more on the other side of that corridor than green grass and tall trees. I see it in your eyes."

Jake spit out the last word and jerked forward in his chair.

"How 'bout you calm yourself down and describe what happened to you in a bit more detail?" Leonard raised both eyebrows. "Hmm?"

Jake stared and slowed his breathing. The old man could slam the door on this conversation in a second, and provoking him was a good way to make that happen sooner rather than later. There was more that Leonard knew, there had to be. But Jake couldn't force it out of him.

Jake sat back in his chair and told the story from the moment he saw the first flash till he made his way back through the corridor and climbed into his kayak. Leonard's only reaction during the telling was a few slight nods and an occasional *hmm*.

When Jake finished, Leonard folded his hands across his lap and said, "What is that place, Jacob?"

Jake clenched his stomach and fought down the urge to shout that this was exactly why he sat in front of Leonard at the moment, because he didn't know the answer. *Stay calm. Read the label on the bottle.* The lettering on Leonard's was clear. He didn't want to give Jake direct answers. The old man enjoyed a dance of conversation where he led with questions he likely knew the answers to.

"I'm not sure."

"You may not be sure, but I think you have at least formed a theory."

"I think it could be a fragment of heaven. Or Eden. Somehow it's a spot on this earth God has made that is untouched by the fall of man and creation that broke from its original design."

Leonard nodded slowly, never taking his eyes off Jake. "Yes, that works for me."

"Is that what it is?"

"I don't know for certain. But that's what I've always suspected." Leonard slowly tapped the tips of his fingers together awhile before he spoke again. "But that's not the critical question. The critical question is, do you want to go back?"

Jake didn't hesitate. "Yes."

"Why?" Leonard cocked his head and drilled Jake with his eyes. "What would you accomplish next time that didn't happen this time? What will you do to make the healing happen?"

"I don't know. But I'll keep fighting till I figure it out."

"Ah, yes." Leonard tapped his fingers together again. "That's good. That's the spirit you'll need."

"Why?"

"Because I don't think your next visit will be quite so easy."

"How do you know that? Tell me what you know about the corridor, Leonard."

Leonard smacked the armrests of his chair twice and leaned forward. "It's been good seeing you today, Jake."

"Answer me one more question."

"I might." Leonard scooted to the edge of his seat.

"Do you think if I can find my way to the other side again, that I'll be healed?"

Leonard snatched a shelled walnut out of a box that sat to the right of his chair and tossed it to Jake, then grabbed one for himself. "I suppose you've figured out this is a solo trip, right? That corridor's only wide enough for one person at a time."

"That's why Susie and I didn't find anything a few days ago."

"Yep."

"If get through again, will I be healed?"

"Can't you take a hint?" Leonard spit out a bit of his walnut and glared at Jake. "Ask a different question."

"No."

"You're a stubborn little stallion, aren't you?"

"I think you recognize yourself."

Leonard turned and muttered under his breath, soft enough that Jake knew the old man didn't think he'd be heard. "More than you know."

Jake let the comment go. It was enough to realize Leonard saw himself in Jake, and he knew Leonard wouldn't explain the comment if Jake confronted him.

"How bad do you want it?" Leonard stood and folded his arms. "What's it worth to you?"

"Everything."

"In that case, if I was betting my life on it? I'd say yes."

It wasn't the answer Jake expected, at least not with that degree of conviction, and it fanned the ember of hope inside him that refused to be snuffed out.

"I'll see ya, Jake."

Leonard didn't wait for Jake to respond. He ambled across his deck over to his door and stepped through it without looking back.

Jake sat on Leonard's deck and stared at the willow branches in front of him almost close enough to touch. He promised himself he'd be touching the curtain of willow branches at the end of the corridor again before this time tomorrow.

21

P eter's voice boomed out of the family room inside the house later that morning, loud enough that Jake, sitting on the deck, couldn't pretend he didn't hear the summons.

"Gather now, everyone. Let's get all those willing to join me in the living room. Here we go, here we go now."

Jake set down his book and pushed off his chair. By the time he reached his feet, Susie and Andrew had ambled over from the far corner of the deck and eased up next to him.

"I don't think this is an optional invitation," Andrew said.

"Lucky guess," Susie muttered.

They ambled into the living room. Andrew and Susie took the love seat next to the fireplace, Jake settled onto the couch.

"ATV day, baby!" Peter stood in the middle of the cabin's living room and did a dance that made him look like a hula dancer with epilepsy.

Camille laughed and said, "You do realize you look like a complete moron, don't you, dear?"

"Oh yeah, oh yeah, sing with me now, 'ATV day, baby, everyone's going now, we don't mean maybe.'"

Ari strolled into the living room and plopped down next to Jake on the couch. He tried to ignore the fact her leg touched his and she didn't move away. He pulled at his jeans and shifted a few inches to his right. If Ari noticed, she didn't show it. She pointed at Peter as she leaned toward Jake, her shoulder against his. "I've never seen him do that dance in the office."

Susie pulled out her phone and started filming. "This is going to be viral gold."

Peter immediately stopped, and Camille gave Susie a quick nod. "Thank you. It's the only thing that can quash his spastic gyrations."

"You love it and you know it, Cam." Peter grinned at his wife.

"What life would be without you, Peter, could only be imagined by sad poets," Camille said.

Peter pointed at her and winked. "Don't you know it."

Ari again leaned toward Jake, and their shoulders touched for the second time. "He's never like this at work."

"Then you are a blessed woman."

Ari laughed as Peter wagged a finger at Jake. "Hey! Only the privileged get to see Peter the Dancing Machine."

"What's the plan, Pete?" Andrew asked.

"We'll take your van so we can all go together, if that's okay with you and Susie."

Andrew nodded as Peter glanced at his watch, then announced, "Ten-oh-five now. We're outta here at ten fifteen."

During the hour-and-a-half drive out to the coast, Peter kept up a steady stream of advice on how they could get the most out of their ATV adventure.

"How many times have you ridden an ATV on the dunes, dear?" Camille smirked.

"Enough."

"Once." Camille held up a finger. "He's gone one time and now he's an expert."

"Okay, okay." Peter grinned and held up his hands in defense. "It's true, I've only been once, but I've watched a lot of videos on YouTube. Besides, if Clark 2.0 is going, I gotta go."

"Clark 2.0?" Ari said. "I thought it was just Clark."

"It's Clark 2.0 when we're going on an adventure together."

"I'm sure there's a story behind that."

"No," Jake muttered. "No story, okay, Peter?"

"Of course there's a story!" Peter laughed. "Three years ago I planned a trip for my now fourteen-year-old son. Taking him on his first backpacking trip. But two weeks before we head out, I break my arm and of course my son's heart as well. The moment I tell Jake he says, 'I'll take him,' and he did. Five days. Gave my son an adventure he still talks about all the time. Made it epic. Pretended they were Lewis and Clark blazing a trail to the Pacific Ocean. That's when I added the 2.0."

Jake kept his gaze fixed on the trees rushing by the van window even though he felt Ari's green eyes on him. That had been a good trip. Great, great kid. He didn't know Peter's son still talked about it. Jake couldn't stop a smile from breaking out.

After a few minutes of silence, Ari said under her breath, "I'm not sure I can do this. I had a . . . I'm really not thinking I'm up for getting out on the sand."

Susie patted her arm. "If you haven't figured it out by now, you're not allowed to get embarrassed in this group. We're just a bunch of misfit toys, and nothing you tell us is going to make us think less of you. So whatever deep, dark ATV secret you're hiding, you can tell us and it won't make a sandy hill of difference. Really."

"Okay."

"Tell, tell, tell, tell, tell." Peter rubbed his hands together and leaned in like a dog about to get a T-bone steak.

Ari laughed and batted at him with the back of her hand.

"When I was thirteen my family rented ATVs and I had a pretty bad wipeout. I broke my ankle and I've been scared of them ever since."

"That's it? That's the big dark secret? Come on, it has to be something worse than that."

She smiled. "Sorry, that's it."

"Go slow," Andrew said. "It'll be great."

"Well said," Peter chimed in.

Susie tipped her head back and stared at the van's ceiling. "Men, they're so darn sensitive."

Jake tried not to stare at Ari as they gathered outside the van, but he couldn't help himself from trying to gauge her true level of comfort. So when she caught him looking at her, he could only blame himself. And when she shuffled over to him, he had to say something.

"I bet you'll do fine." Jake shoved his hands in his front pockets. "I'll keep an eye out for you, and if you get nervous, you know, I'll, uh, try to talk you through it."

She smiled at him twice as long as necessary before responding. "That means a lot. Thank you."

The thick man behind the counter had a face that looked like a petrified rock, and his voice wasn't much more appealing. "You have a reservation? 'Cause you're not getting out there if you don't. We're totally booked today."

"Yes. It should be under Peter Danner."

The man took hold of his computer mouse and thirty seconds later said, "Six of you, huh?"

"That's right."

After they filled out the release forms, the man took their paperwork and turned his raspy voice to a young woman at the other end of the long counter. "I'm going to get these six out on the dunes. Handle things while I'm gone."

The young woman let out an exasperated sigh and continued to work at her computer.

Rock Face led them outside to three rows of ATVs—at least twenty-five in each row—and pointed at the first six in the front row. "Those are yours. Keys are in 'em, gas tanks are full."

Jake and Peter started to walk toward them when Rock Face threw up his hand. "Wait! Back off, Spanky. There's a few ground rules to cover, because even though you all signed those forms, I'm guessing none of you actually read them. Hmm?"

Rock Face raised his eyebrows to an exaggerated degree, but Jake had to admit the man was right, and a quick glance at the others confirmed the man's assumption.

"We have to cover three rules." He held up a finger. "Rule number one. Don't roll your ATV. Lemme repeat that. Don't roll 'em. It's bad for the machines and bad for you. Bad for your physical health and bad for your pocketbook, 'cause if your vehicle gets up on its side, you're slipping me an extra forty bucks before you leave. And don't think you'll clean out the sand and we won't notice. We will notice."

Rock Face held up two fingers. "Rule two. Don't trust your eyes out there."

He held up a photo, walked back and forth in front of the six of them, then smacked it three times with the back of his hand. "Whadda you see? Huh? Huh?"

"Sand," Andrew said as he tried to stifle a laugh.

"Nothing else?"

Peter and Jake peered closer, then shook their heads and fought back a smile.

The man smacked the photo again. "I can't see anything else either, and that's how it's going to look once you're out on the dune, but let me assure you, you're looking at a ridge with a six-foot drop-off in the middle of this picture."

Jake leaned even closer, and as he studied the photo, a razor-thin line in the center of the picture came into focus. "I can see it now."

"Exactly my point." Rock Face held the photo two inches from his face. "Once you focus and get up close, real close, you'll see the break. But you won't spot these till you're right on top of 'em, which means turning or stopping is a serious challenge. Keep your eyes open and the speed down and you'll be fine."

"Third rule." The man held up three fingers. "Have fun."

Jake smirked at Ari. Have fun? He didn't see that requirement coming from Mr. Personality. But Jake definitely intended to take Rock Face's advice.

After they all settled onto their machines, Susie leaned over and whispered in Jake's ear as she glanced at his legs. "You're not going to do something stupid out there, are you?"

"What are you talking about?"

"Do you remember the time when we were kids and you jumped your bike over—"

"Yes, Mom. I remember, thanks. And yes, I'll be careful out there."

Susie slapped him hard on the shoulder as Jake laughed and tried to avoid a second strike.

For the next forty minutes they soared over the dunes. Jake kept an eye on Ari for the first ten minutes or so, but it was obvious whatever fear she carried from her early teens evaporated the instant she got out on the sand.

Jake brought his ATV to a stop somewhere near the center of the vast track of sand and let the joy of the moment fill him. No, he wasn't on a mountain cliff five hundred feet above a raging river, or burning up his lungs racing along a back road trying to beat his personal record in an Ironman, but he was outdoors, feeling the wind whipping against his body, riding the adrenaline shot of being alive.

A moment later, Peter and Andrew pulled up next to him. Peter gave him the same look he'd given hundreds of times over the course of their friendship, but never since the incident. It was a look of challenge, a look that shouted the games were about to begin.

"Wanna have some fun with Andrew and me?"

"Without question."

"See that flag out there about a quarter mile away? There and back. Don't worry about the blind drops. I've checked it out twice, and as long as we stay within fifteen feet on either side of us, straight to the flag and back, we'll be slick. All fine and flat."

"Good," Jake said. "I'm not thinking rolling one of these would be any fun for body or wallet."

"Agreed," Andrew said.

"Losers buy the winner dinner?" Peter grinned.

"Deal," Jake and Andrew said.

"We go on three." Peter held up three fingers. "One. Two. Three!"

Jake gunned his engine, and his ATV shot forward on just his two back wheels. "Whooo-hoooo!"

A second later the front tires of his machine thumped back onto the sand and Jake leaned forward, low in his seat. The less wind resistance, the better. He would win this thing. He glanced to his right. Peter was a foot ahead of him, Andrew a foot behind.

For the next quarter mile the lead shifted back and forth every few seconds. Jake couldn't hear Peter's and Andrew's laughter over his own and the roar of the ATVs, but he knew they had to be busting a gut. This was too fun. And far too long in coming.

The flag loomed ahead and Jake maneuvered his ATV to the right. He wanted to attack the corner from a wider angle. All three of them tore into the corner less than a foot apart. The temptation was to throttle back in order to stay tight on the curve and not roll the ATV, but that would slow his machine enough for Peter to increase his lead to a point where Jake couldn't catch him on the return trip.

As he veered to his left, Jake leaned his body out over his machine to fight the centrifugal force. He wouldn't be able to pass Peter on the inside—he was too smart to let Jake take that path—but Jake was counting on Peter to play it safe. He did. Yes.

Jake shot ahead. Once he straightened out, he pointed at Peter, then to the ground. Laughter poured out of him as the rush of victory filled his mind. Stupid to get this worked up about winning a race around a flag on ATVs, but it wasn't the winning that mattered. Pushing himself did. It was the competition. Seeing if he could do better than he expected himself to do in a way that satisfied him like nothing else, a world he hadn't feasted on for over a year and a half.

Maybe he couldn't push his body any longer, but he could push this machine, and push his brain to find the fastest way out and back.

Jake glanced back. Peter was gaining. How? He outweighed Jake by at least thirty pounds, and the machines were the same. Nah, not the same, there wasn't any rule that the shop had to tune these things identically. Simple answer. Peter's was faster. But that didn't mean he would win.

Jake squinted at the hill of sand rising up ahead of them. It had slowed all three of them down on the way out, and he wasn't going to let it do the same thing to him on the way back. He veered slightly to his right hoping Peter and Andrew wouldn't follow. This race would come down to inches, and riding the flatter ground around the rise would provide the margin of victory Jake needed.

Jake glanced to his left. Yes! Peter and Andrew were heading up the rise. Already he was ahead. By the time they came down the other side, he would be ten or fifteen yards ahead. Jake flattened himself as much as possible and kept his throttle wide open. The thrill of triumph started to rise and lift his spirit to a place it had not been in an age. Then the ground dropped out from under him.

Without warning, the sand under his tires disappeared, and he shot out into the air as a truck-sized stone landed in his stomach. Time seemed to crawl forward like a slug as the front of his ATV tilted forward and Jake rose in his seat. But he wasn't sitting any longer. His hands still gripped the handlebars, but his body was now above the ATV and splayed out behind it, like one of those crazy motocross kids doing Superman stunts on their nitro-powered dirt bikes.

Then the seconds seemed to speed up and the front of the ATV smashed into the sand. Jake flipped over the top of the machine, his feet now straight up in the air. The momentum of his body ripped the handlebars from his hands. He twisted and from the corner of his eye saw the ground racing up to crush him. An instant later, his head and shoulder slammed into sand and he rolled to a stop. Sand filled his mouth, eyes, nose, and he spat onto the ground. His shoulder felt like it was on fire. Broken? Maybe. He rotated onto his back and thanked God for the helmet, closed his eyes, and tried to slow his breathing.

Seconds later the roar of an approaching ATV filled his ears, and he opened his eyes to find Peter jumping off his machine. Peter dropped to his knees as Andrew pulled up next to Peter's ATV. Seconds later, Camille, Susie, and Ari arrived.

"Talk to me!" Peter leaned down till his face was a foot from Jake's. "Are you okay?"

"I think so. Might have broken my shoulder."

"That was an idiotic idea. My fault. I never should have sugg—"

"Not your fault. I veered from the route. Totally my screwup."

⸻

Two hours later, Jake walked out of the emergency room they'd found in a town ten miles north on Highway 101.

"How's the shoulder?" Peter stood and strode over to him. "You going to live?"

"Painful, but not broken. Just badly bruised."

Peter dropped his voice. "Was it worth it?"

Jake glanced down the hallway to his right and left. None of the rest of them were there. "Where's everyone else?"

"Went to grab all of us something to eat and get gas."

"Yeah, it was worth it." Jake gave Peter a half smile. "You know it was. I've been dying of thirst and was just handed a gallon of water."

"Enough to quench you for a while?"

Jake didn't have to think about the answer. "No. Not even close."

"Why? I don't get it."

"I love the rush of competition, the adventure, pushing myself, but that wasn't me doing the work, it was a machine. All I did was pull down on a throttle and turn some handlebars back and forth."

"You did more than that. You—"

"You don't have to placate me, Pete. You like the outdoors. Doing a little waterskiing, going on a stroll down a hiking trail. For me it's different. The mountain climbing, the mountain biking, triathlons—that is who I am." Jake popped his fist into his palm. "Who I was. Losing my legs is about more than just yanking me off the dating circuit. It's taken me away from . . . I don't know who I am anymore."

22

After dinner that night, Susie set a drink on the armrest of Jake's deck chair and took a sip of her own as she plunked down next to him. She kicked off her shoes and set her feet on the wooden ottoman in front of her chair. Jake peered at her stony face, but she didn't turn.

"Are you going to say anything?" he asked.

Silence.

"Sooz?"

"Do you find it at all ironic that you teach people how to discover what's on their label, but you have no clue what's on your own?" Susie took another swig of her drink and kept staring straight ahead. "And even if you did, you wouldn't be willing to admit it?"

"I know what's on my label."

"Yeah, sure you do. That's why you had to be an idiot out on the sand today. Proving you're still a stud. You have no idea what's on there."

"I wasn't trying to prove anything, and, uh, yeah, I do know what's on my label. I went down that path nine years ago when I started my company. Did it again two years ago. Went through my own process, with input from close friends. Like you. Or did you forget we did this? I don't teach what I don't know."

"Has anything happened during the past two years that might have changed the label?"

Jake didn't respond.

"Want to know what I think? I think you have a few typos in your text because of certain life events." Susie twisted to face him. "In fact, I think you have more than typos. I think you have whole sentences blacked out and lies written over the top of them. But that's only what you're seeing. I'm still reading the old label, all of which is still true.

"But again, you no longer believe what's written there. You've shut yourself inside your bottle and because of that, you're not only not helping yourself, you're not helping anyone else with their labels either."

"What are you saying? Helping people discover what's on their label is my life."

"Used to be, yeah, used to be. But not anymore." Susie thunked her glass up and down on the armrest of her chair in a slow cadence. "Now it's your job. You've stuffed the 'it's my life' part down deep in a basement you've bolted shut. And as much as I can, I understand why, but if you really want to continue to help people see what's written on their souls, you need to be willing to read what's being written on yours. Not what was written back then, what is being written right now."

"Oh, so here it is. The moment where my little sister comes and lectures me on what I need to do in my life to have it make sense? To get it fixed?"

"Nope."

Susie sat back in her chair and took slow sips of her drink as Jake stared at her.

"I get it. You think your mere presence here will cause me to squirm till I finally talk about what I'm feeling toward Ari and what I should or shouldn't do about it."

"Ari is such a small part of this, but yes, that would be a place to start. Time to risk it."

"You think I should stop hiding. Tell her what happened to me."

"Yes, but not for the reason you think you should."

"Oh really?"

"Yes, really. You believe you need to take the risk of telling her so you can see if she'll reject you. That way you can put yourself out of your misery, one way or another."

"Sounds like the right reason to me."

"I disagree."

"How can I take a bigger risk than that?"

Susie's face was full of hope as she sat up and took Jake's head in her hands and shook it.

"Listen to me, big brother. You're on a journey. No big revelation there. But you think it's to find someone who will look beyond your scars and love you regardless. You think if you do find this mystery woman, her acceptance will restore the place Sienna gouged out of your heart. But that's an external journey, one that ends with a person, whether that's Ari or someone else. I think you have a more complex path you need to follow."

Susie popped Jake's knee with her fist. "You need to tell her so you can stop fixating on her and move on to the deeper thing that you want most in the world. So deep you don't even know what it is."

"But you do."

"No," Susie said. "I'm not saying that. But I am saying you need to get off the path to Ari and onto—"

"The path that leads back to me."

"Yes." Susie patted him on the knee. "Yes, my dear brother, yes. You need to take a journey inside the bottle and forget about what people are seeing on the outside."

"I know what's on the inside. It greets me every day."

"Oh really?"

"Yeah, really." Jake held his breath, then let it out in a slow stream. "You want me to get gut-level honest with you, sis? I mean, really bare-my-soul-to-you-type honest?"

Susie's breathing slowed and she looked at him as intently as she ever had, then gave one slow nod.

"What's inside the bottle is not enough. I'll never be enough. Never."

Susie's eyes never left him as she waited for him to speak again. She didn't need to ask him why. Everything about her was inviting him to dive in. Maybe it was time to take the plunge.

"My mom didn't die in a car accident, Sooz." Jake let out a bitter laugh. "Can't believe after all these years I never told you the truth."

He turned away and stared at the sky as the memory of those days back in the spring of '89 hit him like a hurricane.

"I'm going to the school bus now, Mom."

"Okay, Jakey. Be good."

"I'm trying." He pushed open the screen door and stopped. "Really, I am."

"Try harder." His mom crushed out her cigarette in an ash-tray full of butts and closed her eyes. "You knocked over your milk again last night. How many times is that this month?"

"Twice."

"No. Not twice." His mom opened her eyes and fixed her gaze on him. Cold eyes. Dead eyes. "Not even close to twice. Five times. Five! Too many. You're wearing me out, Jake. You're going to be the death of me, I swear."

"I'm so sorry. It won't—"

"—happen again. I know. I know you're sorry, Jake. I know, I know, I know. And I know 'it won't happen again.' But it will. It will." She closed her eyes again. "You make Mommy so tired sometimes. The mud you tramped in last month, the cuts I have to deal with when you fall off your bike. The mess in the bathroom. And your room. Good golly, Miss Molly! Do you know what that does to me?"

"I stopped riding my bike. And I keep my room clean. All the time. And my side of the bathroom is—"

"Fine!" Jake's mom slapped the table. "But your sister leaves that bathroom a pit." She put another cigarette to her lips and lit it without opening her eyes. "I'm exhausted, Jakey. Just be good."

"I'll vacuum again today when I get home from school."

His mom's head fell back and she opened her eyes and looked at him with a lifeless stare. "If you come home today from school and I'm gone, then you'll wish you'd been a better kid and not so wild all the time. You understand me?"

Jake shuffled up to his mom, his Captain America backpack now feeling like it weighed a thousand pounds. He took his mom's free hand. "Feel better, okay, Mom? And take your pills, okay? Promise me, Mom. Promise? Take your medicine, okay? Please?"

She pulled away and gave him a sick smile and pulled a long drag from the cigarette. "I'll try to remember, but if I forget, you know whose fault it is."

Panic rose in Jake, his breath quickened. "No, don't say that, Mommy. I'm going to be better. I promise."

"I'm kidding." She waved him off and took another long drag.

"Promise that you're kidding and nothing will happen? Promise."

"Just be good, all right? And stop exhausting me all the time."

Now the memories came like flashes of lightning. How every day during the spring of '89 he begged her not to kill herself. How he'd begged his dad to help her. The flowers he plucked for her out in the field behind their home. The times he sat his parents down and tried to get them to talk to each other.

Ten years old and trying to get his dad to stop controlling every second of her life. Trying to get them to have a conversation that was about more than his dad telling his mom exactly what to do, and his mom looking at him with her dead eyes.

"I think if you guys would talk about things together, it would be really, really good. And then you can listen to what each of you is saying to each other, then maybe . . . I mean, if you'd really listen . . . and then one of you would go first to try to listen and then—"

"Okay, Jaker. That's pretty sweet of you to try." His dad gave that plastic smile that really meant shut up and lifted Jake off the couch. "But Palmer children don't talk to their parents that way, do you understand? You're not my counselor, young man."

"I'm just trying to . . . Mom needs you to—"

"Jaker?" His dad's eyes went hard like they always did before he was about to slap Jake, and Jake went silent. "There's ways we do things around here, and ways we don't do things. If you can't figure out which is which, we'll need to have another kind of conversation, which you won't like very much."

"Okay, Dad."

The decades-older Jake stared at Susie, her face full of sorrow, eyes wide.

"What happened, Jake?"

"I got off the school bus that day and had all these plans to make my mom feel better. Was going to vacuum the whole house. Then dust. Then sing this song that made her feel better. It always worked, this simple little silly song I made up that made her laugh. That made all her sadness go away, if only for that moment."

Jake's voice sounded hollow in his ears and his mind drifted away as if someone else was speaking. "I was the one that found her. Didn't know what to do. Finally remembered to call 911.

"I waited for the ambulance to come and cried every tear I had. Then I stood in the corner of the room, frozen, and watched the paramedics try to revive her. They worked for so long, at least it seemed like such a long time. But even at that age, I knew it was pointless. She was gone, just a dead body. And as I stared at her I realized something. I knew something in my gut that I've never forgotten."

"What did you know?"

"I realized I was the only one who could have saved her. And I didn't."

"That's not true, Jake." Susie took his hand.

"Yeah, it is. If I'd been enough, if I'd been what she wanted. If I'd been a better kid, if I'd only come through. I could have prevented it. I know I could have. If only I'd . . ."

"What? What else could you have done?"

Jake stared at Susie, her eyes imploring him to believe the truth, but he didn't know what that was. "I could have done something."

Susie squeezed his hand. "No, you couldn't. You were ten years old. Ten!"

"I could have stayed home from school, I could have been there to stop her."

"You could have dropped out of school at age ten and stayed home every day? Your dad would have allowed that?"

"No, no . . . but I could have . . . I could have . . ."

"Look at me, Jake." Susie took both his hands. "You know what I'm saying is true. You know a ten-year-old kid isn't responsible for his mom and dad. Please tell me you know this."

His mind raced through the times he'd told his mom he loved her in the weeks and days before she'd taken her life. The notes he left for her, scrawled in his ugly ten-year-old handwriting. How he tiptoed into the kitchen and out onto the back patio every morning that spring and stared at the smoke from her cigarette snaking its way up to the heavens and prayed that she'd get well. But it wasn't enough.

"I know it with my head, Sooz, but my heart sees it much, much differently." He dug his fingers into his hair. "I can't go down her road. I won't."

"No, you can't. And you're right, you won't."

"But how do I get the regret out of my head?"

"You have to let that go, Jake. By facing it. You have to."

Jake sighed through clenched teeth. No, he didn't have to.

"Are we done?" Jake started to get up, but Susie pointed at his chair and he sat back down.

"I'm so sorry about your mom, but I need to tell you something because I love you. This might sound harsh in light of what you've just told me, but for the same reason, this is even more important for you to hear.

"You have a decision to make. About what kind of man you are. Are you going to stay on the fringes, circling the deep pain of your life for the rest of your days, or are you going to risk it all and step inside and face whatever you find?"

He frowned at her. "Go inside where?"

"You know exactly where." She poked him in the chest. "In there. Deeper than you've ever gone before."

Jake got up again, and this time Susie didn't try to stop him. He looked down at her and gave two quick nods. "What if I told you that's exactly where I'm going tomorrow morning?"

"I'd ask you what that means."

"I'd tell you I have no idea, but I'm going anyway."

23

As dawn crept over the hills to the east, Jake pushed through the tunnel of trees toward the field. It seemed narrower this time, as if the branches had grown closer in just a few days, the green boughs now brushing his shoulders as he moved forward.

He pushed past the curtain of willow branches at the end of the corridor and stopped. The instant his foot hit the ground on the other side, a surge of adrenaline sent him stumbling to his right. Nothing looked different. The trees, the grasses, the pond, the waterfall were all the same. But he knew the meadow had changed.

This time he felt like he was part of the field. He was in the field but the field was also inside of him. The thought made little sense in his head, but this wasn't a place of the mind—it was of the heart. Peace coursed through his body, mind, and soul, and he had no doubt he was about to be given what he wanted most in the world.

He closed his eyes, breathed deep, then opened them and eased forward. The ground under his feet felt softer, the breeze coming straight at him warmer than his first time here, the calls from the birds in the trees more melodic.

Jake didn't think, didn't need to. He allowed himself to be drawn in without consideration of where his feet would take him. A rabbit scurried out from under the brush like before, but this time it spotted him, stopped, and stared directly at him for a moment before scampering back into the brush and disappearing from sight.

He looked back at the branches of the willow tree now blocking his view of the corridor. The real world had vanished. Real world? This one he now stood in was as real as anything on the other side. His friends back at the house were the ones living in a dream.

Jake turned back and now the meadow did look different. Nothing significant. Little nuances like the color of the sky overhead. A deeper blue. The emerald leaves of the aspen trees more vibrant. He closed his eyes again and strolled forward, breathing air that seemed to make him lighter, that seemed to pour strength into his arms and body and legs. His skin tingled as if it was . . . yes, on fire. But a fire of power and life.

When Jake opened his eyes again, he found himself standing at the edge of the pond. The water seemed clearer than before, the creek feeding it more animated as it cascaded over the glistening boulders, the tall grasses at the pond's edge greener than before.

An otter broke the surface on the other side of the pond and Jake watched the ripples slowly come toward him till they reached his side. As they died he studied his reflection in the water, starting with his face and working his way down his body till he fixed his gaze on his legs. As he stared at the mirror image, Jake shook his head. Not possible. The reflection in the water couldn't be accurate.

Jake staggered back and went down hard when his heel caught on something behind him. He tried to catch his breath—not from the fall but from wonder—sat up, closed his eyes, and begged God to make the reflection real.

When he opened them he stared at his legs, mouth cracked open. They were whole. Perfect. His skin faultless, muscles sinewy and strong. He flexed one leg, then the other. Jake reached toward them in slow motion as if his legs weren't real and if he touched them they would morph back into the repulsive, scarred sticks he'd lived with for the past year and a half.

A finger, then two, then his whole hand. They were real. Laughter started deep inside and spilled into the early morning air like a geyser. Without looking, he reached back and ran his hand over his right calf. Smooth. Perfect. Was it there? His M-Dot? He twisted and looked down. Yes. There, the dark red of the ink, the black outline, both as fresh as the day he'd had it done. Unbelievable.

Wait. Had he been healed completely? Jake leaped to his feet and tore off his shirt. He jerked his head down at the same time his hands fumbled on his hips, his glutes, his upper thighs. Yes!

Jake kicked off his shoes and dove into the pond. Was that okay in this holy place? *More than okay,* his heart shouted. This was a time to immerse himself in the wonder of what God had given him and let God's joy course through his body like a flood. Why had he doubted? Why had he pushed God away for so long?

Forgive me.

He swam toward the other side of the pond. Halfway across, a realization struck him though it should have already been obvious. Not only had his body been healed cosmetically and structurally, his strength had been restored. The muscles he'd worked so hard to develop had returned to what they'd been before. Maybe stronger.

When he reached the other side, Jake pulled himself from the water and took off in a full sprint toward the far side of the meadow, then ran full out in a circle around the entire field. It had to be at least a half mile around. Yes! No worry about his body overheating. When sweat seeped from his lower torso he swiped it onto his fingers and stared at the water and laughed. To sweat again! Seemed strange to celebrate something that had always been such an irritant, but it was so right.

When he reached the tree line where he'd started, Jake jogged to a stop and let his gaze sweep the meadow again and again. Whatever this place was, it was without question a slice of heaven. Why God had created it, who could know? Why did only certain people find it? No idea. All he knew in this moment was a gratitude toward God he couldn't express in words.

"Yes, Lord!" He shouted it with everything inside, his arms thrust to the heavens. Then he fell back—*floated back* would be more accurate—and collapsed onto the lush grass. His arms were wide, his legs splayed out as laughter again poured out of him.

Time slowed till it slipped away. He lay in the meadow and let the wind blanket him. Finally he rose and looked at the corridor that would take him back to his life. Life the way it should be.

Jake shook his head. He was healed. Jake grabbed his legs and squeezed his flexed muscles. Whole. Restored. Time to show the world.

He sprinted back to the pond, scrambled at its edge, picked up and put on his shirt. The pull to stay in this paradise was strong, but the lure of the corridor was stronger. He had to go to his friends, shout to them and the world about what God had done.

Had to find Susie, find Leonard, find Peter, and tell them what had happened. An image of Ari filled his mind. For the first time since he'd met her, Jake allowed his deep feelings to surface. He was drawn to her like he'd never been drawn to another woman. More than anything he wanted to get to know her, see if what he'd imagined in her eyes when she looked at him was real. He could almost believe God had orchestrated their meeting through Peter, and this orchestration was now a resounding new symphony. Now he was whole. Now he could be who he really was with Ari.

She'd already stayed two days longer than originally planned. Maybe she'd be willing to stay a few more. Maybe he would invite her for a long walk as soon as breakfast was over and tell her about his journey.

Jake sprinted back toward the curtain of willow vines and plowed through them ten seconds later. He turned and took a last glance at the meadow, trying to burn an image of it into his mind. But he knew he didn't have to try hard. The memory of this morning would never fade.

He half ran, half walked through the winding tunnel of trees that would lead him back to the water, back to his kayak, back to the cabin. A minute later the ground grew soft. Thirty seconds after that Jake was up to his waist in water, pushing aside the cattails.

As he slogged forward, the cattails seemed to have grown stronger, and he had to push harder to get through them. But soon he reached the spot where they thinned and he was swimming toward his kayak. His strength wavered a bit as he swam, the adrenaline of his encounter with heaven subsiding, but the peace it had given only increased.

How was he to describe what had happened when he got back to the house? He would show his friends, of course, but what words could he find to tell them about the meadow, his restoration, the overwhelming sense of God in that place? Would they believe him? After one look at his legs they would have to. And what if they wanted to come with him next time? Maybe Leonard was wrong. Would he even be allowed to find it again?

Enough. Their questions would come and he held no answers. But if possible he would do everything in his power to bring them all to the corridor.

Just before reaching his kayak, Jake glanced at the spot where Leonard had been when he'd first reached the end of the lake. He didn't expect the old man to be there, and he wasn't. But Jake had hoped he would be. Who to tell first? Had to be Leonard.

Jake hoisted himself into his kayak with more effort than he expected and slid into the seat. The experience had understandably sapped as much energy from him as it had given. It made sense. He hadn't run like that for eons, and even in a place like the meadow, his lungs weren't accustomed to that kind of exertion. Let alone his mind being overwhelmed in a state from the emotional roller coaster. He grinned.

As Jake reached for his paddle he caught a glimpse of his legs. His scarred, burnt legs.

24

Darkness swept over Jake, then through him, into the cracked parts of his soul so deep he had never sensed them before. His gut tightened and he fought to pull in ragged breaths. Sweat broke out on his face and hands, his arms. But not below his waist. Not on his legs. Not on his feet.

His vision went black and he clutched the sides of the kayak to keep from toppling into the water. He gasped for air and tried to keep from looking at his legs, but he couldn't stop himself. What kind of sick joke had God just played on him? Did he enjoy this kind of cruelty? Jake fought to keep his heart from shutting God out as he'd done for a year and a half, to believe God was in this somehow, some way. But how could he? The meadow wasn't heaven, it was hell.

For a moment he wondered if what he'd experienced on the other side of the corridor was real. But only an instant. No! He refused to believe it. It wasn't a dream, wasn't a vision, wasn't some deluded fantasy he'd concocted inside his head. His gaze whipped to the place on his arm where he'd scraped it against a tree during his run. The scratch was there, a thin line of blood hardening. He clutched at it as if to make sure he wasn't seeing things.

Jake twisted in the kayak, his eyes seeking the corridor. But it wasn't there. Vanished. Even the reeds he knew he'd broken to reach the lake looked like they'd never been touched.

"No!"

Jake screamed the word over and over till his voice grew ragged.

"Why, God?" Jake whispered toward the cattails, but the only response was their slight movement as a breeze came in from the east. There would be no answer, even if the corridor didn't exist anywhere but inside his head. No! He wouldn't consider that for a second. He'd been healed. It was real. There had to be something missing, something else God wanted him to do.

Steady. He had to take his time. Think. Make rational decisions. Jake glanced again to the spot where Leonard had bobbed two days ago. Yes. That was the smartest move he could make.

He didn't care if his body would overheat. He'd let it cool in the water as soon as he reached Leonard's. As he covered the distance to the old man's home, Jake tried to pray, but words abandoned him. Or maybe he was too angry to pray. Angry. Stunned. Betrayed.

By the time Jake had taken five strokes forward, the breeze kicked up to a full-out wind, plowing straight into him with gusts up to at least fifteen miles an hour. Perfect. The ideal complement to the horror he'd just been through.

Jake struggled against the wind, his arms sapped of strength, his stamina flagging. But he kept pushing. Leonard would have answers. He had to. Tiny whitecaps danced on the water, sending spray into Jake's eyes and soaking his shirt, but he continued to ignore the burn in his arms and concentrated on steady strokes. Dig in, pull, repeat.

Finally he reached the gentle curve of the land as it swept around to the left, and Leonard's home grew slowly closer. Three minutes later he reached the dock and laid a hand on the gray, weather-worn planks and slowed his breathing. *Relax*. Answers were coming. They had to.

Jake got out of his kayak and slipped into the water next to Leonard's dock. He let the coolness of the water seep into his body for two, three minutes, then pulled himself onto the dilapidated dock. The boards creaked under his feet as he strode across them, but the sound barely registered in Jake's mind.

"Leonard!"

Jake went to the garage and swung open the door. Nothing. Next, the house. He banged on the sliding glass door. No answer. Jake pounded it again. Again, no response. Jake tried the door. Unlocked. He stepped inside.

"Leonard? It's Jake. I have to talk to you."

There was no sign of the man. Not in his garage, house, garden. Yet Leonard's truck and scooter were there. As was his boat. Jake strode around to the side of the house and gazed up at the hill behind Leonard's home.

There. Movement up on the hill two football fields away. Too far away to be certain it was Leonard, but who else would it be? Jake took a deep breath. Yes, the hill was steep and the sun was getting warmer, but if Leonard had made it up there, so could Jake.

He stopped after fifty yards. He'd paddled over from the corridor too hard. There wasn't enough strength left to climb this hill. But his desperate need to get answers drove him upward. In another two minutes his breathing had turned to panting and he stopped. Had to catch his breath, slow down. Leonard wasn't going anywhere.

Maybe he should wait. It wasn't a bad idea. But Jake dismissed the thought after a few seconds. He couldn't wait. He would take it slow. Get there without dying. Then get perspective on what had happened to him in the field.

Jake shielded his eyes against the rising sun and scanned for Leonard. Yes, it was him. In silhouette, but Jake had no doubt.

"Leonard!"

If he heard Jake he gave no indication. Jake called again; again no response. Another forty yards. Then a stop, hands on knees, gasping, waiting for his wind to return. Jake turned and looked across the lake to where his friends would soon be rising to make coffee and breakfast. Not good.

If they were up when he got back, that meant Ari would be up as well. And even though he'd left his pants on the dock, what if she was on the deck above and saw him? What if she was down at the dock?

Stupid. Why was he thinking about something so asinine as her seeing him, when the disaster of the corridor should be at the forefront of his mind?

"Leonard!"

This time the man turned and gazed down on him. But only for a moment, then he turned back to whatever he was working on high above the lake. Jake continued his trek up the side of the hill, pausing just long enough to gather the strength to continue upward. Ten steps. Rest. Fifteen steps. Rest. He couldn't see Leonard any longer as an outcropping of rock blocked his view, but in a few minutes he'd reach the man and demand answers.

Twenty more yards. Come on. The air seemed to thin as he slogged on. One hundred more steps. Keep going. Almost there. And then he was. Jake stepped around the corner of the craggy rock and readied himself to confront his old friend.

But Leonard was gone.

"Leonard! I know you're close. You have to be. Talk to me!"

He scanned the area where the old man had stood minutes earlier. But there was no one. Nothing but browned grass and jagged rocks pushing through the soil in stony patches.

Nothing to do but head back down, return to the house across the lake, and pray they were all still asleep. He glanced at the sun. Probably seven by now, maybe later.

As he trudged back down the hill, all the emotions of the past three hours seeped out of him and left a dull kind of despair that throbbed at the back of his mind. He wasn't looking forward to faking his way through the day, trying to create answers as to what had happened. No explanation would come close to satisfying his aching soul.

When he reached Leonard's dock ten minutes later, Jake slipped back into his kayak and paddled across the lake toward the rental house, dreading what he was about to face.

Someone sat in the spot where he and Peter had talked the first night. Still too far away to tell if they were male or female. A few minutes later he could tell it wasn't Peter or Andrew. Too small for either of them. But no clue yet which of the women it was. If it was Ari, what would he say?

Hey, can you toss me my pants? Once I get them, I'll paddle far enough away that you can't see me, then put them on and paddle back before getting out of my kayak. I'm sure you'll understand, because you see, I'm too embarrassed for you to see me as I really am.

Jake clenched his teeth, paddled forward, and shot up a prayer. "Please let it be Susie. Camille even. Just not Ari."

Another minute and he'd know. He dipped his paddle in the water again and pulled hard. If it was Ari, he'd figure out a way to get ahold of his pants without looking like a moron.

Forty-five seconds later relief flooded him. It was Susie.

"Thank God."

She waved at him. He waved back and eased his pace. His arms were still trashed from the slog between the end of the lake and Leonard's place. When he was still twenty-five yards offshore, she called out, "Where have you been?"

"Just out for some time by myself."

Should he tell her? Without Susie, he wouldn't have ever discovered the meadow. He laughed sarcastically inside. Exactly. Without her he wouldn't have found the corridor and his heart wouldn't currently be in a blender. There would be time to tell her later.

"Hey, are you listening to me?"

Jake looked up. "Yeah."

"Where'd you go for this alone time?" Susie hugged her coffee mug with both hands, face full of anticipation.

Jake glanced up toward the house, even though he couldn't see it through the trees as he pulled up to the shore. "Can you do me a favor?"

"Sure."

"Go grab my pants? They're on the dock." He pointed to the shoreline. "I'm going to get out here."

Susie was gracious enough not to ask him why. She shuffled down to the water's edge and held out her coffee mug. "Hot cider. Want some?"

Jake shook his head.

"You okay?"

"Yeah. I'm good."

She marched off as Jake got out of his kayak and tied it up to a branch hanging over the water. By the time he clambered up the bank and settled into one of the four Adirondack chairs, Susie had returned from the dock with his pants.

"You want these?" She dangled them from her outstretched hand, just far enough away that Jake couldn't grab them.

He leaned forward to take the pants but Susie drew them back. "Oh, you do want them."

"Yes."

"Then tell me."

"Tell you what?"

"Tell me about whatever it is I see in your eyes."

"There's nothing to tell. Went for a long paddle, got some time to think about my mutated life, came back, and here we are."

"Okay." Susie draped the pants over her shoulder and started to walk away. "See you up there."

"Fine. I'll tell you."

Susie stopped.

As he looked at her, one of the few people in the world he still trusted, the mask Jake had been wearing shattered.

"Oh my gosh, you went back, didn't you? Did a little more exploring without me?"

"Why do you say that?"

Susie tilted her head and gave a thin smile. "You'd never make it in the World Series of Poker if I was playing. I know you too well. You held it together for a good three minutes, but that's about your limit."

"All right."

As Susie studied his face, hers slowly shifted from one of curiosity to one of wonder. She set her cider on the arm of her chair as she plopped into the seat, and her voice jumped half an octave. "No, are you serious? You found it, didn't you? You did."

Jake gave an almost imperceptible nod. "I got through."

"What!" Susie clutched both legs and leaned forward, astonishment splayed across her face. "What . . . what . . . what are you saying . . . are you kidding me? Are you kidding me? Tell me, tell me!"

He reached out for his pants. "Give them over first."

Susie handed Jake his pants as her face burst into a full-on smile. "Tell me every detail."

"I don't know where to start, Sooz." Jake slipped the pants

over his trunks and drew the string tight. "It was heaven and hell. More of the latter than the former."

"How can it have been . . . both?"

Jake started to tell her, then stopped and drove his teeth into his lower lip. It was one thing to shell out the facts of a remarkable discovery, but another whole can of meatballs to describe the agony of having your greatest hope be crushed just as it was about to be gloriously reborn.

"What's wrong?"

"I'm not sure I want to relive the pain."

"This is me, Jake. You know sharing it will be a kind of catharsis. You need to talk to someone about it. I don't know if I can offer anything, but I can listen."

Jake locked his hands behind his head, pressed his elbows together, then let his arms fall to his sides. "I got healed, Sooz. I mean completely healed. Everything from my waist down was restored. No, I'm not kidding."

Susie's lips parted and her gaze slowly moved from Jake's eyes to his legs.

He snorted out a bitter laugh. "Didn't take. So fun to have God toy with me."

"What . . . what happened? Everything."

Jake told her about finding the corridor, then finding it again and the story of the healing. "I'm sorry I didn't tell you earlier. I should have. I just—"

"I'm so sorry, Jake. It makes no sense."

"I know."

"Are you going back?"

"Yeah. Tomorrow morning." He gazed at her. "You want to go, don't you?"

"In a heartbeat."

"All right, then it's done. We go back together. Now that I know where it is, we can find it again—doesn't matter what Leonard says."

"But I can't."

"What? Why not?"

"That was my dream, Jake, the one I told you about. I dreamed about the corridor. That you went through. I had an overwhelming sense there was danger there, but also incredible hope. I didn't see what happened in the end, but one thing was certain: you were there alone and no one else was supposed to be with you."

He started to protest, but before he could, the sound of footsteps along the path from the dock stopped him.

"Hey, guys." Peter and Camille stepped into the clearing. "Ready for breakfast?"

"Sure," Susie said.

Susie glanced at Jake and told him with her eyes she wouldn't say anything to anyone.

"What about you, Clark?"

Breakfast? Go up and pretend that everything was normal? Nah.

"I think I'm going to take the day to get out of here, spend some time thinking about life. Need it."

Camille frowned. "How are you going to drive the boat today if you're not here? You have to drive the boat."

Jake stood and shuffled past Peter and Camille. "Nope. Don't."

"You okay, Jake?" Peter's voice floated toward him as he strode away. Jake flashed a thumbs-up but didn't turn around.

He spent the rest of the day exploring the roads in the area, finding nothing remotely interesting, but that might have been influenced by the fact that he couldn't get his mind off the corridor for more than two or three minutes at a time.

By the time he arrived back at the house late that night, the only person up was Ari. She sat out on the deck reading a book under the star-blotted sky. In another age he would have joined her. For a short time that morning he had stepped into that other age. And if there was any way to figure out how to make the healing stay, that age would come again.

Sleep that night came in starts and stops, but when his cell phone alarm buzzed at four the next morning, he was ready to roll.

25

Jake was about to push off from the dock at four fifteen when a voice floated down on him from somewhere on the stairs and he froze.

"Wait up!"

No. Please no. Heat shot through him. It was Ari. Halfway down the stairs.

His body went numb, as if he'd taken a swim in Novocain. Where was she when he'd left the house? He'd heard nothing as he got ready to go and prepared a snack in the kitchen. Heard nothing on the stairs as he slipped into his kayak. But now she appeared out of the predawn light like a ninja.

She clipped down the rest of the stairs till she reached the boating storage shed and reached for the kayak hanging on the back of it. She pushed up, but only one end of the kayak moved. They weren't heavy, so one of the cords holding the kayak in place must have been caught on something.

"Would you like to give me a little help here?" Ari stayed focused on the kayak.

"Did you see me?"

"See you what?"

Jake's heart throbbed in his ears. He tried to speak casually, but the question came out like he'd just stolen the last brownie at church camp. "See me get into my kayak as you came down."

She frowned at him as she struggled with the kayak. "What? See you, what do you mean see you? I see you right now. I saw you sitting in your kayak. Of course I saw you."

"Did you see me get in?"

Ari let her kayak go and it knocked against the boathouse. The boom was loud enough to reach the house sixty steps above them. She scowled at him and shook her head.

"Did I see you get into your kayak? That's the pressing question on your mind right now."

Jake pulled back and tightened the grip on his paddle. "Yeah."

Ari rolled her eyes as she untangled the cord, regripped the kayak, and lifted it off the wall.

"Is that illegal in these parts? Watching someone get into a kayak?"

"No, I just . . . I just wondered how far behind me you were."

She hefted the vessel over her head and clomped down the three stairs next to the shed and then down the ramp that led onto the dock. Ari set her kayak on the dock, squatted, and smiled at him. "You're a strange one, Jake Palmer."

Jake took a furtive glance to see if there was a chance of her seeing his legs. No. Safe. For now. What was wrong with him? All he needed was to stop caring what she would think. Stop letting every moment of her presence fill him with a stupid spark of excitement. Sure. Easy. Might as well grab a sponge and mop up the water coming over Niagara Falls.

"You mind having a guest this morning?" She smiled at him as she put on a dark red life jacket.

"Um, well . . ."

"Great." She grinned as she studied him. "I wouldn't want to intrude if you didn't want me here."

Her eyes told Jake she'd be coming no matter what he said. Didn't mean he couldn't try.

"You sure you want to come? My life is extremely boring these days. I kid you not. I'd feel really bad if my droning on and on about nothing made you fall asleep and you ended up in the water. It's cold."

"I see." Ari eased her kayak off the dock and into the water. She slid into it like she'd grown up around kayaks, despite her comments when they'd first met about being new to the sport, and smiled at him again. She shifted her life jacket, tightened it, and plucked her paddle from the edge of the dock. "Where are we going?"

Jake stared at her, dumbfounded. "Uh, I was trying to hint that I was thinking about being alone."

Ari stretched out her arm, snagged Jake's kayak, and pulled herself parallel. "You know what I think, Jacob Palmer? I think you like being around me. I think you have a civil war going on inside right now. One side wants to be alone, the other is almost excited I showed up here unannounced this morning. And I think one side has already won the battle—that is, if you're man enough to admit it."

Ari tilted her head and bathed him in one of her nova-bright smiles and Jake's heart stuttered. Not fair. Bad enough that she nailed him, worse that he couldn't bring himself to shove her away.

"But hey, if I'm wrong, let me know and whatever direction you head, I'll go the other way. No hard feelings whatsoever. Just give me the word. My ears are wide open."

Jake gripped his paddle tighter. Through gritted teeth he muttered, "A few minutes might be okay."

"Thanks, Jake." Ari flipped her dark hair back over her shoulders, pushed off from him, and took five quick strokes that propelled her across the dark water.

"I promise I won't ask any penetrating questions about why you've built a glass wall around yourself that you think no one can see into."

Oh yeah. Loving this. As if things couldn't get any worse, she zings me with that frameable one-liner. Why didn't she come right out and say she knew his secret? That she'd seen his legs as he clambered into his kayak?

Jake sighed, shoved himself forward, and dug into the water hard. Twelve strokes later he passed her. For the next three or four minutes there was no sound but the dip of his paddle into the water, no sensation other than the drops of water that ran down his black paddle with each stroke, then freed themselves and splashed onto the nylon skirt covering his legs.

Another ten hard strokes and he rested his paddle on his kayak and let himself coast into the unmarred surface of the lake. The sound of Ari's paddle carving the water drifted toward him, but he didn't look back, didn't look to his right when she came alongside him.

"I could be wrong."

"About what?"

"Both. The wanting me to be with you and the glass wall. So say the word, and I'll peel off and head for the other end of the lake."

Jake formed the words in his mind, but his heart hijacked them and he let out a deep sigh through tight lips.

"I'll take that as an invitation to stay."

All over the lake, the surface of the water popped as fish fed on flies darting too close to the surface.

The sun rose over the top of the mountain and their shadows—millions of miles long—shot out in front of them, their arms in unison as their paddles tore into the glass. Jake dug harder into the water and pulled ahead, but only for an instant as Ari matched his pace and they fell into synchronized strokes. The rotation of their paddles and the ripple of the water as they cut two paths through it would have been a rush if he hadn't been distracted with the task of cursing his stupid heart.

He dug deeper. So did she. His body started heating up from the exertion, but he didn't care. Jake increased his pace and his breath came in bursts. He glanced at her and spotted a bead of sweat on her brow. So she wasn't Superwoman after all.

He braced himself for her to kick into conversation, to ask him all kinds of penetrating questions he'd ignore or stumble through answering, but their first five minutes passed in silence. Then ten. Then twenty. By this time they were within sight of the end of the lake and the thick cluster of weeping willows that guarded the corridor.

What had he been thinking? This was the last place he wanted to be with someone else. And if he had to bring someone, Ari would be the last on the list. And what if she spotted Leonard? There was a good chance he'd be here, hidden, waiting and watching.

Jake stopped paddling and his kayak slowed, then drifted away from Ari. She lifted her paddle and slowed as well.

"What's at the end of the lake?"

"Why do you ask?"

"Because I can see it on your face. I think it's where you're going after we part company."

Her always bright eyes turned dark and seemed to pierce into the deepest parts of his soul. Jake clenched his jaw, hating himself for feeling so vulnerable. So weak. So exposed.

"What do you want, Ari?" Jake growled.

"The same thing you want."

"You want to tell me what that is?"

"All who call themselves humans want the same thing. We want to be known. Fully. Fully known and, despite being known to our core, fully loved. We want to be in a place where all our fear, our shame, our worries have no hold on us."

Jake didn't respond. Ari looked at him as if he were a kid about to figure out the secret to a card trick.

"I don't even know you, Jake. But I see something more than what's on your label. I see something so powerful rattling around inside your bottle, yet I don't think you have any idea what it is. But I do pray you find it."

With that, Ari paddled hard to the left, and within minutes she was gone.

26

This time finding the corridor was almost impossible. Jake knew where it was, but there was no light this time, no flashing to show the way. The reeds seemed thicker than when he'd been here yesterday, almost as if the corridor was playing tricks on him. It took Jake more than an hour to slice through the cattails and find the path. And the tunnel of trees had closed in enough that he had to walk sideways.

But Jake finally pushed the willow curtain aside and stepped into the meadow. His expectations scattered like seeds as he took in the glory of the field for the third time. Fear. Hope. Frustration. Exhilaration. Belief. Doubt. All fighting to be embraced. Would he be healed again? Maybe. Would it last? No, he couldn't let himself believe that even for a moment. Was he willing to be healed for just a moment, to feel the power course through his body again, even if it crashed and burned the moment he left? Without question.

He stood on the edge of the field staring at the meadow, trees, waterfall, their colors even more vibrant than last time. It seemed the grasses and trees had grown slightly taller in the past day.

He wandered farther into the field and made his way toward the pond. The sun appeared to be brighter here. If this place was a slice of heaven, maybe it contained more light than what the sun threw off. God is light. Maybe this place reflected the light of his presence. But the field wasn't heaven for Jake any longer; it was a place of aching for what he couldn't have.

But then a surge of adrenaline rushed through him, and even before he looked at his legs he knew they were restored again. Jake ran his fingers over his perfect skin, not sure whether to laugh or scream. He allowed himself a sprint forward, legs pumping like pistons, lungs burning, and the air of this Eden filling him with unquenchable life. But it was a cruel joke, and there was no point in putting off the agony he would have to face as his legs returned to their true state.

He shouted at God, the field, the trees, the waterfall, but there was no response. No voices, no impressions inside his head, no answers, no direction. But maybe, just maybe, it would be different this time. He'd fought hard and well to find his way back. Wasn't that what Leonard had said? Wasn't that the key to having the healing remain? Time to find out.

Jake strode toward the screen of willow branches, jaw tight, fists clenched. This time, even before he reached the curtain, he felt his legs go weak. Jake fought the compulsion to look down but gave in after only seconds. He stopped and screamed as he confronted the blotchy reds and whites of his contorted legs.

He sank to his knees, ignoring the pain of his skin stretching far more than it comfortably could. That pain was nothing compared to the pain once again searing his heart. He hadn't realized how much he'd believed this time would be different. How could he not? Hope knows no boundaries.

Jake sucked in air through his teeth and reached for the willow vines, already thinking of the questions he would ask Leonard, because he had no doubt the old man knew far more than he was revealing. But before he could step through, a voice from far away stopped him cold.

"You've chosen to leave so soon?"

Jake whipped around and scanned the field for the source of the voice. It came from the other side, but he saw no one. But a second later the figure of a man emerged from between the apple trees to the right and strolled toward him.

Jake's heart rate should have spiked, but something extremely familiar about the man, or maybe it was this place, made his appearance seem almost expected. He was about six feet tall, with a lean, muscular build. Blond hair reached his shoulders. Early thirties? Late twenties? Hard to tell.

"Hello, Jacob Palmer," the man said as he approached. "It is indeed a high pleasure to encounter you here."

The man's clothes would have fit in at a medieval fair, and yet they weren't tacky. They were strong, bold, if that was the right word. His shirt and pants were cut to flow as he walked. The dark green fabric seemed perfect against the lush surroundings.

The clothes, combined with the way the man moved, gave him the air of a regal warrior. Ten feet from Jake, the man stopped, hands on his hips.

"Do I know you?" Jake stared at the man.

"Of course you do." He gave Jake an inquisitive smile and

looked to the side as if to present his profile, then pounded his chest twice with a fist. "Don't you feel it right here?"

That was exactly where Jake felt it.

"Who are you?"

"A friend."

"Does my friend have a name?"

"Let us choose the name Ryan, that should work quite adequately. If you are in accord, of course."

"Who are you?"

"A guide."

Ryan strolled around Jake, not getting any closer, but Jake had the sensation the man was closing in. Jake eased to his right, matching his pace. They circled in their slow dance, their eyes never leaving each other. Jake felt no fear, no sense of foreboding. If anything, he felt a strange kind of comfort and confidence. He repeated his earlier question.

"Who are you?"

"You have inquired twice now as to my identity, and twice I have answered. That is enough for the moment."

"A friend. A guide. That isn't an answer."

Jake had met this man. No doubt of that. Spent time with him. A great deal of time. But not in the waking world. In a dream then, yes? But it wasn't a dream. Jake's dreams had always been filled with an ever-shifting cast of players, and none of them returned for a visit more than two or three times. Ryan, or whatever his name really was, had been a recurring player in Jake's subconscious for decades. From somewhere deep in his past, he was certain. But from where?

"You say I know you. I don't. But you do remind me of someone."

"Yes. Quite." Ryan stopped circling, placed his hands behind his back, and tilted his chin up. "As we just discussed, we know each other, so it follows that you would remember me."

"No, I don't know you." Jake stepped back two paces. "Or remember you."

The man's amused, cryptic smile was his only response.

"If I do know you, then from where?"

"This place"—Ryan moved his upturned palm slowly back and forth—"is beyond the realm of earth. I'm sure you've figured that out by now, given the condition of your body, so why couldn't more than one miracle occur here?"

An instant later a story and an image from a story flashed into Jake's mind.

"You can't be him. He doesn't exist."

The man shook his head, a kind but sympathetic look on his face, as if he were dealing with a toddler. "Instead of allowing your mind to convince your heart that what is happening here isn't real, why don't you let go and continue to believe. It will serve you better."

"When I was a child, I read The Chronicles of Narnia. My favorite story out of all of them was *The Silver Chair*. The fourth in the series, where Prince Rilian didn't know who he was any longer. Enchanted. Deceived."

"Yes." Ryan's face grew serious. "Believe, Jacob."

"You look just like I pictured he would when I read that book as a child. Your clothes. Your hair, your height, weight. Even your tone of voice. Everything."

"That would certainly follow." Ryan moved to his left till he reached the apple trees he'd appeared from. He plucked an apple off a tree. He took a bite. After a few moments of chewing, he said, "Delectable. Have you sampled one of these Galas? Perchance you won't want to. I would certainly suggest you carefully consider the ramifications of tasting this fruit. For I fear it would spoil you for any other apple the rest of your days."

Jake stared at Ryan with a fascination. His mind warred with that young-boy part of him that still believed in fairy tales. Who was this guy? An actor? An angel in disguise? His mind finally, fully cracking?

"What do you mean, 'that would follow'?" Jake narrowed his eyes. "Are you saying you're Rilian from *The Silver Chair*?"

"No. I am not." Ryan tossed the apple to the base of the tree and winked at Jake. "Not in the least."

"But you're saying you're real."

Ryan bounded forward so quickly Jake didn't have time to respond. The man stood two feet from Jake and extended his arm. "Take my forearm and I shall take yours."

Jake grabbed Ryan's sinewy arm hard, and his was squeezed the same in return.

"Is that the arm of imagination?" He released Jake's arm and grinned. "I think not."

"But you're saying you came from my imaginings of a fictional character created on a page?"

"You're not able to embrace that conviction?" Ryan tilted his head. "You cannot take hold of the idea that a fictional character can come to life?"

"Good. Now you're hearing me." Jake took two steps back. "No, I'm not tracking with the idea that a character in a book can come to life."

"Why not? It happens quite often in the movies and TV shows that the men and women of your world have created."

"That's my point. They might come to life within the boundaries of a story. Movies. TV. Books. That's made-up. Pretend. It doesn't happen—"

"Here? Ah, yes, therein lies the crux of your lack of faith." Ryan spread his arms wide and his gaze swept over the field. "Here you have reached a realm where there are no boundaries. But you fail to believe this."

Jake shook his head and pushed out a breath as if the action could blow his confusion away. "I have faith. I know there's a spiritual realm, and I know there are things I can't explain, but this is not even close to reality."

Ryan glanced from one side of the field to the other, a puzzled look on his face. "Your statement retains no hold on my mind. This"—he again swept his hands over the field—"is extremely close to reality. The first time you came to be on this side, were the meadow, the trees, the pond the same as they are now?"

"No."

"Your eyes are now open, able to see much more closely the way things truly are."

"Including having a man talking to me who claims to be a character out of a childhood story?"

"You misunderstand. I am certainly not claiming to be that. I am not that character at all."

"Characters who exist in novels do not jump off the page and become real. Even here."

"Even if I did claim to be Rilian, again you would be in error. The character Rilian does not exist between the pages of a book. At all. The words of a book are only ink stains shaped in a way that you understand them. A person who cannot read English would only see unfamiliar markings and have no idea those markings described a character, a place, an emotion, or anything else."

He pointed at Jake's head. "No, the only place any character in any book truly exists is in the imagination and, if you come to love that character, in your heart. You cannot tell me your imagination isn't real. We both know it is."

"Of course my imagination is real. But the things in my imagination don't jump out of my brain into a field at the end of a lake."

"On the contrary, the event you mention has just occurred." Ryan gave a sweeping bow. "I am the evidence that the image you saw in your mind's eye has indeed manifested itself in this realm."

"Impossible."

"But I am not the only evidence. Nay. The rest exists inside you, because you cannot deny I am the exact replica of what you created inside your mind and heart."

"Then where do we go from here?"

"I'm here to help you." Ryan again thumped his chest with a fist. "Help you attain what your soul craves the most."

"I don't understand." Jake narrowed his eyes. "I made it through. I've been given what I want the most in the world. But when I leave, it vanishes."

"I am your friend, Jake Palmer. And I will move as much of

heaven as I can to help bring about what you want, but I cannot do it alone. You are the key."

"What are you saying?"

"Have faith." Ryan began to back away in long, quick steps. "Do not give up, Jacob. You can do this."

"Do what?" Jake jogged after him, but Ryan raised his hand and Jake staggered to a halt.

"No. Our time together has come to an end. But I do bid you come again tomorrow morning. It is then that our adventures together shall begin."

Ryan turned and strode behind a tree.

"Wait!"

When Jake reached it, the man, or whatever he was, had vanished. A ten-minute search throughout the field ended in futility. There was no Ryan, no evidence he'd ever been in the meadow. Was Ryan more right than Jake knew? Was Ryan a figment of his imagination and nothing more? Or better said, a psychotic hallucination?

Jake didn't care. He'd wanted answers. Didn't get them. But he did get an invitation he would accept in the morning. One way or another, he would get the resolution that Leonard refused to give.

27

The rest of the day, he played the meeting with Ryan over in his mind, searching for clues. Jake debated whether to talk to Susie about it, but after lunch she made the decision for him.

"So, did you go back?" She cornered him after lunch down on the grass to the left of the deck.

Jake glanced behind her. No one else around.

"Yeah."

"Anything new?" Susie sat beside him on the thick lawn. "I see a sliver of hope in your eyes."

"True, but at the same time, it got even more bizarre."

"Oh?"

"Remember reading The Chronicles of Narnia when we were kids?"

"Sure."

"Do you remember my favorite?"

"The Silver Chair."

"There's a copy of it in my room. Must have been the owner's daughter's room. Lots of kids' books."

"I'm sure there's a point to this," Susie said as she raised her eyebrows.

"You want the headline version, huh?"

Susie waved her hands. "Sorry, but Peter and Camille said they were coming down to set up cowboy golf sometime before dinner, and I'd really like to hear the rest of the story before they arrive and interrupt."

"Right." Jake glanced over her shoulder up at the deck. Safe for a few more minutes at least. "This is the part where you say I'm nuts."

"I will not." Susie held up three fingers, a mock-serious look on her face. "Scout's honor."

"You weren't a Boy Scout. You weren't even a Girl Scout."

Susie motioned with her thumb toward the house, and Jake hit the highlights of his encounter with a person he'd made up inside his head, inspired by Lewis's fictional character. When he finished he searched Susie's eyes.

"Well?"

"You're nuts. Yes, definitely." She circled her forefinger around her ear. "Loco. Wacko town, city, and country. I'm so glad I'm not a scout and have to go back on my promise."

Jake fell back and laughed. "You crack me up."

"Okay, let's get serious." Susie grabbed his forearm. "What did this figment of your imagination mean when he said, 'It is then that our adventures together shall begin'? And do you—I'm not trying to insult you here—really think any of it happened, or could it have all been inside your head?"

"All joking aside, I'm not crazy, Sooz."

"I'm not saying you are. I'm just exploring all possibilities."

"You're saying it's possible I'm nuts."

"Jake! Focus."

"I'm not saying it's real. Maybe it was just a vision. Or I went to sleep at the end of the lake and it was simply the most vivid dream of my life. But I don't believe that for a second. I'm not crazy, and what I experienced down there was every bit as real to me as sitting right here, right now, talking to you."

"And a character you created in your head, literally a figment of your imagination, shows up and pretends to be your friend and wants to take you through some kind of soul-searching journey that will get your legs and stomach healed up good as new."

"Yeah. Something like that."

"Good. Now we're on solid ground." Susie grinned and started to ask another question, but the sound of footsteps approaching stopped her. Peter and Camille again wrecked the moment.

By the time dinner came, Jake was ready for a distraction, which the coming evening would provide in spades. One of Jake's favorite nights of their annual trip was about to begin.

———

Toward the end of dinner, Camille glanced at her watch and announced, "Quick reminder that our annual poker tournament starts in thirty-five minutes. Don't be late. And be ready to change into the appropriate attire at the end if necessary."

"Appropriate attire?" Ari glanced around the table, a questioning smile on her face.

Andrew grinned. "Sounds like no one has told you the stakes of this poker tournament."

"Didn't I tell you about this?" Peter picked up his plate and strolled toward the kitchen. "Whoops. Sorry."

"We don't play for money like regular people?"

Susie chuckled and said, "I think you've figured out by now we are definitely not regular people."

"Not money?" Ari raised her eyebrows and glanced at Andrew. "Losers have to jump up and down in front of the whole group, perform some kind of dance?"

"Even those kinds of stakes are far too low. Think higher."

Ari again glanced around the table till her gaze came to rest on Susie, who put her hands together and mimed a person diving.

"Oh no. No, no, no, no, no. That's not going to work for me."

"What isn't?"

"Jumping into the lake at night. Dark water and I don't get along."

Peter grinned. "Then I'd say you have great incentive not to be among the five losers."

"There's only one winner?"

Andrew scrunched up his face and in his best Scottish accent said, "In the end, there can only be one!"

No one laughed.

"Oh, come on. You can't tell me I'm the only *Highlander* fan in this group."

"*Highlander?*" Camille asked.

"Yeah." Andrew glanced around, a disgusted look on his face. "*Highlander.* About a group of immortals roaming the earth for centuries, killing each other off, taking each other's powers? You gotta see these movies, and . . . oh, forget it."

Susie patted him on the hand. "Excellent suggestion, sweetie. We will."

Now everyone cracked up and Andrew wiggled his fingers as if to say, fine, bring it on. After the laughter died down, Peter focused on Ari.

"Yes. One winner. The rest have to go for that swim."

"Rules?" Ari said.

"It's call-your-own-game poker, no limit, and as I just said, we play till there's only one at the table holding all the chips."

Ari's face turned a shade whiter as she poked at the chocolate-swirl cheesecake in front of her. "I'd love to be part of the tournament, but I'm not sure it would be fair to me. I've never played poker."

Jake studied her face for a few seconds before glancing at the rest of the group and saying, "You know what I think? I think we have a formidable opponent here who has already started playing with a well-executed but ultimately disastrous bluff."

He locked his eyes on Ari, and he struggled to keep a smile from breaking out on his face. She returned the stare, her emerald eyes firing off shots of both challenge and surprise. Ari pressed her lips together and massaged them like she was about to speak, but she held her tongue, eyes now full of fire.

"Well?" Jake kept his gaze fixed on Ari, and as he did, the look in her eyes shifted from one of challenge to one of laughter.

Jake had heard you could learn more about the deep parts of another person by looking into their eyes for one minute than by

conversing with them for ten. As twenty seconds of looking into
Ari's eyes passed, he had little doubt the saying was true.

Finally, Jake winked and said, "Tell me I'm wrong."

Ari's eyes narrowed. She glanced at her cheesecake, lifted a
bite to her mouth, and popped it in. After a few seconds of chewing, she swallowed and once again lasered her eyes on Jake.

"I'm going to know all your tells within an hour, and you're
going down. Hard. Get ready for a swim, Jake Palmer."

Laughter erupted from all of them, and for a few seconds the
only thing Jake felt was the lightness of the moment and great
gratitude for the gift of friends. As they stood to take their plates
into the kitchen, Susie motioned toward Jake with her thumb and
said, "You do know Jake has won this tournament five out of nine
years, right? He's decent at the game."

Ari stared straight at Jake when she answered. "He's going to
need to be."

"Whoa!" Susie laughed and bobbed her head. "What are you
trying to say?"

"Most people are shocked when I tell them this, but I used to
really be into the game. I even won a few local money tournaments."

Peter came around from his side of the table carrying his plate
and Camille's. "You're kidding."

"Jake better hope I am."

28

Forty minutes later the six of them sat around the dinner table, each with a stack of thirty-five blue chips, thirty-five red, and thirty-five white.

Andrew shuffled the cards as Peter reviewed the rules with Ari. "As I mentioned at the dinner table, we play call your own game, so do whatever you want. If we don't know the game, we'll be happy to learn it. No handouts to another player if they go bust. White chips are worth a buck, red chips are two bucks, and blue chips are five."

After an hour and fifty minutes, it was clear Ari wasn't bluffing about having played before. She, Camille, and Jake were the only ones still in the game. Camille was dealing, the game was Five Card Draw, deuces wild. Camille had a barely perceptible smile in the corner of her mouth. Jake had already folded.

Ari stared at her cards as she rubbed them between her thumbs and forefingers. Her face was stone, her eyes passive. Finally she set her cards on the table, looked at Camille, and blinked once.

"I'll see your seventy-five and raise you twenty-five." She started to slide her chips into the center, then stopped halfway there and a split-second nervous look flashed over her face. "No, hold that thought, I'll raise you another forty-five."

It was a beautiful play, one Jake wouldn't have fallen for, but only because he'd studied the game. She wasn't bluffing, he was certain, but Jake doubted Camille would see that. She'd seen the nervous look and had to think Ari was trying to buy the pot.

"Fourty-five?"

Ari nodded.

Camille studied her pile, as did Jake. If she called, it would leave her with only twenty or so white chips, ten or so reds, and fewer than five blues. She fiddled with the top of the piles for a few seconds, then flicked her gaze at Peter, a barely perceptible smile on her face. It vanished a millisecond after it appeared. She wrapped her hands around her chips and gave a thin-lipped smile.

"Your forty-five, and I'll raise you everything I have left. It'll cost you one-twenty to stay in."

Ari's expression was blank; her only movement was from her eyes as her gaze moved in a triangle from her cards, to her chips, to Camille's face, and then back again. Finally, she slowly counted out her chips and slid them into the center. "I'll call."

Barely contained triumph spilled out on Camille's face as she turned over her cards one at a time, snapping each one down. Queen of spades. Another snap, another queen. This time, diamonds. The third card was the queen of hearts. She picked up the last two cards and turned them over as one. Two kings.

"Full house. Ladies over cowboys." She sat back with a smirk on her face and held out both hands to Ari, inviting her to reveal her cards.

Ari offered no drawn-out dramatics. She simply picked up all five cards and turned them over. Four threes and an ace. She didn't react as shouts and laughter erupted around the table.

Susie slapped her hands on the table and laughed. "Oh my gosh, I love it. I love it! I totally thought you were bluffing! Wow!"

"No! Are you kidding?" Peter stared at Ari's four of a kind, then leaned toward his wife. "I thought for sure you had her."

"Well played." Andrew offered Ari five quick claps.

As Susie, Andrew, and Peter focused on Camille, Ari gave Jake a quick look and winked, her face still a mask of stone. A moment later a slight smile surfaced. Ari hesitated a few seconds, then reached out and pulled the massive pile of chips toward her.

"Nice job," Camille's mouth said, but the look in her eyes could have sliced through steel.

Ari didn't react. She thanked Camille and turned to the job of stacking her chips. Andrew did a mini drumroll on the edge of the table and lowered his voice. "And then . . . there were two."

Jake stared across the table at Ari. She picked up a chip without looking at it and rolled it across her fingers. Her gaze stayed fixed on him, her eyes goading him, the slight smile on her face filled with mischievousness. If she had any obvious tells, he hadn't spotted them. It was as if the face of the woman he'd watched and gotten to know over the past four days had vanished, replaced by an actor who enjoyed pushing buttons people didn't even know they had.

She had the gift of all great poker players, the ability to slide inside herself and reveal no emotion on her face, no tic, no clue as to what was really going on in her mind.

"You ready, Jake? Need a break?"

He shook his head.

Susie raised her hand. "Maybe you marathoners don't need a break, but us regular people do."

Peter nodded. "No argument here. Let's take ten to get snacks, bathroom break, et cetera."

Fifteen minutes later, they all sat around the table ready to celebrate the thrill of victory for one of them, and the agony of defeat for the others. Jake's adrenaline was pinging into the red zone. This was competition the way he liked it. He wouldn't back down for a second, and he knew Ari wouldn't either.

"Your deal." Andrew handed the deck to Ari, then frowned at Peter. "Isn't it against the rules for a first-timer to get this far?"

Peter laughed as Ari took the cards and gave them a series of one-handed cuts. Jake raised his eyebrows and looked at Peter. He laughed again and shrugged as if to say, "I had no idea."

Ari finished with three riffle shuffles and two overhand shuffles, then held the deck five inches above the center of the myrtlewood table and dropped the cards. They landed with a loud slap on Jake's side.

"Cut?"

He waved her off. "I'm good."

She made the diving motion with her hands that Susie had made earlier. "Would you like to concede right now, or should I go ahead and deal?"

Jake responded by craning his neck around the room, then looking under the table and glancing toward the couches that sat in the adjoining family room.

"What are you looking for?"

"Just hoping your swimsuit is close by, because very soon you're going to be getting wet."

Ari scooped up the cards and dealt two facedown in front of each of them, picked up hers, and smiled over the top. "Where's yours?"

Heat rose to Jake's face. How could he have been so stupid? The annual poker tournament was so ingrained in his mind, and he was so used to winning, he hadn't considered the fact he might lose. How strange it would seem to Ari if he jumped in with shirt, shoes, and socks on. There was only one option. Win.

Jake stared at the two cards and asked, "What's the game?" But his gut had already told him what the game would be.

"Seven Card Stud."

Great. His least favorite game, because the poker gods never smiled on him when he played it. A game where you could get suckered into a hefty layout of chips because of a promise of strong cards that never seemed to come to him in the end. Sure, he could always fold, but he wasn't playing not to lose, he was playing to win.

He was positive none of his disappointment reached his face. Tells? He didn't have any tells.

"You good with that?" Ari studied his face. "We can play something else if you want."

Jake's only response was to pick up his first two down cards and raise them to his chest for a quick peek. A seven of diamonds and a four of clubs.

Two and a half minutes later, he had one hundred seventy-five dollars in the pot and a potentially Ari-crushing set of cards lying faceup on the table. But he needed the right card in the hole. If he lost this hand, it would take hours to come back.

His up cards were a five of clubs, a three of clubs, a two of clubs, and a jack of spades. One card to go. All he needed was that six, and the straight-flush train would take him down the victory parade.

Ari held the deck up—"Last card"—and dealt Jake's card. It spun in a perfect three-sixty and stopped on top of the last of his three faceup cards.

Jake reached for the card, knowing how he was going to react even before he saw it. He would flash an almost unnoticeable smile, counting on the fact Ari would pick up on it. Didn't matter if he got the six or not, the smile would sell the perception that he did.

He lifted the corner, spotted the king of hearts, and released the smile. Then shut it down, back to the stoic expression he'd had all along. Now to go in for the kill.

Wait for it . . .

"Your bet, Jake."

Jake fixed his eyes on Ari as he pushed all his chips to the center of the table. Her only reaction was an infinitesimal narrowing of her eyes as she moved her hands behind her chips.

"You sure you want to get out on his dance floor?" Peter asked.

"Positive." Ari shoved every single one of her chips to the middle of the table. "I call."

"Wow," Andrew said under his breath as he shook his head and leaned close to Susie. "What is she thinking?"

He said it so softly Jake barely caught it. He glanced across the table. Based on her stony face, Ari hadn't heard Andrew. Of course she'd proven all night that her nonreactions didn't mean anything.

"What do you mean what is she thinking?" Susie poked Andrew in the side. "You don't think Ari knows what she's doing?"

"Now why'd you blurt that out?" Andrew pointed at Ari. "I didn't say that for Ari to hear, I was saying it to you. Just you."

"Don't worry, Susie. I have good ears. I heard it." She winked at Andrew, then folded her hands on the table and turned her eyes to Jake.

Susie waved her hand in front of Andrew as if to dismiss him. "Pay no attention to my misinformed husband. You go, Ari."

Ari cocked her head at Andrew. "Why do you think I've made a bad move?"

Andrew set his fists on the table. "You're obviously good enough at poker to know the answer yourself."

"But I'm not." Susie glanced between Andrew and Ari. "What's wrong with her going all in?"

"She doesn't need to. She's wearing Jake down. She has more than double the amount of chips he does. It will take time, but she'll take him eventually. To risk it all on one hand isn't smart."

Susie turned to Ari. "Is he right?"

"Yes and no." She smiled at Jake, then looked back to Susie. "He's right because the odds are in my favor to eventually win. He's wrong because I know Jake is bluffing."

"How do you know?"

Ari hesitated, as if ready to give a lengthy explanation, but in the end simply said, "Because I know him." She smiled at Jake. "Well?"

Jake picked up the king, joined it with the two cards in his hand, and tossed them onto the table faceup. Laughter erupted from everyone but Ari and him.

"She did it!"

"You were right!"

"The king is dead, long live the queen!"

After the ribbing and congratulations died down, Jake held out his hand to Ari. "Well done."

Ari nodded, and the thinnest of smiles formed in the corners of her mouth.

"All right, it is time, ladies, gents, and everyone else! We'll gather out on the deck in ten minutes and head down to the lake for a quick late-night dip." Peter rubbed his arms as if trying to warm up. "Hopefully Ari won't laugh too loudly, and of course she promises to take loads of pictures of the consequences of our defeat."

"Don't you mean she promises *not* to take any pictures?" Susie asked.

"Yeah, that's what I meant."

Jake gritted his teeth as they all shuffled away from the table. He was going to look stupid again, dressed in his T-shirt, tennis shoes, and linen pants instead of a swimsuit like normal people. But he wasn't normal. He was a freak. So what? Why did he still care so much what Ari would think? Why not show her who he was underneath and get it over with?

He watched the normals head for their rooms to change. At least he'd get a few minutes on the deck alone to wrestle with his evenly matched emotions. Show her? Not show her. Exhausting.

Jake stepped onto the deck and looked up. Whoops. Stupid. He wasn't alone. Of course Ari was out here already. She didn't have to change, she was staying dry. Jake fought an impulse to spin 180 degrees and walk back inside.

"You're not going in?" She waved her fingers up and down as she glanced at his clothes. "I thought there was only one winner. Second place doesn't have to go swimming either?"

Her mouth asked the question, her eyes told him she already knew the answer. She was playful. Had to give her that.

"Oh, don't worry, I'm getting in."

"That's quite a swimsuit you have on."

"Thanks, I designed it myself."

"Long pants? Socks and sneakers still on? Shirt too? Are you serious?"

"Yeah." Again the urge to spin and jog back inside till the others came out.

"Why would you go in with all your clothes on?"

"Your victory was so well played, I think you deserve seeing the spectacle of me going in like this."

Jake prayed his face didn't betray the lie and smiled as if that would cover up his bluff. From her reaction, he tried to tell himself it worked. But a deeper part of him confessed that the woman at the poker table who had looked through him as if he were a window would see through the glass this time as well.

"How 'bout telling me the real reason."

"Long story. No time." Jake pointed at the cabin. "They'll all be out in a second."

Ari's smile unnerved Jake, but what came next did an even better job.

"You know, I never liked the gambling part of the game. A few of my better acquaintances got hooked on slinging the cards and lost everything that mattered." She stared up at the star-strewn sky.

"I'm sorry."

"At the level I played, it wasn't about the cards, it wasn't about the gambling, it wasn't about winning or losing. At least for me."

"Then why play? What's so fascinating about the game?"

"You know exactly what it is." Ari peered at him as the corners of her mouth turned up. "Poker is all about learning to read other people's labels. It's about being able to look at their face, their body language, and to be able to gaze into their eyes and see what is going on behind the facade, be it a chatterbox player, a stone face, playing naive, whatever mask they choose to put on."

Ari turned to him and zeroed in on Jake with those piercing eyes. "It's learning how to see inside other people's bottles to what's really going on."

Jake felt like Ari was telling him she'd known everything about him from the moment she walked into the cabin that first night. A question sputtered out of his mouth before he could stop.

"What do you see inside my bottle?"

"Probably more than you want me to." She folded her arms. "But I might be wrong, so what if we find out right now. What's your bluff, Jake Palmer? The one in life that you're hoping no one will ever know about?"

Before Jake could open his mouth to object, Susie, Andrew, Peter, and Camille traipsed onto the deck.

"Nice suit, Jake," Camille said.

Ari looked down and Jake gritted his teeth. Before he could say anything, Susie stepped in.

"I can't believe I agree to that stupid game every year." She laughed. "I know I'm going to swim."

"It's going to be so refreshing!" Andrew flexed his muscles in a mock bodybuilder pose. "Good for the soul."

Ari held Jake's gaze throughout the exchange, then started down the stairs. She knew he wouldn't have answered her question even if he hadn't been saved by the arrival of the others.

"I can't believe you let me win my first summer here," Ari called out over her shoulder.

Peter laughed. "If we never invite you back, you know why."

Two minutes later they were all gathered on the dock, standing in a line a few feet from the water.

"Ready?" Susie grinned.

An overwhelming desire to strip off his pants hit Jake and he clutched his waistband with both hands. But an image of disgust on his ex-wife's face flashed into his mind and he buried the urge. The instant Susie cried, "Go!" Jake heaved himself across the few feet of dock, then leaped as much as he was able into the air.

The instant before the lake buried him he caught Ari staring at him, compassion in her eyes. Then the darkness closed over him and he sank. The water at the bottom was colder than the surface layer warmed by the sun, and part of Jake wanted to stay down there forever. But more of him wanted to fight to fix his life, and he knew without a shred of doubt that the corridor held the key. Now he'd met the key master, and tomorrow morning, he would do whatever was within his power to get Ryan to open the door to the kingdom.

29

Just as the sun crept above the mountains to the east, Jake strode into the field and glanced around it, looking for Ryan. There, near the orchard. When Jake reached him, Ryan glanced up at the sky. "It is an excellent day for a run. Your soul will be greatly stirred by it."

"A run?"

"Yes, you need this."

"Need what? What do you mean, run? Sprint? Jog? Here? I've done that already."

"Our quest this morning is to travel to a river canyon that contains a Class V rapid."

"Yeah, right. Like that's going to happen." Jake guffawed. "Even if it did, what would flinging myself down an unnavigable rapid have to do with me getting my legs and stomach back permanently?"

"Everything. Will you come?"

Ryan stared at Jake from under his eyebrows, and Jake couldn't decide if the look in Ryan's eyes was simple challenge or sprinkled with malevolence as well.

"Can I be injured in here?"

"In where?"

Jake poked his finger at the meadow, the sky, the surrounding hills.

Ryan cocked his head. "Even now your eyes have not yet been opened to the truth."

"What truth?"

"The truth that this corridor doesn't take you inside anywhere. The opposite of this is that which is true. The corridor takes you outside."

"What do you mean?"

"This world contains more reality than the one of your daily existence by a quantum amount."

"Then we are in a different world here."

"No. Not at all." Ryan rubbed his chin. "How shall I explain this? This is the same world, but here you can see beyond the shadows. Behind them. Here you can see the light and the darkness as they truly are. You can see the hidden things of the heart and soul. You can see the creation as it was meant to be. You've seen it already. The meadow, the trees, the pond, the waterfall. Here, things are as they were designed in the beginning, before the revolution."

"Revolution? You mean rebellion. The rebellion of Satan and his angels against God."

Ryan narrowed his eyes and continued. "You don't see all, not yet. But in time, your eyes will acclimate. Here, Jacob Palmer, you can taste life as God intended it to be savored, and today, on the river, we will partake in a feast you will long remember."

Jake didn't answer, just peered at Ryan and tried to see the man beneath the surface, as he'd learned to do with such precision over the past nine years. But Ryan wasn't a man. Of that, Jake was ninety-nine percent certain.

He was convinced Ryan was not a physical manifestation of a character Jake had created in his head as a kid. Because if that was the case, then this whole thing—getting through the corridor, the meadow, his legs and body being healed—was all inside his head, which meant Jake was going insane and had no clue it was happening. Certainly that wasn't the case. Was it? Eighty percent sure.

Which left him to ponder option C, that Ryan was some type of spiritual being, which Jake had never truly believed in. Symbolic? Sure. But he'd never set foot in the camp that believed there was a spiritual realm as real as the physical one. God? Yes. His Son and the Holy Spirit. Without question. But not real-life angels and demons. Yet here he was, bantering with a man who fit the most neatly into category three.

"Are you coming or not?" Ryan glanced at the sky again. "If yes, we must proceed."

"Yes."

"Excellent." Ryan strode past him and pushed into the apple orchard behind Jake.

Ryan passed ten or eleven trees, turned right, and disappeared from sight. Jake didn't hesitate. If he was going on the ride of insanity, there was no point in holding back. He stuck his water shoe in Ryan's footprint at the base of the tree and turned right.

Instantly his surroundings changed and he found himself

sitting in a kayak in a sun-drenched river. Hawks overhead cried as if announcing their arrival, and the smell of wildflowers drifted past them.

"What in the—"

"Fix your rapt attention on the way the current ebbs and flows." Ryan pointed down the river. "The easiest route through a rapid is to follow the water flow. The majority of the water flows into the deepest part of the riverbed, which forms a V, which you'll see when you get closer to the rapid. Stay in the V.

"Study the river like it's a moving map, because that's exactly what it is. Look for holes, rocks, eddies, logs—"

"I appreciate the lesson, but I've been kayaking on a river before."

"Five times, and never more than a mild Class III. If we're going to shoot a Class V together, there's nothing wrong with going over the fundamentals."

Adrenaline and fear doused Jake. "I thought you were kidding. There's no way I'm ready to do a Class V rapid."

"Don't tell me you haven't thought about it. You've paddled that kayak around this lake enough to make you itch for a river. You've read enough thrill-seeker kayaking articles to whet your appetite. Indeed, you're salivating. Yes?"

Jake stared at Ryan. "How do you know—"

"I must halt your speech, Jacob." Ryan winked at him. "You don't want me to think you're asking a stupid question, do you?"

Jake stared at Ryan, probably with an idiotic expression on his face. "You know Leonard."

"Of course."

"How—"

"Come now, Jacob." Ryan winked again. "If you have taken hold of the notion that this place is a slice of heaven on earth, then certainly you can believe I have the capability to see beyond this realm."

"I'm still in the process of taking hold."

"Fair enough."

Jake turned his attention to the river. Not a ripple in it for at least one hundred yards. Beyond that, it turned a corner with no hint of what lay beyond. Ryan backpaddled to stay in place, and Jake matched his stroke.

"Let us move over to the shore, secure our crafts, and scout ahead so you may see what we are about to face."

"Now?" Jake studied the smooth water flowing downstream like liquid glass. "I don't see even the hint of a rapid for at least the length of a football field."

"The river has a way of lulling one into complacency when dangers of severe consequence lie in wait just out of one's vision. And once in a chute, it can be difficult or impossible to climb out." Ryan pointed down the river. "One of the main dangers of this river is rolling into rapids that appear benign. You must recognize those sections as having to be scouted."

They paddled away from the center of the river and pulled their kayaks onto the thin strip of sand on the bank and clambered out. Jake's legs were still strong, maybe even stronger than they'd been in the meadow. He didn't care if this was heaven or Colorado or somewhere in between. Feeling the surge of power in his legs and stomach again was paradise.

"Where are we?" Jake squeezed his thighs. "Still in the meadow? Is this real?"

"Have you forgotten already what I told you when you first arrived this morning?" Ryan frowned. "Where we are is on the river."

"What river? There isn't a river like this anywhere near the lake."

"The corridor is a doorway, and in kind there are other doorways, byways into other realms. It was this way in the beginning, and is so in this realm."

Jake glanced around, the splendor of the heightened colors and sounds filling his senses. "I could get used to the world being like this."

"Come." Ryan motioned for Jake to follow and they stepped onto a narrow path that led them along the river. Thirty paces forward the path shot up a thirty-degree incline. Three minutes later they stood on a rock outcropping looking down.

One hundred feet below, thundering white rapids cascaded through narrow slots in the rocks. "That's where your smooth water goes after it turns the bend. Our options for traversing this section are limited to one: portage up and around. It is not runable by any human." Ryan grinned at him. "Do not fret, on the other side is a section we can run."

They jogged back down the trail to their kayaks, hoisted them over their heads, and started the slog back up the trail. When they reached a spot on the trail just beyond where they'd stood ten minutes earlier, thick brush and deadfall crowded the path. Ryan didn't seem to notice, and they bushwhacked through it at a torrid pace.

Their descent slowed as they navigated fallen trees along the meager path, but within fifteen minutes they'd dropped the 150 or so feet and stood looking at a frothy section of the river. Massive jagged rocks the size of large buses had fallen into the water ages ago from the vertical cliffs above them. Ryan set his kayak down on a relatively smooth section of rock, then reached in and hoisted out a dark green throw bag. He pawed through it and pulled out carabiners, pulleys, and webbing, examined the items, then shoved them back into the bag.

"What is all that for?"

Ryan pointed at three massive boulders downstream. "See those boulders? Ones like that create spaces called sieves, where water flows underground. Getting stuck in one of them is a fair distance from enjoyable, and 'tis an encounter we will focus on avoiding. But if we do get drawn under, it is quite advisable to have made preparations."

"Then don't I need a bag of the same things?"

"If I am unfortunate enough to be drawn under the water and detained there, do you have the experience to use the tools I just showed you?"

"No, but—"

"Then there is no sense in my weighing you down with items that would only serve to hinder your journey down the river." Ryan smiled, but it was grim.

"Then don't go under," Jake said.

Ryan's smile lightened. But only slightly. "Agreed."

"But if I do?"

"I will be there for you."

"Can I drown here?"

"Ah, yes, back to your question from so long ago this morning." Ryan laughed and a look that Jake didn't like flashed in his eyes. "I don't mean to make light of your question, but if you are not certain of the danger, I encourage you to slip into the river here and hold your head under till you lose consciousness. I believe that will convince you."

"So I can drown."

"Most assuredly, yes. But please do not. I'm quite fond of you, Jacob."

"I'm still processing the idea that any of this is real."

"You will be fine."

"That's incredibly comforting." Jake picked up his paddle and adjusted the handles. "But I'm not sure I'm willing to hang my life on your faith."

"Why is that?"

"This doesn't happen every day." He motioned at his legs and stomach. "And I don't know too many people who walk into a meadow, meet a prince from their imagination, and a few minutes later end up on a river hundreds of miles away."

"You live in such a limited realm, Jacob Palmer." Ryan smiled. "It won't always be so."

It was hard to concentrate on Ryan's words, not only because of the low rumble of the water ahead. He couldn't shake the image of his kayak shooting underneath a boulder where there was no chance of escape, with him inside it.

Jake stared at the logs strewn across the rocks like massive shattered chopsticks. Slivers of green brush and the occasional fallen tree masked the danger they were about to face.

"Jake? Did you hear me?"

He squinted at Ryan. "What?"

"It's time." Ryan slid his kayak into the water, then motioned at Jake's. "Let us sail forth into the adventure before us."

"I can't get this picture out of my head that I'm going to wind up underneath one of those boulders, pinned against the rock with the weight of the whole river pressing down on me, the air slowly seeping out of my lungs."

Ryan paddled upriver to avoid being taken downstream. "You do not have to do this. But if you do, I will be with you."

"Yes, I do have to do this." Jake's heart hammered in his chest.

"Why?"

"You know why. It's the reason you set this up, the reason you brought me here."

"Speak the words."

Jake ground his teeth together. "I have to know if I'm enough, if I have what it takes to do this."

"Anything else?"

"Let's go."

He strode to the edge of the river, strapped on his helmet, and clambered into his craft. Ryan nodded at him, eyes solemn, and pushed off.

"Follow my path and you'll be fine. And remember, panic is your enemy. Never stop paddling. And get ready for an experience you'll never forget."

Jake nodded and tried to slow his jackhammering heart. Not possible.

Within twenty-five yards the river narrowed, and they skirted a fallen tree with less than a foot of space. The river, smooth moments ago, began to churn. By the time thirty more seconds had passed, the water was a pulsating cauldron. After sixty, the thunder of the Class V rapids they were about to hit drowned out any other sound.

Ryan turned to him, shouting, his voice barely audible over the water. "There's no scouting or walking around this slot." Ryan's face turned grim. "It's unique because we cannot avoid it. There is no opportunity for a portage. We simply must run it."

"What's it called?"

A thin smile now. "Leap of Faith."

"Of course it is."

"You can't see what it looks like till you're in it, and by that time you won't be able to choose your line. Trust me when I tell you to start on right and angle left. From the eddy, it looks like we will drop onto jagged rocks, but do not allow doubt to cloud your mind. I promise, you will land on white water as if landing on a feather pillow."

Ryan continued, his voice strong and steady. "The churn will send you immediately to the left. You'll get pushed into a wall, then through a rock garden, and you just go with it on faith."

"You've run it?"

"Many times."

"And I can handle it?"

"I believe you can, yes."

"No guarantees though?"

"You know this truth. It isn't necessary for me to speak it to you."

"What truth?"

"Hear this, Jacob Palmer." Ryan's face brightened as if he was

JAMES L. RUBART

giving a message of great import. "Nothing worth having, in this life or the one to come, is free of risk."

With that, Ryan pushed off. Jake hesitated only for a moment before following. Two strokes, three, then he shot into the slot, and the water in front of him vanished as he was launched, the roar of the river slamming into his ears.

The bottom of his kayak seemed to float for a second, then the bottom dropped out and he hurtled down the narrow slot like a stone. A second and a half felt like an age, but an instant later a wall of water on both sides swallowed Jake and he went under. So much for the feather-soft landing.

Ten, maybe fifteen seconds later—it felt more like sixty—Jake popped to the surface, gasping for air. Then, exactly as Ryan had said, Jake was pushed left, then through the rock garden. Relief flooded Jake. He'd made it. But an instant later, panic shot through him.

Two massive boulders loomed in front of him, fifteen feet ahead. They filled both sides of the river. Smooth, glistening walls shot up fifty feet on each side, and the only path through was a narrow slit in the rock not more than three feet wide. Why hadn't Ryan briefed him!

Move! Jake's only chance was to shoot that slot and hope his kayak was narrow enough to get through. He could do it. Had to do it. *Dig. Harder.* He wasn't going to make it. Yes! He was. But what Jake hadn't counted on was a trough in the river four feet deep. Jake jammed his paddle into the water and pulled with all his strength to avoid the hole, but it was too late. His kayak flipped and Jake went under. And this time he didn't pop back up.

30

For a moment, light filtered through the churning water. A second later it vanished and darkness filled Jake's vision. The water drove him down, spinning him like a cyclone. There was no way to know if he was looking up or down, left or right. As he spun, the massive power of the water pushed him downstream. His only hope was to be pushed under the boulders, out the other side, and back into the light, where his life jacket would take him to the surface.

Somehow he'd had the presence of mind to fill his lungs just before he went under, but he'd also taken in water, so the pressure to cough pounded at his brain. He had to ignore the feeling. If he could, he'd be all right. Even though his fear was screaming that he didn't have enough air, he did have enough. How long had he been under? Five seconds? Ten. Plenty of air in his lungs.

When he'd been training, he could hold his breath for two and a half minutes, and in here, where his body had been more than restored, it was likely longer. *Stay calm. Have to stay calm.* He was moving, the water shoving him forward, faster. It would be over in seconds.

But a moment later the river thrust him down and to the right and then to the bottom of the river. Pinned him against a boulder. Jake reached out to grab hold of a crack, a stone, a log, anything on the riverbed he could use to pull himself free, but the current of water surging against him was like hardening concrete.

With what little strength he had left, he had to try. He stretched out his arm as far as possible, but all he felt was slick rock. Despair clutched him around the throat like a noose. He was going to die here in the river, and none of his friends would ever find him. No, there had to be a way out. He refused to drown here.

Wait! At his feet, something protruded. Didn't matter what. He pushed his feet against it and he moved. Not far. Inches, but enough. Then almost a foot. Yes. His feet had found a jagged crack in the boulder. If it ran in the right direction, he could push himself all the way free.

Jake dragged his feet forward and set them again. Push off. Another two feet. Again. Again. The pressure of the flowing water increased, now helping him as he inched along. Now all he needed to do was believe. Believe that however the river escaped the boulders above there would be enough room for Jake to go with it. Leap of faith.

His arms began to tingle, then his legs and the rest of him. No! He argued with his body, screaming in his mind that he had enough oxygen in his bloodstream to survive at least another minute. Even more.

He was going to make it. Hold on. Just a few more seconds. But just before hope started to fill him, something caught his foot. No! A stone. A log. But Jake's heart skipped a beat as he realized it wasn't a stone, log, or any other obstacle that would be found in a river. Because none of those things would take hold of his ankle and squeeze with a strength that was inhuman.

The shock of feeling a hand around his foot almost expelled all the air from Jake's lungs. He yanked his foot as hard as he could, but the gesture did nothing to loosen the grip of whoever, or whatever, had hold of him. Jake attacked it with his other foot. Again, it would have been easier to kick the boulder out of the way than to dislodge the fingers wrapped around his leg.

All hope vanished. There was no way out. Whatever had him in a death grip would never let go. But just before Jake let the air from his lungs burst out, he sensed a body next to him in the river.

Half a second later, the grip on his ankle slackened. Another half second and whatever had him let go completely. Then strong hands grabbed his sides and shoved him hard. An instant later he was free of the boulder and shooting downstream. A hint of light, then more. Then he burst through the surface of the water as the sun almost blinded him with her brightness.

Jake pulled in huge gasps of air, wheezing and hacking as he floundered on the water. Then the same strong hands he'd felt while under the water pulled him to the left, to shore. Jake collapsed on the sandy bank and closed his eyes. He would thank his rescuer in a minute. For the moment he simply wanted to breathe in and out like it was the most normal thing in the world.

Jake's racking coughs slowly subsided. His lungs burned and his body felt as wrung out as it had ever been, but he felt strength seeping back into his legs, arms, and torso. Finally he wobbled to his hands and knees and glanced at the person beside him.

Of course. It was Ryan, deep concern etched into his face. Jake stared at him as he continued to draw long breaths. After another minute he sat up, knees pointing to the sky, and wrapped his arms around his legs.

"Are you well, Jacob?"

Jake stared at Ryan and puffed out a disgusted laugh. "Well? Am I well? I just came within inches of dying. No, I'm not well right now."

Ryan stayed silent, his eyes fixed on Jake.

"Who was that?" Jake kicked at the paddle at his feet and ignored the pain that shot through his big toe. "And how did you get him out of there and where did he vanish to? He didn't have time to get out of the river and skip away before you dragged me onto the shore."

"He did have time. You were under longer than you know."

"How long?"

"A minute and a half of the clock passed after I reached down to take hold of you." Ryan's eyes grew intense. "Another two passed. More than an adequate amount of time for a man to slip away."

"But he wasn't a man, was he?" Jake squinted against the brightness, searching Ryan's face for any hint of confirmation. "You know, don't you?"

"I cannot reveal to you the identity of the man who put you in a position of drowning."

"You can't, or you won't?"

Ryan turned his attention to the river.

"It wasn't human, was it?"

"No." Ryan's face was pale. "It was not."

"It almost killed me. You saved my life." Jake slumped forward on his elbows. "Why was it after me?"

"There are forces in this universe that desire life, and others that are twisted, their only desire the destruction of all that is good."

"But you were stronger." Jake's heart rate had settled to its normal pace, but his mind still felt like it was racing at the speed of light. "Thank you."

Ryan squeezed Jake's shoulder.

"Are you all right?" The worry on Ryan's face deepened.

Jake didn't answer.

"Are you, Jacob?"

"Once again, I wasn't enough."

"Yet you are alive."

"Only because of you."

"It's time to go." Ryan gave Jake's shoulder another squeeze, then stood.

Jake wobbled to his feet. "That was insane. I thought my life was over."

As Jake stared into Ryan's eyes they flitted with what? Defiance? Anger? The man, or whatever he was, had just saved his life, and yet there was a spark of something Jake wasn't entirely comfortable with.

"And you, Ryan? Are you well?"

"I don't like what happened here."

"That's two of us." Jake looked upstream at the boulders that had almost taken his life. "How do we get back?"

Ryan motioned toward a thin path that led to a stand of pine trees fifty or sixty yards away. "Through there is the way back. Are you ready? Or do you need a bit longer?"

"I'm good." Jake stumbled a few steps forward.

"I can tell." Ryan smiled.

After they pushed through the trees and stepped through whatever kind of doorway they created, Jake looked at the sun and said, "How long have we been gone? Four hours? Five?"

"Yes and no."

"What does that mean?"

"It will seem as if only minutes have passed when you get back."

"What?"

"Have you not noticed this yet?"

"Noticed what?"

"That the time you arrive and the time you leave seem to be close to the same."

"Yeah, but my first few times I haven't stayed that long."

"What is the longest time you've spent in the meadow before returning back to the lake?"

"Half an hour, maybe forty-five minutes."

Ryan nodded. "Not long. And I would suspect that given your level of rumination on what happened to you here, you haven't examined the clock after you've returned to the house you're staying in."

Jake frowned. No, he hadn't. "Maybe I haven't looked at a clock, but time has passed. The sun is higher in the sky."

"The time it takes you to get to the entrance of the corridor, the trek across the water, and the trek back when you return, yes, of course that takes time. And yes, time passes while you are in the meadow and other realms within it, but not at the same rate."

"Then how do I know anything really happened? How do I know I'm not simply having visions that fill my mind for a few moments, that fool me into thinking it's real?"

"There is no truth in that question. Remember, Jacob, emotions do not dictate truth. Truth dictates truth. You have been given a remarkable gift. Do not let unnecessary distractions keep you from embracing it fully."

"So this is real." Jake swept his hand over the field.

Ryan dipped his chin and stared at Jake from under his eyebrows. "Tonight, when the water you ingested into your lungs is working its way out of your body, ask yourself if it's in your mind or if it is real."

Jake reached out his hand. Ryan stared at it for a moment before taking it.

"Thank you, Ryan. For saving my life."

"It was my honor, Jacob."

"I need to confess something to you."

"Oh?" Ryan's eyebrows moved up a touch.

"I didn't trust you. Not fully. Not till you saved me in the river. Forgive me for that."

Ryan's face softened and a smile broke out. "Ah, Jacob. There's no need to confess or ask for my pardon. I sensed the hesitation in you and did not once consider it an affront. Instead, I counted it as wisdom.

"Come, Jake Palmer, you did well today. It is time for us to return you to the cabin where your friends await your return."

Ryan clasped Jake's shoulder as they strode back to the curtain of willow branches. "Tomorrow we will fight again. It will not be as easy as today. I suggest you attempt to acquire adequate rest between now and then, both physical and emotional."

Jake stared at Ryan. "Not as easy?"

"No."

"Are you kidding? I almost die and you're saying tomorrow is going to be harder?"

"This journey you have chosen to undertake is not one of ease. It surprises me that you have not yet embraced this truth."

"I knew this was going to be hard. Leonard said the same. But he didn't say I was going to die in the process."

Ryan smiled. "This was not your day to die."

31

By the time Jake reached his kayak, a familiar voice called out to him.

"Tell me what happened."

Leonard.

Jake paddled over and pointed a finger at him. "Tell me something. How do you always know the day and time I'm going to be here?"

Leonard adjusted his sunglasses and focused on the cattails to Jake's right. "I have no idea when you're going to show up here."

"Really?"

"Yes."

"Then explain to me why you're here sitting in the shallows almost every time I exit the corridor."

"Simple."

"Tell me."

"Don't be an idiot, Palmer."

"It's not a stupid question, Leonard." Jake dipped his paddle in the water and pulled a stroke closer to the old man.

"You can't figure it out, huh?" Leonard blew out a soft breath, took off his glasses, and looked at Jake with tired eyes. "I come here every morning. Every morning of the year. Spring. Summer. Fall. Winter. I'm here without fail. I've been coming here every morning for the past forty years."

Leonard looked away, and when he turned back, the sadness in the man's eyes was so deep it struck Jake like a gong. An instant later it was replaced by a steely resolve.

"So let's drop that and get on to you."

"Why?" Jake paddled even closer. "Why do you come here every morning?"

"Now you are asking a stupid question. You know why."

And in a flash, Jake did. Leonard came here every morning searching for the corridor. For a way in. So he could get what he wanted most in the world, just like Jake, just like any man or woman would. But why believe in something that had proven to be false for so many years?

"Why do you keep searching for it? Why do you still believe it's real?"

Leonard stared in the direction of the reeds where Jake had exited and spoke more to the cattails than to Jake. "I made a choice."

"What choice?"

"Same one you're going to have to make soon."

"Tell me."

Leonard leaned forward and pulled in the rope attached to his tiny anchor. Not that he needed it in the still waters at the end of the lake, but it was probably a habit born of years of fishing on Willow Lake in conditions not so benign.

"Lemme tell you something, Palmer." He hoisted the anchor

into the boat. "I like you. So there's a big part of me that wants to tell you what I know, but I think you should probably figure that out on your own, and since I'm not sure if I'm right, I'm going to keep my mouth shut."

"Why do I need to figure it out on my own?"

"It's the way it is."

"How do you know these things?"

"I don't 'know these things' like I just told you. I don't know what's right and what's wrong. I only know what happened to me. Maybe with you it will be different."

"What will be different?"

Leonard finished securing the anchor in the bow of his boat and gripped its sides. "Don't make the same mistake I did. Press in. Face it when it comes."

Jake dug hard into the water and propelled himself across the five feet that separated him from Leonard, then took hold of the old man's rowboat and spoke through gritted teeth.

"I need to know everything I can about the corridor and what does and can go on in there, and you know everything about it."

Leonard clasped his hands together, and his eyes once again turned in the direction of the cattails. "I don't know much, son."

"I know you do."

"So little. I know so very little about that place."

"But you've been there, Leonard, haven't you?" Jake shook the rowboat, but Leonard stay fixed in his seat as if he were on dry ground. "Answer me. You've been there, I know this."

"Yes." The old man's eyes turned to stone and he flicked his chin at Jake. "But no one gets a do-over on the corridor tour."

"What happened?"

Leonard grabbed Jake's hand, yanked it off the rowboat and shoved himself away. "Leave it alone, Slick."

"Tell me, Leonard. What was the wrong choice you made?"

Leonard growled and dipped his oars in the water and pulled hard. Ten seconds later he'd pushed through the thin outer layer of reeds and faded from sight.

———∞———

At lunch out on the deck, Susie slapped both hands on the table and said to everyone, "I've been thinking about something since poker last night. Since this is a group that likes to go deep, I want to invite you to go deep as we sit in this paradise with a crystal lake in front of us and a cloudless sky overhead."

"Wow. Poetic." Peter grinned. "I can tell this is going to be good."

"You know it." Susie winked at Peter. "I'm going to ask a question, and the first thing that comes to mind is what you have to answer with."

Susie locked eyes with each of them before continuing. "Everyone in?"

Everyone around the table nodded except Jake. But Susie either didn't see or ignored him. Jake would bet his life on the latter.

"Great! Like I said, I've been thinking about the poker game. Specifically the bluff Ari pulled off on Camille, and her ability to see that Jake was bluffing when he went all in.

"What is bluffing but pretending?" Susie spread her hands on the table. "Saying something is real when it isn't. Putting up a false pretense and trying to get everyone else to believe it. But it's not just poker, it's life, too, right? We all wear masks and desperately hope no one will peek underneath. And yet there's a big part of us that wants to take off the mask. That would be freedom."

Jake's stomach tightened as Susie continued.

"We trust each other, have shared deep hurts and wonderful triumphs. So what I want to do is have all of us tell what our biggest bluff is, the one we desperately hope no one finds out about."

Susie sat back and Jake watched her watch the faces of her friends. When she reached him, Susie glanced away. He guessed the look in his eyes wasn't the warmest at the moment.

"Okay, now that I've given time for that first thought to roll around in your brain for a few moments, let's get started." She laughed and said, "And since I'm the idiot who came up with this stupid idea, I'll go first. But before I do, please know I have this in my hand."

She pulled the wooden baton out from under her leg and waved it in the air. "I will give it next to whoever isn't nice to me when I tell you my bluff."

She pressed her lips together, looked toward the trees to the west, and gave a quick nod. "People say I have a nice figure, and I do work at it, but there's more to the story. When I was in the tweener years, I got pudgy, and my dad teased me about it. *Teasing* is putting it nicely. I decided right then I would never ever, never ever ever get heavy. I've never had an eating disorder, but I still hated the bumps on my legs that I couldn't get rid of no matter what I did."

Susie let her head fall back and a soft groan floated toward the sky. "I can't believe I'm going to confess this, it's so completely embarrassing. Why did this have to be the first thing that popped into my mind? Arrrgh! Fine. Fine, fine. You want to know. You really want to know? I had liposuction. There, I said it. You happy? I had liposuction on my upper legs and part of my butt."

She dropped the baton onto the table and covered her face with her hands. Andrew put his arm around her shoulder and drew her into his chest.

"Well spoken, love."

"That's so cool." Camille leaned forward. "Where'd you have it done?"

Susie laughed and shook her head. "I love you, Camille."

Andrew waved his forefinger. "Who's next?"

Susie grinned and shoved the baton to her left. "Why, look at that, dear. It looks like it's right in front of you."

Andrew rolled his eyes and said, "I pretend I don't like dessert, but I really do."

The joke fell flat, and Andrew's gaze dropped to the table. He looked like he was trying to hide his thick frame behind his chicken-salad sandwich.

"The one I don't want to admit even to myself, let alone you guys, is the one that came to mind immediately, so that's of course the one I have to let out. Right? Of course right."

Susie squeezed his hand, her face full of knowing and compassion. Andrew rapped the table twice with the baton and continued.

"Growing up, my dad hammered me if I ever said, 'I don't know.' He drilled into me the idea that you always had to have an answer anytime, anywhere, for anyone who asked a question. He told me I had to answer with conviction and strength.

"I grew to believe telling someone 'I don't know' is the worst response possible. I haven't said those words since age thirteen. Even if I don't know the answer, I give one." Andrew glanced around the table, then focused on his chips again. "I'm not lying exactly, I'm not trying to deceive anyone. I just come up with an answer, even if I have to guess some of the facts and make some of it up along the way. I fight it and hate myself for doing it, but it's been a tough habit to break."

The confession didn't surprise Jake, just as it wouldn't surprise anyone around the table except Ari. Jake had known it for years. And instead of making him think less of Andrew, the admission made his respect for the man grow. No one commented, but they didn't need to. Their faces spoke of acceptance and grace with more power than their words could have. From the expression of peace on Andrew's face, he caught his friends' sentiment. *And the truth shall set you free.*

"Who are you going to hand the baton to?" Susie asked.

Andrew pointed it at Peter. "You're up, my man."

"Wow." Peter leaned forward, elbows on the table, and let out a nervous laugh. "I didn't think this would be so hard."

After the laughter died down, Peter rubbed his temples. "I say the second thing that came to mind, right?"

"Go ahead," Andrew said. "Keep stalling, we have all night."

Peter groaned and threw his head back. When he brought it forward again, his eyes were somber. "If you ask anyone at the office they'll tell you I'm nuts about the NBA. I'm in three NBA fantasy leagues. I can quote you stats on the leading players on every team and predict the next superstar coming out of college with amazing accuracy. I'm not so good at football, but I can keep up with most guys when it comes to the NFL and college ball. But it's all a front. I hate basketball. I hate football. I really don't like sports."

Andrew's eyes went wide but he didn't say anything.

"When I was young, I was always tall for my age. Ever since the age of eight my uncles and older cousins would sing, 'Peter, Peter, you're so tall, why don't you play basketball?' When it came to football, they said I'd make a great tight end once I put on weight. The QB could throw the ball so high I was the only one who could catch it. I wanted to be one of the guys, so I tried out for both sports and I was horrible in each of them. Worse in basketball.

"There it is, folks." Peter opened his palms. "My bluff. I'm the great pretender. I'm not macho. I never will be."

"Way to go, Pete." Andrew smacked him in the arm. "You're such a stud. Always were, always will be in my book."

After the others offered their support as well, Peter pointed the baton at Jake's chest. "Your turn, Clark."

Jake chuckled and said, "Since you said Ari could take the fifth anytime this week, and she has agreed to play this game, I'm going to borrow her pass."

"Ehhhhh! Sorry, pal." Peter knocked on the table in front of him. "That's only good for Ari, not the rest of us."

"But what about that amendment to the summer-gathering constitution about being single? Don't I recall that if someone is single, they don't have to—"

"Oh, come on, Jake," Camille spouted. "Ari is going to go and she barely knows us, but you're not willing to go?"

Jake considered lying, but he'd end up confessing the lie later anyway. As his heart hammered away inside his chest, he tried to figure out a way to escape. In the end, he made a lame excuse about having to use the bathroom and didn't return.

Susie found him fifteen minutes later down on the dock. "Nice exit."

"I'm not proud of it."

"I wouldn't be either."

He glanced at her, then went back to watching the lake. "Why'd you do that to me?"

"I did it to all of us." She pointed back toward the cabin with her thumb. "Everyone played, even Ari. Everyone but you."

"I'm not ready."

"Because it would mean telling Ari about the incident?"

Jake didn't need to confirm Susie's assertion. Of course that's what it was. He looked at her and spoke the words he knew she wanted to hear. "I'll tell her tomorrow."

"No you won't."

"What?" Jake whipped his head toward her. "You don't think I have the guts to do it? If I say I'm going to tell her tomorrow, I will tell her tomorrow."

"I believe you." Susie's face grew serious. "But since she's leaving this evening, tomorrow will be too late."

"What?" Jake lurched forward. "I thought she'd decided to stay the full ten days."

"Guess not."

"Why didn't you tell me?"

"I just did." Susie motioned up toward the cabin. "I just found out."

"I have to talk to her. Have to."

"Why?"

"It doesn't make sense."

"What doesn't?"

"This is crazy, it's only been a week, but I think I'm in . . ." Jake trailed off, unable to say the words.

"Yes. You most certainly are." Susie clapped him on the shoulders. "Go."

Jake held his breath. "Any idea where she is?"

"Out on the grass overlooking the lake, last I saw."

Jake was headed toward the stairs leading up to the house when Susie's voice stopped him. "Hey."

"Yeah?"

"It will go better than you think, my dear brother."

Jake walked onto the deck praying Susie was right, but knowing there was a high probability she was dead wrong.

32

Jake spotted Ari in the northwest corner of the property, lying in a hammock, an open book across her chest. The back of her head faced him and he halted six or seven yards before he reached her. Did he really want to step into this confessional booth? No. Not at all. But he had to tell her. If there was any chance of a future for the two of them, he had to tell her now.

He eased forward, not sure why he kept his feet from making any sound on the grass leading up to the hammock. When he got two feet from the back of the hammock, he swung to his right, stopped, and looked down at her. Ari's eyes were closed, her hands folded over her stomach.

"Ari?"

She didn't startle but simply shifted her head toward him, opened her eyes, and said, "Hello, Jacob Palmer," as if she'd been expecting him.

"Susie tells me you're leaving soon."

"Yeah, I've had a wonderful time, but I need to get back." Ari glanced at her watch. "Probably in twenty or thirty minutes. But

I wanted to soak up a few more moments here in this paradise before I go."

"If you don't mind, I'd like to take a few of those moments to talk. Just a few things I need to say."

"Of course. Take as much time as you need."

"Things I need to say about us."

"Us?" Ari sat up in the hammock and swung her legs over the side. "There's an us?"

Jake went over to the fire pit, grabbed a chair, and came back. He set the chair a few feet from the hammock, sat, and rested his elbows on his knees. "Yeah. Us. But before we talk about us, I want to talk about me."

"I'll talk about anything you want to."

"I want to talk about what I've been hiding from you all week. My bluff."

Ari nodded and pushed off the grass so the hammock swung gently back and forth.

Jake waved his finger in front of his shirt and pants. "There's a reason I jumped into the lake after poker with all my clothes on."

"Kind of figured there was." Ari put a finger on her lips. "I have to confess, I asked Peter as well as Susie."

The confession didn't bother Jake. "They didn't tell you, did they?"

"Good friends, those two. They know how to hold a secret."

Jake nodded.

"Forgive me." Ari leaned forward and a breeze ruffled her hair.

"For wanting to know my deep, dark secret?"

"Yes."

"You don't need forgiveness for that or for asking. I would have done the same."

"Thanks, but still, I'm sorry."

Jake stood and shuffled a few feet toward the lake. The breeze was making tiny ripples on the surface of the water, marring the usual mirror image he'd come to expect at this hour of the day.

"That's why I'm here. To tell you what it is." Jake stayed fixed on the lake. "But now that the moment is here . . ."

"Your choice."

"I've already made the decision." Jake turned and fixed his gaze on Ari. Peering into those sea-green eyes kicked his heart into a double-time beat. This was harder than he thought it would be.

"No, the question isn't whether I'm going to tell you, it's where to start."

"Anywhere."

He eased back into his chair, nodded once, then began. "You never asked why my wife divorced me."

"It's not something I need to know."

"Yeah, you do."

"Okay."

"She was repulsed by me. By my appearance."

"Oh?"

Ari's eyes widened, but she didn't look surprised. For some reason that put Jake at ease, as if nothing he said could make her flinch. A kind of peace seemed to float out of her eyes and seep into his mind and heart. And somehow he knew it was all going to be okay.

"A year and a half ago I tried to be a hero. It didn't work out."

He stopped and groped in his mind for the words that would tell her what happened in the most efficient way possible. Faster the better. Jake hadn't told the story to anyone for a year and a half, and he didn't enjoy pulling it out of the drawer and dusting it off.

"I was burned. Pretty badly. Everything from here down." He placed the side of his hand under his rib cage. "Legs, backside, front side, ankles, feet, everything."

Ari's face showed no expression, no hint whether this revelation surprised her or confirmed something she already suspected. She said nothing, so Jake continued.

"My lifelong dream of being a leg model was crushed, and—"

"You don't have to make a joke out of this, Jake."

He nodded. "One day my wife walks in and tells me she can't handle the sight of me any longer." He allowed the emotion of Sienna's blow to come over him. "She'd already filed. Three months later the divorce was final.

"For some strange reason it's made me hesitant to go on dates or think about getting involved with anyone ever again. Weird, right?"

Compassion filled Ari's eyes. Was she feeling sorry for him? He didn't want her pity, didn't need it. There was little more to say. The moment to reveal himself had arrived. Jake took hold of the hem of his shirt and closed his eyes. No way he'd risk seeing her face when she reacted to the mass of charred flesh under his clothes.

Jake took a quick breath and lifted the fabric, but Ari spoke in a commanding voice.

"Stop."

Jake did.

"I don't need to see your scars, Jake."

"I think you do. If there's going to be any kind of—"

"Jake? Stop. Listen again. I don't need to see. This I promise you." Ari leaned forward, her eyes burning with intensity. "When I was seven years old, my father was burned in a fire that started in my bedroom. I was lighting matches, and the fringe of a tiny tablecloth that covered my nightstand caught on fire. It was my fault. I . . ."

Ari's eyes grew moist, but after a moment, she shook her head and regained her composure.

"No wonder." Jake tilted his head back and sighed. "Now I get it. That's why Peter invited—"

"No." Ari shook her head, then tucked her dark hair behind both ears. "It's not. Peter doesn't know the story of my father. He has no idea. I've never told him. Few people do know about it. But my father's story is the reason why I think I understand you more than you know. Just as you are, my father was a handsome man and had great difficulty showing anyone what had happened to him."

Jake sat stunned. "You've known the whole time."

Ari nodded, so slight Jake wasn't sure he'd seen it.

"I didn't fool you for even a moment."

"It was tough not to notice you always wore pants or nylon sweats at a place where swimsuits and shorts are more the norm. So yes, I suspected. And you're right, I more than suspected. I figured it out after the first day. The stories of your being a triathlete and mountain climber in the past, but not anymore . . . so yes, I knew. The way you walk, just like my father. Barely noticeable, but if you've grown up with it all your life, you know what it is."

"But you didn't back off . . . you've tried to get to know me . . . you've—"

"I like you, Jake. And I think you probably now realize a few burns, or even a hundred burns on someone's body, has no impact whatsoever on how I feel about them."

Jake stared at her, stunned by the revelation, and shot through with adrenaline as he also realized that she accepted him. Fully. If they did grow to love each other, there would be no rejection this time, no looks of revulsion, no guessing whether love was seeping away because of his appearance.

An intoxicating amount of hope buried him, and he struggled not to burst out laughing. As he stared at her, blinking with amazement at God's kindness, Ari rose from her chair and knelt on the soft grass at his feet.

"May I?" She pointed at the bottom of his cream-colored linen pants, her eyes questioning.

"What?" Jake peered down at her. "I thought you said you didn't need to see—"

"I don't need to. But I want to, if it's all right with you."

"Yes. Of course."

She gently removed his left shoe, then his sock, and set them to the side. Then she lifted his pant leg three, maybe four inches. The corners of her mouth turned up into a soft smile as she gazed at the lower part of his leg for ten, twenty, thirty seconds.

Ari held out her hand, pointed at his leg, and again asked, "May I?"

Jake nodded, heart slamming in his chest like he'd just completed an Ironman. In what seemed like slow motion, Ari reached out and ran her fingers along his ankle, over the top of his foot in a circle once, twice, and then underneath on his sole. Her countenance was tinged with tenderness and a sadness Jake didn't understand. Time stretched as he waited for her to look at him again.

When she did there was moisture in her eyes. "So temporary, these costumes we wear." She placed both her hands on his foot and gazed at him. "You won't get to carry these symbols of freedom much longer, you know."

"Freedom?"

"How tragic to live a life where you are loved for what you are instead of who you are. You were given freedom from that curse—if you choose to live in it."

Jake fixed his eyes on her, not sure how to respond.

"As I was saying, a day is coming soon where we will discard these costumes and put on our true clothes and wear them for ages that do not end."

Jake could only nod.

"No more hiding, Jake. If you want to live, you cannot hide any longer."

He took her hand and squeezed it. She squeezed back, then released his hand, stood, and settled back into the hammock.

"I'd like to see you again," he said. "Soon. See where you and I might be headed."

"Don't say that, Jake."

"What?"

"Just don't." Ari looked down and shook her head. "There is no us. And there won't be."

Heat shot through Jake. After what had just happened, her

outright acceptance of him, he had expected a significantly different reaction. He leaned back and a puff of disbelief shot out his mouth.

"Wait a minute. I'm not asking to get engaged. I'm simply saying I'd like to have a cup of coffee, get together and take one day at a time, see where things lead."

"No." Ari glanced everywhere but at him. When she finally did look his way, he saw tears gathering in her eyes. "I'm sorry."

"What is going on?" Jake glanced around to make sure their conversation was still private. "Did I imagine what went on between us these past days? Either there was a connection, or I'm crazy."

Ari stepped off the hammock, went over to the fire pit, and brought back a chair. She set it directly across from Jake and sat in it, crossing her legs. By the time she settled in, her eyes were dry and her face had grown cold.

"Jake?" She smiled but it didn't reach her eyes. "I like you. Very much. Was there a spark between us? Yes. I think we both know that, and it would be untruthful of me not to admit it. But when I told you that second night that I wasn't looking for a relationship? It wasn't just a line to be coy or playful. I meant it. It has nothing to do with you other than the fact you're male. If we were in a different time of life and a different set of circumstances, yes, a hesitant maybe. But that time and those circumstances are not now."

In his thirty-seven years of life, Jake had rarely been at a loss for words, but this was a moment where all possible words had vanished from his mind. It made no sense. His burns weren't even a blip of an issue for her. There was no one else in her life. She'd been widowed for three years. On top of all that, she all but came out and confessed her feelings for him. So what was the problem?

"I don't understand," he finally sputtered out. "Just a cup of coffee back home. Daytime. Anytime."

She smiled at him, eyes as bright as he'd seen them. "I wish you great joy and much freedom, Jake."

Ari rose from her chair, went over to the hammock, and picked up her book. Then she sauntered back to Jake, leaned down, and whispered in his ear.

"Please, respect my wishes." She kissed him lightly on the cheek. "Good-bye, Jake Palmer."

With that, Ari strolled back to the deck, through the french doors, and vanished from Jake's life.

33

Jake glanced to the east early the next morning as he slid the canoe into the water. Felt right to take it instead of one of the kayaks. Change of pace. New beginning. Adventure with Ryan coming. He was still stunned over his conversation with Ari, but he was determined to let it go. Not so easy, but what other choice was there?

Probably another ten minutes before the sun crawled over the low mountains to the east and lit up the lake like molten gold. The dull gray that hung in the sky was a perfect reflection of Jake's mood. Would he get over Ari? Yes. Did he want whatever was waiting for him at the end of the lake? Yes. Did he believe the world at the other end of the corridor was real? Maybe. Ryan? Still impossible, yet Jake knew he wasn't crazy and he didn't think what he'd encountered was a vision. Ockham's Razor: Of two possible explanations, the simplest one was most likely true.

With little warning, the first rays of dawn burrowed into his neck, and in that moment, his mood lightened. Maybe all of it was a dream, but a dream where he was restored—where he could run again and be healed permanently—was worth fighting for.

This time he spotted the shimmer at the end of the corridor while he was still seventy yards away. Its brightness grew as he eased through the water, and the sun inched down the cattails as if choreographed to fully illuminate the entrance at the exact time he reached it. The sight should have filled him with exhilaration, but a flag of caution fluttered at the back of his mind.

As Jake crawled out of the canoe and slipped into the chilly water, the cry of a blue heron ten yards to his left startled him. The bird jerked its head back and forth as if puzzled by what Jake was about to do. What *was* he about to do? Place his trust in a . . . uh . . . man he knew but didn't know? Choose to believe that whatever journey he was on would lead to light in the end?

He stretched out his arms and stroked through the water. The debate could rage in his head all day. Right now there was only action or inaction, and he hadn't come here to ponder. As he got closer to the entrance, the sliver of him that still doubted melted away, and laughter spilled out of his mouth as the light swirling around the tunnel of willow tree vines invited him to tango.

He pushed through the corridor, the path so narrow now that the trees on both sides brushed his back and chest as he stepped along sideways. But he barely noticed the inconvenience as his soul filled with the anticipation of his legs and stomach growing strong, of sprinting through the field again, of facing whatever challenge Ryan could toss at him and finding triumph in the end. This time, his body was restored ten yards before he reached the vine curtain. The earliest healing so far.

Confidence flowed into his mind and he swept the willow branches aside with boldness. But as soon as he stepped through, he gasped and lurched backward. There was nothing beyond the vine curtain but blackness.

He staggered back another step, fear surging through him. Where . . . what happened to the meadow? Another step back, his arms clutching at a handful of the vines, the only thing keeping him from falling backward onto the path. Then a confident voice rang out. Strong. From the other side of the curtain.

"Your actions bring confusion to my mind. Why are you leaving? Did we not agree yesterday to continue your journey this morning?"

Ryan. A moment later he pulled the vines aside and stepped into the corridor. His gray-blue eyes were intense, yet a hint of laughter moved across them.

"I was . . . when I pulled back the willow vines, I couldn't see anything."

"Yes, that is true." Ryan glanced behind him. "Quite black. It will take your eyes a moment to adjust to the darkness we are about to step into."

"Darkness?"

"Yes, did you not hear me?"

"Yeah, I heard. Ears are working fine this morning." Jake pointed over Ryan's shoulder. "I have to say, that doesn't look anything like the meadow."

"You are late." Ryan zeroed in on Jake and his voice had a sharpness to it. "The morning grows old. I suggest we start on our journey and no longer waste time on questions that can be answered along the way."

Jake swallowed and gave one nod. Ryan nodded back, then

pushed through the vines and stepped into only he knew what. Jake lunged forward to push through the vine curtain. If he was about to fling himself into a world of darkness, he would be right behind Ryan when he did it.

Once he stepped through, he saw that the blackness was less grim than he'd first thought. A few moments later, his eyes did adjust, and he found himself standing inside a small cave. Enough light streamed in from the corridor to make the outline of Ryan's body visible.

"Where are we?"

In the dim light, all Jake could see was Ryan's hand pointing to the right of them. "Over there is a stone slide with the ability to deliver us to the bottom of this cave in less than a minute. However, given our assumed mutual desire to avoid broken limbs and cuts and gouges upon face and hand, I suggest we take the stairs to our left."

Jake trudged over to the stairs in the far left corner of the cave and studied them. He'd been in his grandma's apartment complex last week. The stairs that led from the lower level to the one above were designed for the elderly, easy to navigate, each step only a few inches higher than the one before, so walking up and down was simple.

The stairs before him now were designed for the antithesis of his grandmother. Each step was at least a foot-and-a-half high, and describing them as semiflat would be generous. Describing them as barely wider than a shoe would again be generous. And of course no handrail to steady a descent. Impossible to traverse these stairs with his burnt legs, they would still present a challenge to his restored ones.

JAMES L. RUBART

"Are you ready?"

Jake pointed into the inky blackness below. "We're going down there?"

"Yes. Don't fall. You would die."

Ryan's laugh was not kind and it sent trepidation through Jake.

"I'm not liking that plan."

"No, we couldn't have that happen, could we?"

Ryan chuckled again. He took the first step as if walking through the field with one of the orchard's Gala apples in his hand. Jake followed, all of his concentration on reaching the bottom alive.

By the time he reached the last stair, sweat had broken out on every inch of his body, but the sensation was exhilarating. To once again feel his skin the way it was supposed to be, to feel the sweat and the coolness of the cave on it, to feel the sensation of his feet on the steps, brought life to him.

"Well done. That cannot have been easy for you."

Ryan plucked a torch off the wall of the cave and strode toward the opening on the other side of the landing. A faint blue light ebbed beyond the curved passageway, and something about it struck Jake as familiar.

He followed Ryan through the breach in the cave wall and found himself standing on a kind of underground beach. Gray sand mixed with silt and a few pebbles, and a lake lapped at the shoreline as if trying to make itself known even in the absence of tides or wind.

A rough-hewn, narrow wooden boat big enough for three or four men sat halfway in, halfway out of the water. From the stern hung a lantern, which cast the dim, gray-blue light Jake had seen from the bottom of the stairs. A surge of memories rose in him. The boat, the shoreline, the curve of the caverns as they rose out of sight above them were all familiar. He'd been here. Not in real life, but in his imagination.

"I know where we are." He stared at Ryan, almost expecting the man to dissolve into the air.

"Oh?" He stared at Jake with playful eyes.

"'Many sink down, but few return to the sunlit lands.'"

"I would certainly hope so, if it is indeed your favorite of the Chronicles." Ryan winked and motioned toward the crude wooden boat, resting halfway on the sand. "So *The Silver Chair* truly was your favorite."

"I've read it more than a dozen times." Jake let his gaze sweep 180 degrees. "It's exactly as I imagined it."

"I should think so." Ryan pulled hard on the oars. "You created this."

"What do you mean—"

"Just as you created me and brought me to life, you created this. Without you, this version of Underland wouldn't exist."

"That makes no sense. I had nothing to do with this. I expected to step through the curtain into the field, not into a suffocating cavern."

"And a noble job of creation it is, indeed."

Again the thought struck Jake that the corridor, Ryan, the kayaking experience, all of it was nothing more than a delusion he'd concocted inside his own brain. That he was breaking down emotionally from the loss of who he was before. In Susie's words, the fact he was now living two lives had finally shattered his mind.

"Let me ask again, is any of this real? Or am I slowly going insane and just don't know it?"

The question was a ludicrous one. If he was going crazy, asking Ryan this question would essentially be asking himself to figure out a question he would have no way of answering truthfully.

"We must go, Jake. Again, these are questions that can be answered as we traverse the water."

Ryan got into the boat and Jake followed. They shoved off into the darkness, no sound except the oars on the jet-black water.

"We're going to her kingdom, aren't we?"

"Not exactly."

"What do you mean 'not exactly'?"

"We're going to your imagination's version of what that kingdom looks like. Don't ask this question again. It grows tiresome."

He stared at Ryan, whose face was distorted in the dim blue light from the boat's lantern. Ryan's tone sent a chill snaking down Jake's spine. He wasn't dreaming, wasn't going crazy. Not a chance. All of this was real. If only he could convince himself.

As if sensing Jake's apprehension, Ryan said softly, "From your holy book: *No eye has seen, no ear has heard, no heart has imagined.* Yet you doubt all that is happening to you. Might I inquire as to why?"

"This is impossible."

"With God all things are possible."

Jake didn't respond. He needed a moment to figure this out. But that was probably the point. There was no logic that could make him believe. The only answer was faith. Faith that whatever kind of bizarre journey he was on at the moment, it was exactly where he was supposed to be. And that in the end, answers would come.

As he stared into the darkness, he pulled up his memories of the book. They would soon reach the witch's kingdom where Rilian was held prisoner. Where the great lion Aslan and the children, Jill and Eustace, and the Marsh-wiggle Puddleglum set Prince Rilian free from ten years of dark enchantment.

"We're almost there." Ryan's voice seemed to come from all around Jake.

"If this is my imagination, how do you know that?"

Ryan didn't answer, but thirty seconds later, the dark kingdom Jake remembered from the book emerged out of the darkness. Towers with murky light in the windows rose in the center of a city made of stone. But there were no oddly shaped gnomes as he had remembered. Only empty streets and silence.

Before he had time to consider the implications of what that meant, Ryan stood on dry ground, beckoning Jake to join him. Jake got out and they climbed the stairs in the center of the city. They would lead to the chamber where Prince Rilian in the story had been tied to his silver chair for the hour when the enchantment could not hold him prisoner.

As they reached the door leading to the room that had contained the chair, Ryan lurched forward and stopped his fall with an outstretched hand against the thick dark-gray stone next to the door. He blew out a long breath and raised his face upward, eyes closed.

"What's wrong?"

"I know you cannot understand how I can be truly real, since

I've explained that you created me. Consequently, you cannot imagine how I could have emotions similar to those that humans have. I, however, do not need to imagine myself having feelings of sorrow. At this moment, I am remembering what occurred here many years ago."

"In the way I saw you reacting when I read the stories as a child."

"Yes."

Something broke inside Jake. Whether any of this was real, he felt true compassion for this being called Ryan who stood before him. "I'm sorry. This can't be an easy moment for you."

"It is not." Ryan pushed off the wall and clasped Jake's shoulder. "But it is good. One that ends in triumph. And it is right. This is the site of a freedom you learned from when you were young, and that is a good thing." Ryan reached out for the door. "Are you ready?"

"Yes." Jake hesitated, then asked, "Are you?"

Ryan didn't answer. Instead he pushed the door open and stepped inside. Jake entered and stood next to Ryan and glanced around the chamber. The size, or lack of size, struck him. He'd expected it to be bigger. The sensation was familiar to anyone who had returned to a childhood home or playground or ball field. He was returning to a children's story that wasn't real. But Jake knew if he let the truth in his heart take center stage, that story would prove to be more real than many things in his life.

Ryan moved around the room like a cat. His footsteps were light, his pace steady. When he neared the center of the chamber, he leaned in and circled as if upon seeing the chair sitting there, he needed to examine it up close. After he'd paced around it three times, he straightened and focused his eyes on Jake.

"In this room, in this spot, on that wretched chair, Prince Rilian knew who he was for one hour each day. But for twenty-three he did not know. He forgot. The enchantment took hold of him and he could not see through the darkness during those hours. In those hours he was inside, to use your analogy, his bottle. Deceived. He could not read the label."

Ryan pointed at Jake. As he did, something in the being's eyes shifted. From intense to malevolent. A smile played on the corners of his mouth, but not even a millimeter of mirth reached his eyes. Jake's heart rate doubled as Ryan stared at him, eyes on fire.

Ryan's gaze darted to his right. Along the floor, hidden in the shadows, lay a short sword. Two strides and Ryan stood over it. Another moment and he held it in his hand, his eyes again fixed on Jake. Ryan slowly lifted the sword till it was pointed at Jake's chest.

"What are you doing? What is wrong with you?"

"Wrong? Nothing." Ryan slid his foot forward.

Ten feet was all that separated them. Seven feet from the tip of the sword.

"You're making me nervous."

"Oh? This isn't the way you remember the story going?" Ryan was on his toes now, bouncing slowly.

"What's going on, Ryan?"

Ryan's only response was to cover the ground between them faster than Jake thought possible. Another flash of movement and the tip of the sword hovered half an inch from Jake's heart. Ryan's breathing now came through clenched teeth.

Jake tried to back up but slammed against the stone wall behind him. Ryan advanced, the sword touching Jake's clothes. Now the point pressed into the skin beneath his compression shirt. Sweat broke out on Jake's forehead and his heart slammed against his rib cage. Ryan had gone nuts. Jake had to think, figure out a way of escape.

But if he got away from Ryan, where would he go? Ryan knew this realm. Jake, on the other hand, knew nothing about the paths and tunnels that would lead him to the surface. His only chance was to talk Ryan down.

"Again, why are you doing this?"

"It is necessary."

"Necessary for what? What do you want from me?"

"I want the same thing you do."

"I don't know what I want."

"You want the truth. You want to be free. Isn't that what you came here for?"

"Free from what?"

"What is your chair, Jacob Palmer? The one that holds you in an enchantment so powerful you cannot break free? One that has held you all the days of your life? Think!"

"Killing me isn't going to help me figure that out."

"'From the days of John the Baptist until now the kingdom of heaven suffers violence, and violent men take it by force.' From your book of Matthew."

Ryan's eyes grew wilder. He pushed the sword harder against Jake's chest, and it broke the skin. He felt blood ooze into his shirt as Ryan's face contorted. A moment later, the world went black.

34

When Jake opened his eyes he stood at the bottom of a long, steep road enclosed by a tunnel.

Ryan stood next to him, eyes bright. No sword, no strange look in his eyes. It was the man who had saved his life and spoken wisdom with every word.

"Jake?" Ryan's face looked puzzled. "Are you with me?"

"Yeah, I . . ." Jake shook his head and stared at Ryan. "What did you say?"

"I asked if you're ready to return to the sunlit lands."

"Yeah, sure. I mean . . . sure." He pointed behind him toward the dark castle. "How did we get here?"

"We walked." Ryan frowned. "Are you quite well?"

A breeze brushed his face for the first time since he'd entered the underground kingdom. Along with the light wind came the smell of grass and cattails.

"Yeah, I'm good."

They hiked up the dim road without speaking for the better part of thirty minutes. Finally they came around a bend and sunlight burst through an opening in the tunnel the size of a small door. Jake blinked against the brightness, which was almost blinding compared to the dim light he'd been in for the past—two hours? Three?

Jake slowed and let the light wrap around him like a blanket. He stood in the opening and drank in the trees and the pond and the meadow. He was back. And now that he was back in the light, he was going to get answers.

"What happened down there?"

"Pray tell, what do you mean?"

"You attacked me." Jake narrowed his eyes. "Why did you do it?"

"Attacked?" Ryan's lips pushed together and confusion contorted the rest of his face. "I don't understand that of which you ask, Jake Palmer."

Jake stepped across the meadow's thick grass and stuck his face within inches of Ryan's. "You understand exactly what I'm talking about."

Ryan danced back, hands up, the corners of his mouth twitching as if ready to break into a smile.

"Please tell me what I understand, Jacob. My ears would welcome your view of what happened in the throne room."

"Throne room? That wasn't a throne room; it was a torture chamber."

Ryan's only response was a raised eyebrow.

Jake rubbed his fingers over the spot where Ryan's sword had penetrated his skin, then lifted them. "See this blood? This tells me you were more than making a point. You either lost it down there, or you're playing a game with my life that you've told me nothing about. Why did you do it?"

"I explained this already, Jacob. Because it was necessary."

"That tells me nothing."

"I have sympathy for your plight, but that is as much as I can reveal at this time."

Again the look of mirth in Ryan's eyes and the hint of a smile at the corners of his mouth, but seconds later the hint broke into outright laughter. The mirth turned to disdain.

"Tell me."

"As great as my desire is to explain in detail what is truly transpiring here—and that desire is indeed great in the moment—I cannot do so. My deep apologies."

The laughter died down, but the mockery in Ryan's eyes did not. A slow rage built inside Jake, fueled by the mind games, the shock and fear of being stabbed in Underland, the answers that weren't answers, all mixing into a Molotov cocktail that was about to explode.

"What is wrong with you?" Jake stepped forward, hands balled into fists. "Why are you putting me through this?"

"There is nothing ever wrong with a bit of amusement. In fact, it can be a balm to the soul."

As Ryan continued to dance like a boxer in front of Jake, something broke inside. Without a sound he sprinted toward Ryan, drove a shoulder into his stomach, lifted him high, and slammed his body to the ground.

Ryan's air whooshed out of him, but Jake didn't hold back. He jammed his knee into Ryan's ribs and placed his hands around the being's throat. As Ryan gasped for air, Jake shouted, "Tell me!" over and over again.

Ryan grabbed Jake's forearm in an iron grip. Jake clasped Ryan's wrist and tried to yank it off, but it was like trying to bend a steel bar. With one swift move, Ryan wrenched Jake off of him and rolled to the right. A second later he was on his feet staring down at Jake.

"Well, that was enjoyable." Ryan laughed again as he brushed the dirt off his dark green clothes. "But I think we should be finished, wouldn't you agree?"

Jake struggled to his knees, staring up, heart pounding with fear. He rubbed his arm where Ryan had taken hold of it. Jake knew the grip well. It was the exact same one he'd felt the day before in the river. The one that had held him down.

The one that had wanted him to die.

Jake staggered back, blinking, shaking his head. "No, it's not true. It can't be."

But the truth was undeniable and blazed its way into Jake's heart. He gave little shakes of his head as he stared at Ryan.

"It was you."

Jake stumbled back another two steps and went down, the revelation almost too much to take.

"Of course it was me." Ryan lifted his hands and clapped once. Twice. Three times. He continued to clap, a second between each strike, as he started a slow circle around Jake.

"Clever, don't you think? Almost killing you, then pretending to be your rescuer? In here I have all the power, and I thought that a fun little exercise for us to take part in." Ryan laughed, a high, mocking laugh that slid down Jake's back like ice. "But what took you so long? I anticipated you figuring it out before now. Is it possible that Leonard is right, that you are quite stupid?"

Jake's mind spun, searching for answers. "Why would you do that to me?"

"It's quite complicated."

He staggered to his feet and rotated, his eyes fixed on Ryan, who continued to circle around Jake. "Try me. Let's see if my little pea brain can track with you."

"You are one who can bring much light to the people of this world. If you figure out this journey of healing you're on, you'll bring that much more light to everyone around you." Ryan tightened his circle and Jake moved to his right, mirroring Ryan, two prizefighters staring each other down, evaluating strengths and weaknesses.

"And you don't want that to happen."

"To get there, to find the healing you crave, there are obstacles you must overcome."

"And you're going to try to stop me from succeeding."

"Not try, Jake." More laughter. "I don't have to try."

"Who are you?"

But Jake already knew the answer. Ryan had already spoken the truth yesterday on the bank of the river. *There are forces in this universe that desire life, and others that are twisted, their only desire the destruction of all that is good.*

"How can you be here? If this is a slice of heaven, how can you be in this realm?"

"Your holy book speaks of Satan being in the throne room of God." Ryan smirked. "Any other questions, Jacob?"

"What do you want from me?"

They continued to circle, Ryan with his palms together. "That, I can tell you. The answer is quite simple. I want you to die."

Jake took short breaths through his nose and pushed them out through his mouth. *Steady.* He didn't doubt Ryan's words. The conviction in his eyes only heightened Jake's belief, but something was off. Something that made no sense. An instant later it cut through his mind like a shaft of light. Revelation swept over Jake and he realized why he hadn't died in the river.

"You're not allowed to kill me, are you?" Jake puffed out a mirthless laugh. "You would have done it in the river if you could have. But you didn't. You held me under that water long enough to bring me to the edge of death, but you weren't allowed to seal the deal.

"You were doing whatever you could to scare me off. Keep me from coming back. You crave the idea of seeing me shredded. Want to drive fear in my mind, anchor it down, and keep me in the prison I've lived in for the past year and a half."

Ryan's face was stone. No emotion. No reaction to Jake's words.

"I'm right, aren't I?" Jake balled his hands into fists. "You don't want me to have healing or restoration, to gain back what I lost. You don't have all the power you claim to wield. Just as Satan had to ask permission to sift Peter, there are rules, restrictions that hold you in check."

"The old man might be wrong." Ryan smirked again.

"You just said there were obstacles for me to overcome. What are they?"

"You'll never pass the final test, Jake. Give up now. Life will go better for you. Leave the meadow and never come back. At least you'll live."

"Tell me what I have to do."

Ryan stopped circling and drilled his gaze into Jake, but Jake held his ground. Ryan couldn't kill him. Whatever this being threw at him, Jake would find a way to overcome.

"Tomorrow, meet here if you dare." Ryan pointed at the meadow. "Right here, and you will have one chance. If you survive, you will have the healing you desire. Healing that will stay with you when you leave this realm. You have my word. But know this also. The restrictions placed upon me to this point? They will be lifted if we meet again."

"We will meet again."

"Then know this in the depth of your soul." Ryan advanced three steps, then four toward Jake. "I've seen the future. If you come back, Jacob Palmer? You will die."

35

Jake's mind was still reeling as he hauled himself into his canoe. *Have to talk to Leonard.* He glanced frantically around the little cove, among the reeds, anywhere the old man might be. Nothing. *Always here? Every morning? Then why not today?*

After ten more minutes of futile searching, Jake headed for Leonard's house. Jake found him forty minutes later sitting in a lawn chair, staring at his garden. A second chair sat next to Leonard. Obviously he'd been expecting Jake.

"You weren't there this morning."

"Nah. Something in my gut told me you'd need a chance to calm down before we talked. That your visit wouldn't be the most pleasant. I thought the paddle back would give you a chance to clear your head."

"It's still a mud pit." Jake sat and gripped the arms of his chair hard. "Which is why I'm here."

"Then we're both here for the same reason."

"You told me the promise of the corridor comes with a price. And my time to pay is coming. What did you have to pay, Leonard?"

Leonard's eyes grew misty as he gazed up at the clouds. He held the position long enough for Jake to wonder if he'd decided to stop talking. But he finally brought his head back down and fixed his eyes on Jake.

"I was married for fourteen years to my third wife, but this time it was different. This time my marriage was a sappy, stupid, fairy-tale marriage where we never fought and loved each other more each day. She was light and life all bottled up in a concentrated form so potent that a few drops a day were all I could take. Any more and I would have died of happiness."

Jake frowned at him in surprise and Leonard waved his hands as if he could wipe the look off Jake's face.

"I know, I sound like a moron. Or like a chatterbox from a little-girl movie."

"No. You don't. You sound like you had a love as rare as gold."

Leonard turned away and Jake guessed the old man was wiping the tears off his cheeks. When he righted himself, his face was stoic again. "Go ahead, I know you want to ask what happened to this pink-cotton-candy-puffy-cloud bliss."

"I do."

"Pretty simple. Same thing millions have been through. She started coughing one day. Lasted long enough to go to the doctor, who told us if she was lucky she'd live a year. She died three months later."

Leonard gripped the sides of his chair and his arms shook.

"I came here to Willow Lake a year after she passed away. All I wanted was to be alone. But as fate would have it, I talked to a local who told me a fairy tale about the lake, and for reasons I still can't explain, I became obsessed with seeing if the legend was more than a folk tale.

"I didn't believe, but it gave me something to do to put a salve on my broken soul."

"Because the thing you wanted most in the world was to see her, be with her again."

Leonard's glare seemed to ask why Jake wasted the air in his lungs to make such an obvious statement. He dropped his gaze and Jake thought he might not start up again, but after an age, he scuffed the sod at his feet and continued.

"I knew it was impossible to see her again, truly see her again. She was gone and wasn't coming back. And I knew there was no chance of there being a path anywhere on this earth that would take me to the place where she would be."

Leonard's head swung slowly back and forth. "But I searched the end of the lake like I was searching for my own life, like if I didn't find the path to the field, I would die.

"That impression grew till I had no doubt the corridor was real and I had no doubt I'd find it. Only a matter of time. I still didn't think I'd find Anna on the other side, but that didn't slow my search in the least. It gave me a purpose, a passion, an obsession really."

Leonard lifted his head and peered at Jake from under his brows.

"But when you finally did find the corridor, to your utter astonishment, you found her as well."

"Baw!" Leonard waved his hand at Jake as if swatting flies. "You can't find the corridor. You can only put yourself in a position for it to find you."

So true.

"Was she there?"

"Yes and no."

Again, Leonard paused and seemed to vanish into a world inside his head. Jake imagined his elderly friend was revisiting moments experienced forty years earlier.

"Even now I don't know if she was really there or if what I saw was a vision or just a figment I made up in my mind or an angel who looked like her. Did it matter to me?"

Leonard drilled his gaze on Jake as if he truly wanted an answer to this question. Jake gave a tiny shake of his head.

"You're right, it didn't matter, because whatever it was, it was real and it was her. We talked about things only she and I would know. We walked around that meadow full of the thickest grass I've ever seen, around that pond of crystal water, and I allowed myself to sink into the greatest joy I've ever known before or since. I was blown to bits in the hurricane of her presence.

"We lay down together, backs up against a gnarled apple tree, and I fell asleep in that field. When I woke, she was gone." Leonard shook his head as his chin drooped again to his chest. "She was gone."

"And?" With his eyes, Jake begged Leonard to continue. "What then?"

Leonard looked up and glared at Jake with narrowed eyes. "You like this, don't you, Jacob?"

"What?"

"Seeing me wallow in this sickening sorrow."

"No."

"Sure you do. You want answers and you're willing to drag regrets from an old man." Leonard jabbed a finger at him and his voice grew louder. "Well, you're going to have to work for the answers. You're going to have to face the crucible yourself. Because if you don't, you'll end up like me."

By this time Leonard was shouting, and it took all of Jake's focus to stay calm. Whatever choice Leonard had made years ago had been eating his soul from the inside ever since. Finally his words petered out. He settled and seemed to shrink at least three inches into the lawn chair.

The truth was so obvious Jake scolded himself for not figuring it out earlier. "You can't get back, can you?"

Leonard didn't answer. Didn't move. Just stared at Jake with those steel-gray eyes. He didn't have to answer.

"That's why you're there every morning after all these years. You're trying to find the corridor again. But you can't. You're locked out somehow. You got what you wanted most in the world—you found her, talked to her—but then something happened that blew it all apart. Something that has kept you from getting back in all these years."

"Maybe you're not so stupid after all."

"Then give me the gift of a full education." Jake leaned forward, his heart thumping. "What choice did you make? What did you do or not do that shut you out?"

Leonard's gaze roamed the sky as he spilled out the rest of his story.

"After Anna vanished, I waited two days for her to return. Then a man appeared in the meadow. Called me by name.

Claimed I knew him, and that he knew me. He stood on the other side of the pond beckoning me to join him. So I did.

"Something about him was so familiar I was instantly drawn to him. A bit older than me, midforties by his look, knew things about me only God could know. I was wary—something about his eyes—but I listened to him because the things he said boggled my mind.

"Then he showed me things that stretched my beliefs further than I thought possible. It didn't take me long to figure out he was not a man, but a spiritual being of incredible power. And that's when he began to crawl under my skin. I saw things in his eyes I didn't like.

"The next day I came again, and again Anna wasn't there, but the man was. His talk was still full of honey, but at certain moments I saw his eyes grow so cold I was frightened. But even so, I asked where Anna was and if I would see her again that day. The man's answer was sharp. 'Tomorrow you will have the chance to fully grasp what you want most.'

"Of course I returned the next day, found the corridor as easily as I had the first three times, and when I met the man, I naturally asked when I would be united with Anna."

Leonard stopped talking and watched a dragonfly land on the apple box next to him. It seemed the dragonfly was looking at the elderly man, wanting him to continue the story, and when Leonard spoke again, it was to the dragonfly and not Jake.

"The being I called Arthur answered with a wave of his hand. Instantly Anna stood behind him, her eyes wide with fear. Arthur pulled two long knives out of his belt and laid out the rules quickly.

"'A blade for you, a blade for me. We fight to the death. If you win, Anna is yours. If I win, she is mine, and you will be gone from the meadow forever.'

"I tried to tell myself it was a joke, but Arthur leaped forward and sliced his blade through my forearm. Not deep, he was only sending a message about how real this battle would be, and how serious his declaration was.

"I'd never learned how to handle a knife, but I didn't see much choice. The fight was over minutes after it began. There I was, kneeling on the ground, trying to stop the blood seeping from my wounds. As the ground beside me darkened with my blood, I staggered up and tossed my blade at his feet."

Leonard pulled up his sleeves. Long, thick scars ran up and down his arms. He ran his finger along the longest one, glanced at Jake, then returned to the story.

"'Is that all you have?' Arthur mocked me with scorn in his voice. 'Where is your courage? Your valor? Will you not die for the one you love?'

"'I'll be back,' I shouted to Anna as I staggered toward the corridor. But before I could push aside the willow branches, Arthur called out in a voice that haunts me in my dreams.

"'If you leave here now, you'll never return, and you will never see Anna again.'

"I didn't believe him. I'd been to the corridor every day for four days in a row. I knew I could find it again." Leonard sighed.

"Part of me did believe him. But I convinced myself I could get back with my shotgun and kill Arthur and be with Anna forever. I looked at Anna and told her I loved her and that nothing would stop me from coming back for her, then pushed through the branches. I never saw her again."

Jake didn't speak. Didn't move. Simply waited for the revelation to settle. It all made sense now. Why Leonard seemed to have a love-hate relationship with the corridor. Why he seemed to want to help Jake one moment and thwart him the next. His friend was shattered by what he had done, or what he hadn't done. Part of Leonard wanted to see Jake find what he wanted most in the world; another part believed he would be sending Jake to his destruction. Destruction no matter which path he chose.

"She was my prize, the one I lived for. I never figured out how someone so beautiful, so kind, so perfect would love me. But she did. And I gave up on her. Gave up on us."

"Could you have beaten him?"

"My mind says no. Logic shouted it would have been impossible. I was bleeding out. Cut in six different places. The doctors said if I'd gotten to the hospital any later I wouldn't have made it."

Leonard let out a bitter laugh. "They asked if I had cut myself. That was of course the only explanation for what happened. Apparently I was incoherent. Kept babbling about the corridor and the meadow where I'd seen my dead wife and fought a man with knives."

Again, Jake let the emotions of the moment subside. He handed his blue water bottle to Leonard. Leonard took a long drink before handing it back.

"But there's only one thought that I've never doubted. For forty years now I've never wavered in this belief."

Leonard peered at Jake with haunted eyes. "I should have

stayed, Jacob Palmer. I should have continued to fight. Maybe I could have beaten him, figured out a way to win. At least I would have tried. At least I wouldn't have had to live these past forty years wondering *what if?* I should have realized Arthur was telling the truth and if I left, I would never return."

"How could you have realized that?" Jake said. "You didn't even know what the place was. Didn't know what kind of powers you were dealing with. Didn't know—and don't know—if what you and I have both experienced is all inside our heads. You don't know if those scars on your arms and legs came from your own hand. But you do know one thing. You knew that dying there in that meadow back in 1976 wouldn't have accomplished anything. And—"

"Oh, I know that, do I?" Leonard glared at Jake with fire in his eyes. "I know that it would have done nothing? Let me tell you something, boy. Let me describe for you what I do know for certain: I know that if I hadn't given up, if I'd died that day in that field on the other side of the corridor, I wouldn't be sitting here in a battered old-man body, drowning in a lake of my own regret day after day after day."

They sat in the silence for more than five minutes. Maybe longer. The sun continued to creep up their bodies, and the warmth of it somehow sparked hope inside Jake. But hope for what?

"What should I do, Leonard?"

"You can beat him, Jake. I believe it with everything in me. I don't know how, and I can't even start to explain why I believe that so strongly. But I do, right down here." Leonard patted his stomach and clenched his jaw.

"I don't think you'd be let into that place just to end up dead. I know that's not a lot to go on. It's almost nothing to go on. And I know I'm the one who never went back, who stayed on the sidelines. But I've had a lot of years to think about what I didn't do, and I'm not going to let this drop till I tell you how I feel and what I think your choice should be. Couldn't live with myself if I didn't, you understand?"

"How do I defeat a being that is obviously stronger than me? He's in control of what goes on inside the corridor, can bend reality to his will . . . how can I win?"

"I don't know. But I have to believe there's a way. I think you want to believe there's a way as well. Ultimately it's your choice to return, but let me ask you something."

Leonard stopped and peered at Jake for so long, he wondered if his old friend had decided not to ask the question.

"Even if you do die in there, and Ryan wins this war, what will you regret more? Giving up the shot to have your legs and stomach back, staying nice and safe and cozy in the life you're now living, or facing whatever this final test is and letting your chips fall where they may?"

"How do I even know that Ryan told the truth when he said there were rules he had to follow? How do I know he wasn't lying when he said that if I pass the tests, my restoration will remain?"

"You don't. Of course you don't."

For the first time since Jake had met the old man, Leonard leaned over and placed both his hands on Jake's shoulders and squeezed them tightly.

"But I think there's a piece inside you, a small piece way deep down, that knows what Ryan has spoken to you is true. And I think among all the Jake Palmers you've tried to be in your life, the real one wants this battle, whatever it is, more than anything he's ever wanted."

36

Jake stood on the edge of the dock staring down into the black water that night, racking his brain for the answer to whether he should launch himself into the unknown in the morning. He'd avoided Camille, of course, but also Andrew and Peter, even Susie. He needed the time to process, to think, to come to some sort of decision. But nothing had come. Then, just as a resolution to stay away from the end of the lake started to take shape, a deep voice from behind floated toward him.

"We gotta talk, Jake."

He turned to find Andrew standing at the bottom of the stairs.

"Andrew."

"There are a few things you need to hear."

Jake returned to gazing into the depths of the lake. "I appreciate the thought, but company is not what I need right now."

"Remember six years back when our pipes cracked and insurance didn't cover the cost, and outta the blue you fly out and help me redo the floor and paint and recarpet the place?"

"Yeah."

"You showed up for me. Now I'm showing up for you."

Andrew clomped down the ramp that connected to the dock. He stopped after he reached the planks faded white from years of harsh summer light and cold, wet winters. He spread his legs shoulder width and pulled his arms across his chest. "It's time to step up, my dear brother."

"I need to figure this out on my own."

"That's exactly what you don't need."

"Yeah, it is."

A gust of wind blew Andrew's thick hair off his forehead, revealing a deep scar that ran just below his hairline. Jake blinked. In all the years of knowing Andrew, Jake had never seen it. Instantly Jake realized why Andrew always wore hats when it was windy.

"Where'd you get . . ."

Andrew pulled his hair back and pointed at the scar. "This? You want to know about this, Jake? You want to know why I've never told you about this or how this happened in all the years we've known each other? You want to know why I keep it hidden? You think you're ready to hear the story?"

Andrew took another two steps forward.

"When I was a kid, my dad's brother was always friendly to me. And then one day he got a little too friendly. It went on for six months till one time something came over me and I fought and I broke free and sprinted away, but I tripped and cracked my head on a table and gave myself this forever reminder of those days."

Jake's friend came closer, till they stood within three feet of each other.

"I never told anyone but Susie, because for years I believed it was my fault, and the shame of those six months kept me hidden so deep in the shadows I didn't know the sun existed. But last year I took a step toward the light. Got some counseling. Worked through it. Susie has been my rock through the whole thing. And I'm free, Jake. Like I've never been before."

Andrew threw his big arm around Jake's neck the way he had in the bedroom a few days earlier.

"You're the label guy, so let me read a few things on your bottle. You inspire people. You encourage them. Bring them light. You're a three-in-the-morning-phone-call friend. You show people what freedom can look like, then lead them down that path.

"But Jake, baby, you're not free yourself. You're in a cage. So while I don't know what you're going through, I do know that it's time you face whatever is keeping you in the shadows. It's time to do whatever it takes."

Jake grabbed Andrew's forearm and squeezed tightly.

"One more thing."

"Sure," Jake said.

"I see it in your eyes. The war raging deep inside. And fear. I just want to say, whatever it is, don't back down. Trust this God of ours, and fight with all you have. Not for anyone else. Fight this battle with everything you have, for Jacob Palmer."

37

For the fifth time in ten days, Jake slid into the waters at the end of Willow Lake. The water felt colder, and he wished he'd waited for the sun to rise farther and warm him more before starting, but what was the point? This would either end well or end in death. No sense in dragging it out. And no matter what happened, he would take Andrew's counsel and trust God. There was no one else to turn to. In the moment he made that choice, a peace came over Jake he hadn't known since before the incident.

He pulled forward with a breaststroke, his breathing steady, his thoughts the opposite. Would he make it? Was he ready for this war? Ryan's words pinged through his mind. *If you survive, you will have the healing you desire. Healing that will stay with you when you leave this realm. You have my word. But know this also. The restrictions placed upon me up until this point? They will be lifted if we meet again.*

The width of the corridor had tapered down yet again. Now it was so narrow Jake had to push hard through the trees, even turned sideways. When he reached the end of the path, he pushed aside the willow branches and stepped onto the edge of the meadow. Nothing moved. No bird called, no blade of grass bent to the wind. Calm now, but the storm would come.

Seconds later, Ryan appeared fifty yards away, next to the pond, arms folded.

Jake didn't hesitate. He strode toward Ryan and slowly raised his hand and pointed at his enemy. "You're not all-powerful. There is only One who is. I can overcome today. I will overcome with his strength. So let the games begin."

"Yes." Ryan's stone expression didn't change. "Let us begin."

"What will it be, Ryan? Knives like you did with Leonard?"

"Knives? How archaic," Ryan scoffed. "Battles fought with guns, swords, knives are so stark. Devoid of nuance. No, for you, Jacob, I have something different. A battle where you'll be forced to fight against the turn of a phrase, against psychological feints and parries, against what brutalized you in days gone by."

Ryan grinned. "You'll have the chance to fight three battles you have previously lost. Three battles that represent the type you've longed to fight a second time, to prove you can do it right, fix things, and finally be enough for them."

"Who?"

"You don't need to ask, do you?" Ryan smiled, eyes cold. "You already know."

"My mom. My dad. Sienna."

"Oh, very good, very, very good, Jake. Once again, you impress me."

"Whatever you throw at me today using those three, I can overcome it. You won't defeat me."

"I will not have to. I have no doubt you will bring defeat upon yourself."

"How do I know you'll keep your word when I succeed?"

"As Leonard said, you don't. But do you have a choice?"

"Let's get this over with."

"Agreed." Ryan pointed to a narrow path on the far side of the apple orchard. "That's where you'll begin. There is truly nothing to explain. Follow that path. Things will become clear. I'm giving you a great gift, the chance to make things right. To finally be enough. If you can accomplish this, then I promise, you will be healed, and the healing will remain."

"How long do I have?"

Ryan tried to hold back a smile. "As long as you need."

As Jake passed the orchard and stepped onto the path, a groan of agony ripped through the air. Jake broke into a jog. Without question it was his mom's voice. He'd heard that cry of anguish almost every day of his childhood, till she'd taken her own life.

Another guttural groan smothered the woods, and he pushed faster down the narrow path, branches scraping across his legs, arms, face. Ahead, a thick cluster of branches blocked his way completely, but Jake closed his eyes, ducked his head, and pushed hard into the undergrowth. Three paces, maybe four, and he was out the other side. Ten yards in front of him, the path banked to the right. Jake plowed forward, driven by another low groan from up ahead.

As Jake dashed around the corner, the foliage opened up, the path widened, and a home came into view, a perfect replica of the house he grew up in. The low groan he'd heard floated out of the house and seemed to snake around his throat and grab hold. He steeled himself, strode down the gravel path, and stepped through the front door.

The entryway was dark, as was the living room. The groan came from his mom's bedroom and he eased toward the partially open door. The smell of cigarette smoke snaked out of the room. Jake clenched his teeth and walked inside.

Her bedroom was spotless—the influence of his dad lorded over her—but a smell like old wet newspapers filled his nose. His mom lay on the bed on a flowered comforter, a dingy white bathrobe cinched tightly around her gnarled body. A cluster of little orange pill bottles with white tops sat on the nightstand. The glow of the lamp put half his mom's face in silhouette, half in the light. The shock of seeing her again after so many years made Jake's knees wobble, but he held steady.

"Hello, Mom."

"Jakey, is that you?"

"Yeah, Mom. How are you?"

She only groaned in response.

His mom looked older than she'd been when she died. Wrinkles now lined her face, the way he imagined she'd have looked if she hadn't taken her life. The rings under her eyes had grown darker, her skin thinner, as if the years had stretched it to the point where it would tear soon.

"How are you?" Jake repeated.

"I'm tired, Jakey, so tired. I want to go to sleep for a long, long time. I want to go to sleep forever."

"No, Mom, I need you to take care of yourself. I need you to make the choice to live."

Her eyes moistened. "You need me?"

Jake hesitated. "Yes, I need you."

"But you're too busy for me. You're always off playing your baseball, and when you are here you mess things up and make life hard for me."

Not entirely surprising that she saw a child standing in front of her and not an adult.

"No, Mom. That's not true. I'm just a kid being a kid. But right now, you just need to promise me you'll take your medicine. That's all. Promise me."

"There you go." His mom waved her hands at the ceiling. "You're just like your dad, doing what you want to do, directing me around, telling me what to do."

"No, I'm not like Dad. I only want you to get better. Take care of yourself. I know you can do it.

"Mom, look at me. Forgive me for not being there more for you. I was wrong, but I tried and I was only a kid."

Her eyes watered as she ground out her cigarette, tilted her head back, and let the smoke seep from her cracked lips.

"Yes, Jake, you were. It was so hard, I was so alone and I needed you."

"Forgive me, Mom. I wasn't even a teenager yet. I should have been there for you more. But I didn't know how."

"You said that. It doesn't change anything."

"I know. But I want you to hear me. This is important. We can change things this time. I'm here now."

"Will you stay?"

"I don't know how long I'll be able to. But while I'm here, I'll do everything I can to make you feel better."

"Will you?" His mom shifted onto her side, and for the first time since he'd walked through her door, she looked into his eyes. "Will you sing for me? The funny song? You know the one."

Jake knew it. Yes. The one that always helped. The one that always made her laugh, always made her feel better. He racked his mind for the words, the melody.

"Can you, Jakey? Please."

He stared at her, begging the words to come, but there was nothing. He had to remember, had to! It would open her up to his words. And then, like a flash of lightning, it was there.

"Sing it, please? Make me smile. Make me laugh. It would help so much, you know it would help." A toothy smile teetered on her face.

"Okay, Mom."

"Sing it!" His mom pushed herself up, her hands jammed into the white mattress, eyes wild. "Sing it! Sing it! Sing it!"

Jake swallowed and took a step back. "I will. But if I do, you have to promise me something."

She slumped back in bed. "What, Jakey? What do I have to do for you? Always doing something for you. I ask if you'll do something for me, and you end up asking if I can do something for you. Always about you, isn't it? Isn't that the way it's always been? Yes, it has. Always about Jakey. What Jakey wants. What about me, Jakey? What about me!"

"I want to sing the song for you, Mom. I do. But you have to make me a promise. That's all."

"What promise?"

"Live, just live. Just promise to take your pills and live."

His mom's eyes fluttered and she smiled again. A real smile this time, and her eyes cleared.

"You want me to live."

"Yes, more than anything."

"Thank you, Jakey."

She reached out for him and he took her cold, battered hand and began to sing. By the time he finished, her laughter had sent tears of joy down her cheeks, and as grueling as it was to sing that song, Jake felt lighter, freer, because he knew it had worked. It was far less arduous than he'd expected. But that only meant his dad and Sienna would be harder.

After a few minutes of silence, as he watched his mom rock back and forth, eyes closed, a smile on her face, Jake let his hand slide from his mom's and eased toward the door.

When he reached her bedroom door, she opened her eyes. "Thank you for saving me, Jakey."

"You're going to be okay, Mom. I promise."

"I promise too." She glanced at the row of orange bottles on her nightstand. "I love you, Jakey."

"I love you too, Mom."

As Jake strode out the front door of his mom's house, relief flooded through him. Not easy. But he'd done it. Kept his mom from taking her life. Made things right and been enough. Even though part of him accepted that it hadn't happened twenty-five years ago, it had happened now. He'd done what he couldn't do all those years ago. And it counted. One down, two to go.

When he reached the main path, Jake turned left at a fast clip. Get it done. He didn't have to guess who would be next. Had to be his dad, because Ryan would save the toughest for last: Sienna. His parents? He had ideas on how to fix things, be enough for them. But Sienna? Not one iota of a clue. He shook the thought from his mind. Just take care of his dad. Worry about Sienna when he got to her.

As he strode down the wood-chip-covered path, a shout from farther up seemed to fill the sky. His dad's voice. That cheerful, grating voice. No surprise. Jake pressed his palms into his eyes and took in a deep breath. He would be enough, whatever he encountered. He would fix it, do it right this time around. Jake broke into a jog and soon reached a smaller path that would lead to his dad.

The moment he started down it, the sound of hammering reverberated through the woods. As he headed down the trail toward the ringing, something about it unearthed a memory buried deep. Didn't feel like a good one. No surprise.

As he got closer the banging stopped and the sound of a saw biting into wood started. The memory surfaced but was still muddled. But by the time the trees started to thin out, he knew exactly what he was about to face. Harder than what just happened with his mom? Yeah, probably, but Jake had no doubt he could handle it.

Thirty more steps and the tiny path spat him out into a small clearing. No, not a clearing. A lawn. Terraced flower beds to the right. A freshly painted swing set to the left. Jake's backyard from when he was a kid.

Cedar planks were precisely stacked to the right and left of Jake's dad, who was on his knees, saw in hand. His back was to Jake. The old red flannel shirt his dad always wore when working on projects was perfectly tucked in, and his work boots looked like they'd been shined that morning.

Nine? Ten? That's the age Jake had been when his dad stood in their garage and invited Jake to join him in the backyard to build a doghouse. He'd blown it. Bent the nails. Sawed the boards crooked. Didn't line anything up correctly. There were a thousand other times he hadn't been what his dad wanted. Why revisit this one? It didn't matter. All that mattered was making it right.

"Boy oh boy, Jaker," his dad had said that day. "You surely messed it up this time. What in the world am I going to do with you? Let's do it right this time, huh, pard? We always do things right around the Palmer household, don't you know."

The image of his dad's joyless smile hanging over him as he tried again and again and again plastered itself to the wall of Jake's mind. The afternoon had worn on into early evening, but ten-year-old Jake never got it right. But now, that was all going to change.

"Hey, Jaker!" His dad looked up, glanced at his watch, then back to Jake. "Did I get our time wrong, or are you late?"

"I think I'm late."

"Let's not let that happen again, pard, okay? We want to be members of the on-time-all-the-time club, right?"

"Yeah, Dad, we do."

"*We* do?"

"I do."

"Good man. Okay then. Wonderful." His dad motioned at the boards with his saw. "Why don't we dive in and put this structure together."

For the next two hours, Jake did exactly what his dad instructed him to do, not with the skills of a ten-year-old, but with those of a thirty-seven-year-old. His dad kept up his usual stream of banter that was sickeningly cheerful because it wasn't real. His dad was the original velvet hammer, seemingly nice as apple pie, but if you didn't live life exactly as he thought it should be lived, he would smash your thumb and pay no attention to how much it hurt.

When they finished, his dad crawled around on his hands and knees examining the doghouse. "Well, well, well, Jaker! Looks pretty good, pretty doggone good!" His dad laughed at his own joke and relief rose up in Jake. He'd done it. Been enough for his dad, at least this time.

Maybe he hadn't joined ROTC, or gone to work in Alaska on a fish processor, or taken that internship with his dad's integrity-deprived friend down in Texas, but he'd built the doghouse the way his dad wanted.

"Did you hear me, Jaker?" His dad chuckled, hands on hips.

"Sorry, Dad. What was that?"

"You heard, or if you didn't, time to get the wax out of your ears." His dad gave him a lopsided smile.

"I might need to get some wax out."

The smile didn't leave his dad's face, but his eyes were ice. "What I said was, pretty good might be fine for some people, but not for the Palmers. You need to pay attention to your work, Jaker. You can't be sloppy, can't be goofing off." He pointed at the struc-ture. "That's nothing you could ever be proud of."

Jake pointed at the doghouse. "Are you serious? That—"

"Don't say something you'll later regret there, pard." His dad waved his hand over the doghouse. "Tear 'er apart. Let's go again."

Jake rebuilt the house. Again it wasn't good enough. After the third time of tearing apart and rebuilding the doghouse, accompanied by his dad's third berating, Jake broke.

"It's just a doghouse," he growled at his dad. "And it's as near perfect as is possible."

"Nope." His dad waggled his finger. "That's where you're dead wrong, Jaker. It's much more than a doghouse. You're off by a centimeter on this doghouse, it sets you up to be off a centimeter in life. And a centimeter doesn't sound like much when you're ten, but if you keep being off by a centimeter, by the time you're thirty, you're off by miles. Let's go again."

By the seventh time they'd torn the structure apart and rebuilt it, Jake's hands ached like he'd never known. His eyes burned, and the skin of his knees was so tender he couldn't put any weight on them. But he was done. His dad approved Jake's seventh attempt.

Jake shook his dad's hand to say good-bye as he'd done since he was six years old, then wobbled down the tiny trail that led back to the main path. He'd told himself his dad would be more challenging than being enough for his mom. Obviously he was more right than he imagined. Which did not bode well for what was next. Sienna.

38

As he shuffled down the path, Jake rubbed his hands, trying to bring some life back into them, and at the same time trying to guess what he would have to do for Sienna. Jake had always been there for her. Believed in her dreams of becoming a clothing designer. Encouraged her during the lean years. *Don't give up, it's coming, it's coming.* And when success finally rained down on her, he soaked it in with her. Flowers, trips, surprise birthday parties. Their marriage had cracks like any marriage, but nothing even close to major. He'd been everything she wanted him to be. He'd been more than enough. As Jake strode up the path, he scoured his brain for what he hadn't done. There had to be something to make right.

Should be a path leading to her house coming up. There. Thirty yards ahead. He broke into a jog, his knees tender but already feeling better, reached the trail, and slowed to a quick walk. After forty or fifty feet of a gently winding path bordered by pine trees, the trees gave way to a house that sat on top of a two-story boulder. Smooth. No apparent way up. Part of the challenge? Or symbolic? It didn't matter. Jake would find a way up.

He clipped around to the right, running his tender fingers along the surface of the boulder. Nothing. Still smooth, but when he reached the back, he found slots cut into the rock at four- and five-feet intervals. Not easy. Impossible to do with his burnt legs, but in here he would make it, even with them aching from kneeling on the grass for the past five hours. He was more worried about his hands. No clue if he had enough strength in them. Time to find out.

The first slot in the boulder was cut ten feet above him. Jake stepped back five paces, then dug his shoes into the green turf and propelled himself forward at a dead sprint. He leaped up and planted his foot hard on the boulder, praying it would hold. It did, and he launched himself upward. *Stretch hard. Yes!* He grabbed the cut in the rock, then found an imperfection to his right. He tested it with his shoe. Solid. He pushed off again and reached the cut twelve feet up.

From there the boulder flattened to forty-five degrees and the cuts were spaced out evenly every three feet. Jake easily navigated the remaining section of the boulder and stood panting on top, staring back the way he'd come. He couldn't see the spot where his dad was, but his mom's house was just visible through a break in the trees. As he stared at it, it shimmered, then slowly melted into nothing. Yes. Confirmation. It was over. Hope rose inside Jake, and with it, renewed energy. He'd done it. Fixed things with his mom. Same with his dad. Now, the final piece. Sienna. *Deep breath. No time to hesitate.* He pushed open the front door, his heart hammering, and stepped inside.

Sienna sat nestled on a green leather couch, the one they'd

bought together right after getting married. Her feet were up on a coffee table Jake didn't recognize.

"Hey, sweetie," Sienna said.

Jake stood in the entryway and tried to stay calm. It was their house exactly as it had been a week before he'd been burned. A house he hadn't stepped inside for over a year. All the old memories, the good memories, buried him in an avalanche of emotion.

"You okay?"

"I don't know what I'm supposed to do."

The words slipped out before Jake could stop them, but if they confused Sienna, she didn't show it.

"Then let me assist." She patted the couch. "You're supposed to come over here, sit down, and give me a long, passionate kiss."

He stared at her as he shuffled forward, not knowing how to ask what he could do to make things right.

Sienna looked up from her book and set it aside. "You okay?" she said again.

Of course this moment wouldn't be current day. Just as the scenes with his mom and dad had been set in the past, this one would be too.

"Yeah, I'm good."

"Then why do you have a look on your face like you haven't stepped foot in this place for a year and haven't seen me in even longer?"

"It's hard to explain."

"Then don't. Get over here and give me a kiss." She smiled wide and patted the couch again.

Jake didn't move, his feet frozen to the black stone floor. "We're good. You and me. We're good."

"Good?" Sienna stood. "No, we're not good. Not good, not good, not good. We're fantastic."

She picked up a remote from their glass coffee table and pointed it at the fireplace, and flames appeared. "For a bit of ambience."

Jake ignored the repulsion the sight of the flames sent through him. "I have to ask you a question."

"Sure." She sauntered over to him and threw her arms around his neck. "Anything."

"In our life together, where have I not been enough for you?"

"What?" Sienna pulled away, took two steps back, and scrunched up her face. "What are you talking about? You've always been enough for me."

"I'm serious, Sienna. I need to know this. Where have I let you down? Where haven't I come through?"

"You want to know? You really want to know?"

"Please."

She stuck out her hip and pointed at him with mock anger on her face. "I've asked you two times now for a kiss, and you've turned me down both times. There. There's where you've let me down. Not been even close to enough."

"Sienna, please."

Her hips swayed from side to side as she came back to him, sliding her arms around his neck again. "You are really kind to ask, but there's nothing. You've been everything I've ever dreamed of."

Jake wished she were kidding, but this Sienna was serious.

Where could he go from here? If there was no problem, there was no solution, and he was in a stalemate.

"Let me ask you something else then."

"Sure." She motioned toward the green couch. "But could we sit while you ask me?"

"Yeah, no problem."

She took his hand and Jake fought the part of him that screamed this was real. It wasn't. It was only a test. And he would not fail.

As soon as they settled onto the couch, Sienna pulled her knees up on the cool, green leather and stroked Jake's hair. "Okay, sweetie. Ask away."

"If I was in a fire, and I was burned—my torso, my feet, legs, everything from my stomach down—would you still love me?"

"That's never going to happen."

"But if it did."

"Of course I'd still love you."

"I need you to think about this."

"I love you, Jake." She leaned in and gave him a quick kiss. "You. What's inside. The outside, too, of course. I mean, you're gorgeous, but I love *you*." Sienna frowned. "Why don't you tell me why you're asking all these strange questions?"

Jake stared at her for only a second before agreeing. Why not? Maybe if he told her the story, he'd figure out what it was he had to make right. When he finished, she smiled and then a contemplative look came over her face.

"If I could believe, even for a moment, what you're saying— which of course I can't—then I'd tell you exactly what you should do."

"All right."

"You got what you wanted. Your body restored." She pointed at his torso and legs, then opened her arms wide and glanced around the room. "And you have this, all back. And me. Right here."

She took his face and brought their noses together. "So if you have everything you've ever wanted, why would you leave?"

"I can't stay here."

"Why not?"

"It doesn't work that way." He got up and moved to the back of the room, where a picture window overlooked a parkland, and kept his back to Sienna.

"Why not? How do you know? Did you ask your lying, back-stabbing pal Ryan? Have you met someone who tried to stay but couldn't?"

Jake's conversation with Leonard flooded into his mind. Leonard had wanted to stay. Suddenly Sienna's question wasn't insane. Could he stay? Was that what Ryan meant? That the healing would remain if he passed the test, which meant staying indefinitely in the meadow? Was it even possible? And what did that mean for everyone on the other side? Did time stop here forever?

The questions melted away as he turned and stared at Sienna, as beautiful as she'd ever been. The thought of taking her in his arms and feeling the rush of her lips on his filled him. In that moment there was nothing he wanted more. He'd been restored, and this would be the crown jewel in his celebration. Jake moved toward her, a smile on his face, and she began to move toward him.

But just before they reached each other, the truth, unbidden, filled him like the sun breaking through a cloud-soaked summer afternoon. Even though every emotion inside him shouted it was right, staying here with Sienna could not have been more wrong. Jake held up his fingers to stop Sienna from sliding into his arms.

"No, I can't let this happen."

"What are you talking about?"

He stared at her and let a puff of surprise seep out of his mouth. "I thought you would be the hardest by far, and in a way you are, but not in the way I expected. The hard part is to not choose you.

"But being enough for you? Fixing things now? There's nothing to fix, is there? I *was* enough for you. I gave you everything I had, gave you my whole heart, and until I was burned, it was enough. But it's okay, because I left nothing on the table."

"What are you talking about?"

"There's nothing to take out of here except the choice to live in the truth."

"What truth are you talking about?"

"My body was burned, Sienna, whether you believe it or not. It happened. And you rejected me because of it. If I stayed here with you, I would always know that. Know I was living a lie. I came here today to fight for the truth, and that's what I'm going to do. Because I think that was the final test. As much as I wished things could go back to the way they were, the test was to choose the truth instead. It's over. And I've won."

Jake strode toward the door as a smile broke out on his face, followed by laughter. He'd done it.

"Jake! Come back here. Jake!"

Just before walking through the door, he turned his smile to her. "I wish you a good life, Sienna."

By the time Jake reached the ground at the back of the boulder, he was almost giddy. He'd done it, faced his mom, faced his dad, most of all, faced Sienna. And now, to get back through the corridor and leave this place forever.

As he strode around the back of the boulder and onto the trail, he clenched his fists in victory. And then, before he was halfway back to the main path, Ryan stepped into view.

39

Ryan clapped slowly. Each time his hands came together they sounded like a shot, the smirk on his face mocking Jake even before he reached the main path.

"Well done, Jacob."

"It's over, Ryan."

"Yes, yes, yes." Ryan cocked his head as if listening, then held up a finger. "Wait. Wait. Maybe not quite finished."

A voice, not distinguishable, called out from a long ways away. A second later, the voice grew in strength. By the time five seconds had passed, Jake knew who it was.

Ryan jerked his thumb down the trail. "If I'm not mistaken, that sounds like your father calling."

"No. Don't play mind games. I finished that."

Ryan frowned as Jake's dad's voice grew louder. "Apparently not."

"What are you doing?"

"I'm doing nothing. This is about what you need to do. That, and that alone."

"Don't mess with me, Ryan." Jake brought his fists up to chest level.

Ryan peered at Jake's fists and laughed. "There's no need to think of violence. I speak the truth when I agree you were enough for Sienna and that you chose wisely. Congratulations. That part is finished. However, it doesn't appear you're quite finished with your dad."

Jake glared at Ryan and strode toward his father. As he reached the small trail off the main path, his dad's voice boomed through the woods like a cannon.

"Jaker, where are you, pard? Let's get this done!"

Jake jogged down the path, which ended in the same exact place as last time. The perfect doghouse stood where he'd left it, on the edge of his dad's perfect lawn. His dad stood on the deck off the back of the house, hands on hips, a sarcastic smile on his face. As soon as he saw Jake, he pulled open the screen door and stepped inside.

Jake crossed the lawn in five strides, reached the back of the porch, bounded up on the deck, and pushed into the kitchen. His father sat at the far end of the kitchen table, his arms folded. A sheet of yellowed paper lay in front of him next to a red folder.

"Go on ahead and sit down, Jaker, do you mind?"

Jake stood at the end of the table and gritted his teeth against the sickly sweet tone his dad used to ask questions that were not in fact questions.

"What's wrong, Dad?" There was no reason to sit until he knew what he had to do this time.

"Could you go on and grab yourself a chunk of chair there,

Jaker?" His dad extended his hand toward the chair, his eyes like ice.

Jake mashed his lips together to keep from screaming, then said, "What do you want from me?"

"Whadda we have right here?" His father held up the paper and snapped his finger against it.

"I don't know."

"I think you do know, so go ahead and take a bit more of a peek."

Jake leaned forward and squinted at the paper and he knew what it was. Knew why his dad was upset. This same scene had played out in fourth grade, eighth grade, and his junior year in high school.

"Let me fix it." Jake remained standing. "What do you want me to do?"

Wide smile. Arctic eyes. "I want you to sit down, right now. That's what I want you to do."

Jake sat, elbows on the table, legs twitching.

"Let's go ahead and remove those elbows from the table, why don't we? That's not the way Palmers sit at the table, is it?"

Jake pulled his arms into his lap. No shame. He wouldn't allow his mind to go there. Just get this done. Jake repeated the question. "What do you want me to do?"

"Your report card." His dad snapped the paper again. "Says here you got two B-minuses. That's not going to be working for anyone now, is it? Nope, not in a million years. How are you ever going to be enough for a college to take a serious look at you if you can't be enough in grade school?"

Jake glanced at the table's shadow on the kitchen floor. It seemed like it was reaching out to choke him and he swallowed hard. Play the game. Tell him what he needed to hear. Fix it. Be enough.

"I'm sorry, Dad. I messed up. Didn't study hard enough. I won't disappoint you again, I promise. What can I do to make it up to you?"

His dad opened the red folder and pulled out two sheets of white paper. He slid them over to Jake, then tossed him a pencil.

"You're going to take a little test I made up. And if you get any of the answers wrong, you're going to study, then take another test. We're going to do this till you get it right. Put your name on the test, upper right corner on top of the thick line."

Jake snatched up the pencil and started to write his name, but he pressed too hard, snapped off the tip of the pencil, and the shame he'd promised to ignore washed over him. He looked up at his dad without lifting his head.

"Here you go, Jaker." His dad tossed him a pencil sharpener. "Ease up on the pressure there. We don't need to be wasting any of that pencil now, do we?"

Jake blew out a breath from between his teeth as he sharpened the pencil and looked at the questions. Jake fought against the emotions screaming that he was eleven years old again, disappointing his father for not making straight As. He wasn't eleven and this was his chance to fix the past. Had to push through the shame, dig deep, get through it.

The questions were for a fifth grader. He buzzed through them and pushed the paper back at his father. His dad took less than a minute to check Jake's answers. He looked up at Jake but didn't speak. He didn't have to. The tight smile across his face shouted plenty loud.

"One wrong, Jaker. Let's try again."

As his dad pulled another sheet out of the folder, Jake couldn't hold his tongue.

"I'm not a kid," he muttered to himself. "This is ridiculous."

"What did you say?"

Jake's face went hot. How could his dad have heard that?

"You think this is ridiculous? Hmm. Don't believe I'm able to agree with that assessment of your situation, Jake. In fact, I'm not going to believe that sentiment came out of your mouth. No sirree. That would make you stupid. And I don't think my son is stupid, not for a second."

"No, I'm not."

"And you are a kid, Jake. You might think being eleven makes you a man, but it doesn't. Got it?"

Jake nodded.

"I want to hear the words. Do you understand me?"

"Yes, I'm sorry, Dad. I understand you."

"I'm helping you here, Jake. You get in the habit of getting good grades now, it will stay with you the rest of your life. But if you don't figure it out, it'll dog you till the day you die."

"Yes, Dad."

Three tests later, Jake got all the answers right.

"Good work, Jaker." His dad rose from his end of the table, came over to Jake, and clapped him on the shoulder. "Now that wasn't so bad, was it?"

"No, Dad."

"Okay then, head on out the door and we'll see you at supper."

Jake nodded but didn't look up. At least this was grade school and not high school or college. He'd fixed things this time, but what about the other three times he didn't get straight As?

"Are there any other tests, Dad?" Jake stood. "Any others, or is this it?"

"The only one."

Jake pushed through the kitchen door onto the deck and didn't look back. Last test? Maybe. But Jake shuddered as he strode back down the path with the thought it wasn't close to the last fix he would have to make.

He reached the main trail and jogged back down it toward the path to Sienna's house. When he reached it, he started down the tinier path, but stopped halfway down and looked up through the trees. Where he'd expected to find the boulder with their old house on top of it, there was only sky.

Hope surged inside. He truly had fixed that one. He'd fixed his mom. Maybe this last go-around with his dad really was enough. If only he was dumb enough to believe it.

Two minutes later he reached the path that led to where his mom's home had stood. He slowed, then came to a retched halt when a familiar groan floated down the path toward him. Jake shuffled down the trail to find his mom's home had reappeared. Hell's version of déjà vu. When he reached her bedroom, a twisted cackle sputtered out of her mouth.

"I'm glad you came when you did, Jakey. If you hadn't shown up, well, let's just say I don't think I would have been here to greet you if you'd come any later."

"Don't do this, Mom. You promised. We fixed this."

"When did we fix this?" Jake's mom frowned. "Fixed what?"

"I was just here. You promised."

"You haven't been here in ages, Jakey." She peered up at him, confusion bathing her face. "But you can do something to help me right now. Please?"

"What, Mom?" Jake asked, even though he knew what was coming.

"Will you sing me that song you used to sing? You know the one, don't you, Jakey?"

40

By the time Jake finished with his mom, his emotions were as ragged as they'd ever been. He'd sung for over an hour before she promised not to end her life. But there was no guarantee the promise would stick. Ryan had created a house of horrors that Jake might never escape. But it didn't mean he wouldn't try.

Jake stumbled through his mom's front door and down the path toward the main trail, his mind frayed, his body almost as exhausted, but he would not stop till he'd fixed things for good.

"Had enough?"

Ryan's voice. Jake didn't look up. He refused to give Ryan the satisfaction of seeing the absence of hope in his eyes.

"You can't make me go through the same thing again and again. You're breaking your own rules." Now Jake looked up and strode toward Ryan, his anger funneling strength back into his body and mind.

Ryan only smiled, which fueled Jake further.

"You'll never fix everything, Jake. You can't win."

He could. He'd been doing this all his life—with his parents, with Sienna, with friends. He knew the routine, and he could outlast Ryan no matter how many times the scenarios were thrown at him.

He would fix his mom again and again and again. As long as it took. Same with his father. He'd build the doghouse three hundred times if necessary. He'd take the test a thousand times in order to make it right. Sing the insipid song to his mom for centuries if he had to.

He tore off down the path toward his father's backyard and found the doghouse in pieces, and built it again, again endured his father's criticism. Then raced back to his mom's and she promised Jake for the third time that she wouldn't take her life.

Then again taking the tests. Again with his mom. Another two hours building the doghouse. He would not go down. It had to work. He would not falter, not fail. But even as he shouted promises to himself, he knew they were lies. No matter how many times he tried, he would never fix it. Ryan had said Jake would defeat himself and it was true. Eventually he would admit three hundred times, a thousand times, a million times would not be enough.

After he stumbled out of his mom's house for the twenty-fifth time and out to the path that would lead to his dad, he went the opposite direction. He had to recover. Think. Figure a way out, a solution to this insane puzzle.

The path meandered slightly uphill and Jake staggered up it, barely paying attention to his feet. As he pressed on, something moved in his peripheral vision. Jake spun and his eyes darted through the foliage, searching among the trees. There. Again, movement. Jake squinted. Ryan? Yes.

Ryan stood six paces off the path, almost hidden next to a large pine tree. Jake spotted him and in the same moment snagged the front of his shoe on a root. His momentum threw him forward; he lost balance and crashed to the ground. Sharp pain shot into his knees and his elbow.

The sound of Ryan stepping closer through the underbrush thundered in his ears. Jake pushed up to his hands and knees but didn't look up, his gaze fixed on the tiny pine needles on the path. This was the end. He felt it and waited for Ryan to strike him down. But the blow didn't come. The being was taunting him again. No blow was needed. Not even words were necessary. His mere presence squeezed at Jake's head like a press. Jake had been beaten and would always be beaten, no matter how long he stayed on this treadmill.

"What are you doing to me?" Jake drew in ragged breaths. "Why torture me like this? This will never end, will it? What sick pleasure are you getting out of this? Watching me fail again and again. I can't beat you. I admit it. So why not just kill me and end this charade?"

"Rise, Jacob Palmer."

The force of Ryan's words sent a tremor through Jake. There was a strength and authority in his tone Jake couldn't ignore. Jake staggered to his feet and locked eyes with his enemy. There was a look of steel in Ryan's eyes, like a sword ready to strike.

"What are you waiting for?" Jake didn't back down from Ryan's intensity. It drove him harder. "I'm done with this game, this test of yours. It's finished."

"It's not over."

"Yes, it's done."

"You are blind, Jake. Open your eyes."

As the words floated out of Ryan's mouth, Jake's gaze shifted from Ryan's eyes to just over his shoulder. Twenty, maybe thirty yards up the path, Jake spotted a tiny trail off to the right. He stared at it, transfixed, knowing with more conviction than he'd ever known anything that he had to discover whatever was at the end of that path.

⁂

The narrow trail was covered in green moss and slalomed into the trees for forty yards before it curved to the left, out of sight. As Jake started down it, the ache in his muscles subsided, if only a touch, and the frustration started to seep out of his mind.

He reached the curve a minute later, and when he did he saw a small cabin fifty feet ahead made of light-colored wood. It looked new, its thick log walls offset by large windows on each side and a large porch with four chairs.

A waterfall similar to the one that fed the pond sat off to the right, this one higher, wider, with a greater rush of water pouring over the edge. Jake's eyes followed the path of the stream through the woods till he couldn't see it anymore.

The door of the cabin was open. When he reached the porch he stepped up on it, but hesitated before going inside. There was a power here that he'd never experienced, a sensation radically different from the sensations he'd felt at his mom's, dad's, and Sienna's houses. A moment to ready himself, then he stepped inside.

A young boy sat in profile on a thin wooden chair in the center of the room. Sun streamed in from a large window and filled the space with light. A fireplace filled the wall behind the boy, and a redwood table with three chairs around it stood in the far corner. The floor was wood. Rustic but clean.

"Hello?"

"Hello, Jake." The boy didn't turn.

"Who are you?"

"Would you like to join me?" The boy motioned to a chair directly across from him.

Jake eased over into it and stared at the boy. Familiar.

"Do we know each other?"

"Yes."

"Who are you?"

"Before that, there is much for us to talk about." The boy leaned forward, knees on elbows, and grinned. "Only if you want to."

"Sure."

"Can I ask you a question, Jake?"

Jake nodded.

"What is it that you want fixed? What is the one thing you want made right, the deep longing inside you, the one so deep you only hear echoes of its faint calling?"

"I want to be made whole. I want my legs back, my stomach, my feet, all back to the way they were."

The boy shook his head slowly back and forth, not in a wondering way, but with kindness and understanding. "Deeper, Jake. Go deeper."

Jake didn't have to think, didn't have to formulate an answer. He simply spoke from his heart.

"Go back in time. Do life over again. Be whole again. Wipe out the red in my ledger and be what they needed me to be. Be enough."

"They? Who is they?"

"My mom, Sienna, my dad."

"Sienna? I thought you were enough for her. Isn't that what you discovered today?"

"Be enough for another woman."

"Really?" The boy arched an eyebrow. "So you don't believe Ari when she said your burns wouldn't matter to her."

Jake stared at the boy.

"No, I don't think you need to be enough for another woman, I think you need to be enough for your mom and for your dad. That is the root. That is where it all comes from."

"Where what all comes from?"

"You know, Jake. You don't need me to tell you. Go deeper still. I am safe. You can tell me."

He hadn't even officially met this boy, and yet Jake knew what he spoke was true. He could trust this child, so young but so full of wisdom.

"I won't ever be enough for them. Even back then, I couldn't have ever been enough for them." As the words slipped out of his mouth, Jake was stunned by the truth. He looked up at the boy and said, "There's nothing I could have done to be enough. I did it all. Everything I could to make my dad proud. Everything I could to be the son my mom wanted me to be."

"Yes, you did."

"And that's why I was enough for Sienna." Jake shook his head as the revelation poured over him. "But I wasn't even doing it for her. I was doing it for my mom, my dad. To get them to love me."

"Yes, Jake. Yes."

Jake looked up again at the boy, who now had tears in his eyes.

"What would life look like if you could accept yourself, Jake? What would it look like if you realized the fault in your growing up was not yours, but parents who were just children themselves? Parents who tried but simply did not know how to love you because of their own brokenness? What if you realized you are worth being loved not for what you look like, or how powerful your body is, or what you've accomplished, but simply because you are?"

Tears now streamed down the boy's face, accompanied by a radiant smile.

"What if you were to step outside the bottle and show the world who you really are? What if you didn't have to be perfect for anyone? What if you knew you are complete, and perfect, and perfectly loved exactly as you are? What if you knew that the burns you carry are a physical reflection of the burns you carry inside, and that the far greater healing would be of those burns that cover your soul? What if you realized you *are* Superman? Complete, powerful, whole in the Son of God? What if you knew these things, Jake Palmer?"

As the boy spoke each question, understanding rose up in Jake. Not just understanding, but healing. Not just healing, but forgiveness. For his mom, for his dad, for Sienna—but that was nothing compared to the forgiveness that thundered up out of him for himself. For not being enough for his mother and father.

And as he gave himself the gift of unquenchable grace, the tears he'd been fighting to contain exploded out of him and he leaned forward, head in hand, his body racked with sobs from the deepest part of his soul. As he did, the cabin itself seemed to shudder with a freedom and joy that reverberated off the walls.

After a time he felt a hand on his shoulder, the boy's hand, but it felt stronger than a boy's hand should feel. Jake lifted his head and blinked his eyes. The boy was no longer a boy, but a young man, at least four or five years older.

"What?" Jake shook his head. "What is happening?"

The young man smiled, now a hint of facial hair playing on his chin, his jaw strong, eyes even more full of wisdom than before. He held up a finger as if to place Jake's question on hold.

"What do you really want, Jake? The deepest desire of your being."

"This." Jake spread his fingers wide and placed his hands on his chest over his heart. "I want to be whole, here."

The young man nodded. "And?"

"It's happening right now."

The young man nodded again, and as Jake fixed his gaze on him, his face grew from that of a young man to one in his midtwenties. The same dark hair, the same eyes, the same angle of the shoulders. It couldn't be, but it was.

"I don't understand what is happening."

"Yes, you do, Jake." The man laughed, his head thrown back. The sound sent a lightning bolt of joy through Jake's heart. "You know exactly what is happening. I'm growing up. Right before your eyes."

"I created you. Out of my imagination."

The man fixed his eyes on Jake and laughed again, even more powerfully, if that was possible, and it echoed through the small cabin and shot such life into Jake that he thought he might explode.

"Yes and no. I'm as real as you are, Jake. Trust me that this is true. And yet you are right; you did imagine me. But more than imagine me. You've known me as long as you've existed. I've always been here. But you hid me away. Covered me up. Forgot that I existed, even when those around you told you I did. But now those days are over. You have done it, Jake. You have taken the long journey and at last have found me."

Jake stared at the man for eons before he spoke what he'd somehow known seconds after stepping into the cabin. "You are me."

The man nodded as smiles broke out on both their faces.

41

When Jake finally forced himself to leave the cabin and walk back toward the meadow, he tried to convince himself that he didn't have to look at the place where his mom's house had been. *Had been.* Funny how he didn't have a shred of doubt it would be gone—just as he didn't doubt Ryan would be gone—but when he reached the tiny trail that led to her home, he found his feet shuffling over the pine needles once more. He had to see it.

He kept his eyes focused on the path till he reached the point where he knew the house would be in view. When he looked up, he found himself gazing at a massive willow. Jake chuckled. The perfect replacement.

He was right. Gone as if it had never existed. But about Ryan, Jake was wrong.

After he walked through the apple orchard into the meadow, he gazed in a wide arc and spotted Ryan sitting at the base of the waterfall.

Jake approached cautiously, and yet he wasn't sure why. He'd won. Found the healing he'd wanted all his life. Was now living in a freedom he didn't think possible. What could Ryan do to him at this point?

When Jake was ten yards away, Ryan rose to his feet and smiled. A different smile. An old smile. The one Jake had come to know the first two times they'd met.

"Hello, Jacob Palmer. You know what your last name means, don't you? 'Pilgrim.' And you have completed your quest. Well done, Jake. Well done."

Once again, revelation swept over Jake. "You're not . . . you're not . . ."

"Your enemy? No." Ryan chuckled. "No, I am your friend. I always have been. Yes, I was distressed to see the pain my actions caused you, but as I told you that day at the river, they were necessary."

"What?" Jake tried to wrap his mind around Ryan's pronouncement, but it was almost too much to take. "The things you said, the things you admitted to about who you were . . ."

"No, I admitted to none of the things you think I did. I never lied. I only spoke truth. Think back, Jake. There is nothing I told you that wasn't true."

"But you said I would die."

Ryan's smile went wide. "Would you not describe what happened to you in the cabin in a quite real sense as being reborn?"

Jake eased over to the pond and looked down at his reflection. He was indeed a new man, a man reborn. "Without question."

"For something to be reborn, something else has to die."

"Die to the man I was—to the lies, my beliefs, the way I lived my life—in order to become the man I always was destined to be."

"Yes."

"But why? Why did you have to make me think you were my enemy?"

"Because you had to fight to win with everything you had. You had to have a rage burning inside, a determination so deep that you would never quit trying to be enough. You would go back again and again to your mom and dad, and you did. That way, when you had expended everything you had, you would realize the task was utterly impossible. Only then would you be ready to receive the revelation you did inside the cabin.

"I had to force you to go back into your deepest wounds and see them for what they were. If you knew I was for you, you *might* have still agreed to walk into your mom's house, Sienna's home, your dad's backyard. I don't know. But certainly you wouldn't have gone into them with the intensity that you did, with the relentlessness you did, and your heart would not have been in the condition needed to take in the healing."

Ryan motioned toward the lake and they both strolled in that direction. He set his hand on Jake's shoulder as they approached the curtain of willow vines that would usher him into the corridor, onto the lake, and back to his friends. They didn't speak again till they reached the edge of the meadow and stopped, now facing each other.

"I won't be coming back, will I?" Jake reached out and took a few of the willow vines in his hand.

"The corridor has grown narrow, Jacob."

"Too narrow to get through again."

Ryan nodded, sadness in his eyes.

"But the healing will remain." Jake winked.

Ryan's eyes brightened as he laughed. "Oh, yes, your healing will remain."

"Thank you." Jake grabbed Ryan and gave him a fierce hug. "Will I see you again?"

"Your life is but a moment, Jacob. A vapor. And when the vapor is gone, what is eternal will remain, so yes, you will see me again."

<hr />

Jake clambered back into his canoe, and when he'd settled in, he glanced around to see if Leonard was there. No. Not this time. This moment was Jake's to immerse himself in. The sun streamed down on him from just above the mountains to the east out of a cloudless sky, and the lake was glass.

He reached for his legs and ran his perfect hands over his once again blotchy, burnt, scarred legs and smiled. Jake let his head fall back, and he breathed deeply of the late morning air and laughed. Yes. The healing would remain. He would never hide again. Not from himself. Not from anyone.

He dipped his paddle in the water and gave a gentle pull. The bow of his canoe parted the scattered cattails in front of him and he eased through them into open water. Jake didn't hurry back. He wanted time to figure out what he was going to say to Susie, to the others. Maybe nothing. Maybe it was okay to let what had happened settle for a day, a week, a month. He would eventually tell Susie everything. Of course. She was the reason he now felt like he was beginning life over again. But he wouldn't say anything for a while, not for a while.

Jake reached the dock half an hour later and peered up at the deck. Voices floated down to him, but he couldn't make out who was who in the concert of conversation. He secured the canoe to the dock and started up the stairs. A quarter of the way up he heard Susie's contagious laughter, and Andrew's deep, booming voice as well. Peter? Yeah, him too. And then Camille. They were all there. True friends. All of them.

When Jake was twenty or so steps from the deck, Susie appeared at the top and clomped toward him. He stopped and waited for her, a good excuse to catch his breath. She reached him a few seconds later, her eyes wide. "What's going on with you?"

He grabbed her in a bear hug and didn't let go for almost thirty seconds.

"What?" Susie laughed. "What? Tell me."

"I was healed, Sooz. In the corridor. I was healed."

She glanced at his legs and looked back up, confused. "I don't—"

"Don't worry, I'll explain. Soon." He wrapped her up in another quick hug. "But thanks for being the inquisitive, adventurous, weird little sister you've always been."

They tromped back up the stairs and Jake immediately went to Andrew—gave him another fierce hug as only some men can give. "You killed it with your words last night. Nailed me. Inspired me. Pushed me over the edge. Thank you."

Jake released him, and the happy, puzzled look on Andrew's face was priceless. Next, Jake grabbed Peter and Camille, one arm around each of their shoulders.

"Warning. Sappy moment about to erupt." He yanked their heads down and kissed each one of them. "I love you guys."

It seemed like minutes later they were all saying good-bye in the driveway of the cabin, telling each other they needed to come back here next year. Jake agreed but stayed silent about the fact he'd be coming back in less than a week. As soon as he could free himself up from work, he'd be back to have a long conversation with his friend across the lake.

42

Jake pulled into Leonard's driveway at a little past eight the following Friday evening. He didn't think his old friend would be
going to bed for at least another hour, so Jake was surprised there
was no answer when he knocked on the door.

"He said he'd be home today," Jake muttered to himself.

Not in the garage or in the garden. Jake strolled up the slight
incline of Leonard's property, then down the other side toward
the dock. That's where he spotted him, a fishing pole in his hand,
a gray aluminum pail by his side. The bottom edge of the sun
had just hit the horizon to the west and would bathe the end of
the lake in evening gold for a few more minutes. Leonard's form
was a silhouette against the light and could have been a picture
on a greeting card. Jake eased down the gentle slope and strolled
down the narrow path till he reached the walkway that led onto
the dock.

"I thought you never fished off your dock, Leonard."

He didn't move, and for a moment Jake wondered if he'd been
heard. But a second later Leonard turned and glanced at Jake and
said, "I wondered if you were ever coming back."

"I had to do something first, before I saw you again."

"What's that?"

"Get out of the bottle."

Leonard showed his profile and grinned. Then he stood and wobbled toward Jake, and Jake walked out and offered his hand.

"Nah, get your hand out of my face, I'm not that old. And if I do fall in I still know how to swim, probably faster than you."

Jake laughed and made his way back to the bank. They settled onto the bench and Jake said, "Would you like to hear what happened to me in the field?"

"Every detail."

As Jake told of his final visit, Leonard's eyes grew wet, then dry, then wet again. When Jake finished, Leonard simply nodded once and said, "I knew you'd make it. I knew healing would come. Well done, Jake. Well done."

"Who wrote the song, Leonard?"

"What song?"

"Nice try."

"You found it, huh?"

"I'm going to say it was your daughter."

"Lucky guess."

"How long has it been in that piano bench?"

"Long time." Leonard patted his leg. "I'm glad you found it. You're the first one."

"It was my friend Andrew. I'm glad too. None of this would have happened without that song knocking over the first domino. None of it would have happened without you, Leonard. Thank you. You revolutionized my life."

Leonard's only reaction was a gentle smile, but that was more than enough.

After a long pause of doing nothing more than watching the light play tag on the lake, Leonard said, "You think you'll come back to the house next summer?"

"As long as the owners let us." Jake peered across the water at the cabin that had been part of changing his life. "Good memories. As you might imagine, that cabin has become much more than a house to me."

"Yeah, okay, good. That's good, very good news." Leonard rose from the bench and trudged toward his house. "Come on, move, I haven't got all day. Gotta get to bed."

"What're we doing, Leonard?"

"Well I'm not gonna kill you with an ax if that's what you mean. Would've done it long ago if I was going to."

"That's comforting." Jake chuckled.

After they'd stepped through Leonard's sliding glass door into his living room, he waved Jake toward his kitchen table. "I was hoping you were going to say you loved the house."

"Oh yeah?"

"I need a dollar from you."

"What for?"

"Just give it to me." Leonard waved his hand impatiently.

Jake opened his wallet and took out a beat-up dollar. "It's a little—"

Before he could finish, Leonard snatched it out of his hand and stuffed it in his back pocket. "Good. Start signing." Leonard jabbed at a thick document on his kitchen counter. "I drafted it myself, so trust me, there's nothing in there that doesn't play to your favor."

"What am I signing?"

"A simple buy-and-sell agreement." Jake's elderly friend held out a blue pen. "Gotta be in blue 'cause it proves the document wasn't photocopied, something like that."

Jake glanced at Leonard, then picked up the papers. A quick glance told him the agreement was for the sale of a house. After a longer look he fixed his eyes on Leonard and pointed across the lake. "You own that house? You?"

"Yep. Thanks for renting it from me."

"And you're selling it to me." Jake pointed at his chest. "For a dollar?"

"Stupid question."

Jake broke out laughing and even Leonard smiled a bit.

"So I'm buying a place where every time I'm there, it will remind me of the spot where the girl of my dreams rejected me."

"That just means there's someone better out there for you. You'll find her someday. Trust me."

"I believe you."

"Really?"

"Yeah. I finally stepped out of the bottle far enough to read my own label."

"Then maybe it's time you showed the rest of the world."

Jake stared at his friend for over thirty seconds. At the light in his eyes. Or fire. Yes, it was fire. And that was okay. More than okay. Because Leonard was right. And Jake knew exactly how he was going to show the world.

43

Eight weeks later, on a Thursday afternoon, Jake stood backstage at Luce Auditorium in downtown San Diego, his heart pounding inside his chest like a bass drum at a rock concert. Through a slit in the curtain he stared at the mass of bodies milling about the venue.

"Excuse me, Mr. Palmer. You need anything?"

Jake tore his gaze away. A soundman with hair to his shoulders and a Cheshire-cat grin bounced on his toes, waiting for an answer.

"What?"

"You go on in five. Just checking in. Making sure you got everything you need, that your mic is good, all that kind of stuff."

"I'm good."

"You're ready then?"

Jake nodded, against the protest of his churning stomach and the reality that he'd never be ready for this moment. It wasn't one he could practice by videotaping himself. This moment could only come as he stood in front of a live audience.

Seven minutes later, after a quick introduction from the

promoter of his talk, Jake walked into view and basked in a strong welcoming applause. He strolled over to the center of the stage on wobbly legs and gripped the sides of the podium with both hands. As he stared at the crowd, he shot up a quick prayer and began.

"Just before stepping out here, I was asked if I was ready." Jake stared at his fingers gripping and regripping the light wood between his hands. "The honest answer is I'm not ready for this. In fact, I'm more nervous right now than I've ever been. I've given over twenty-five hundred talks during the past nine years, but none of those have prepared me for this moment."

Jake stepped out from behind the podium and stood with feet at shoulder width, hands behind his back. He stared at the back of the room where the wall and ceiling met.

"I'm going to do something this evening I vowed I would never do. In fact, I've been finding excuses not to do it for two months, ever since I promised a friend, as well as myself, that I would. I've had six opportunities in that time, six talks similar to this one, but each time I stayed inside my bottle." Jake smiled and gave a tiny shake of his head as his gaze dropped to the floor in front of his polished black shoes.

"But since I've just confessed to you that I made a promise, it will be difficult to back out now. So fate has chosen you to witness that promise being fulfilled."

A murmur went through the crowd.

"Enough stalling, hmm?"

A smattering of light laughter.

"If you're here, you know that I like to talk about the fact that it's impossible to read what's on the label when we're standing inside the bottle. And we're all standing inside our own bottles. Recently I had the chance to do the impossible and see what was on my label. And now I'd like to show you.

"What you're about to see might be disturbing. If you're squeamish, I'd like to give you permission to leave the room till I'm finished. It will only take a few minutes, and then we'll get back to our regularly scheduled programming."

As Jake spoke, he loosened his tie, then removed the dress shirt covering his white T-shirt. Next, he pointed at his hips and smiled. "Don't worry, this isn't a striptease. I have workout shorts on, so I promise no one will get embarrassed."

He glanced around the room.

"I'm going to take off my shirt first, then my pants." He motioned toward the exits. "Again, if you're squeamish, this is the time to leave."

All of them stayed in their seats. One woman toward the back moved her head slightly to get a better look. No one else moved even an inch. If Jake didn't know better, he'd swear they'd all stopped breathing.

"In order to read the label, we have to step out of the bottle."

Under his breath he said, "For you. For them," as he removed his T-shirt and let it drop to the floor.

"Looking good, Ja—" A woman at the back of the room broke off her shout as her eyes reached his stomach.

"A year and a half ago I was burned in a fire. And I've spent the past year and a half trying to deny the fact, hiding from what I'd become, trying to keep my pain hidden, trying to tell others what's on their labels when I could no longer see my own. Actually I had never seen my own.

"I thought I was worthy of being liked for two reasons. My looks and body, and because I always fixed things, made things right for the people around me. But apparently there's more to me than that. My looks and my ability to help were my shield. I used it so no one could see the real Jake, because I thought the real Jake, the one who lived from his true heart, wasn't enough."

As he spoke, Jake unbuckled his belt and took hold of the top of his zipper. "I was a mountain climber, a mountain biker, a triathlete, a white-water kayaker . . . I was in such good shape a fifty-mile bike ride was a warm-up for me. My best friend calls me Clark, because he thinks I look like Superman with the build to go with it. That was my label. Then it all came crashing down.

"Friends, who we are is not what you see on the outside. This is a costume, a shell, only clothes that are quickly turning to tatters."

Jake held the sides of his pants in both hands, closed his eyes, and let go. The sound of his belt buckle smacking onto the floor of the stage echoed through the room, but that was the only sound. He waited for the gasps of revulsion to come. And they did come. But it didn't matter. He was not his burns or scars. Not the ones outside. And not the ones inside. He'd already stepped outside the bottle, and he knew what was on his label.

After an eternity, Jake opened his eyes. But he didn't find horror or disgust in the eyes of the front row, and he realized the gasps he'd heard weren't revulsion, but surprise. A man in the front row on the far right got up and ambled out of the room. Two

THE LONG JOURNEY TO JAKE PALMER

women toward the back on the right did the same. But their exits barely registered. He even had trouble focusing on the people who stayed, their faces a mix of shock, compassion, and wonder. And hope.

As waves of whispers buzzed through the crowd, Jake pulled his slacks back on as well as his T-shirt. By the time his dress shirt was buttoned again, the crowd had grown silent. After he finished dressing, he paused to collect the emotions churning through his heart. But then again, maybe he didn't need to collect them. Maybe it was okay to let them see. In that moment, he let tears of his own rise to the surface.

"Thank you for allowing me to tell my story." Jake wiped away the tears with the back of his hand. "Once I figure out why it suddenly got so dusty up here, I'll begin my talk and we can—"

"Excuse me." A heavyset woman in the front row stood and with a shaking voice asked, "I'm sorry to interrupt, but would it be possible for me to say something?"

Jake stared at her. He knew the look. Utter terror from standing in front of an audience combined with unquenchable conviction that she had to speak out whatever was inside her. He nodded and lifted his hand toward her. "Please."

Jake lifted the cordless mic off the podium and walked it down to the woman. She took the microphone with trembling hands and gave Jake a frightened little smile.

"I've tried for years to lose weight. I just can't do it. And I've tried to hide it. But there's no way to hide being heavy." She gave Jake another tiny smile. "Clothes can't cover it up. I fantasize about staying in my house all the time. That can't work either. So

I hide inside when people stare, when they don't think I can see them. When they snicker at me. Sticks and stones might break my bones, but words? They'll kill me. And they have ever since I can remember. But today I'm hoping things can change."

She glanced at Jake again, her lip trembling. He winked and smiled.

"I'm burned, Jake, like you are. Maybe not on the outside, but I am on the inside." She bobbed her head at the crowd. "Do you know what I'm trying to say? I bet you do. Even though you don't want to admit it, I bet you do. You understand, right? I'm not alone, I don't think. I can't know what your burn is, or where it comes from, but you're burned, aren't you?"

There was no scuffing of feet. No whispers in the crowd, no movement, and no sound except for the soft hum of the air system overhead. The woman had nailed it better than Jake ever could.

"What if we scrounged up the courage to talk about our burns with each other? I'm scared, really scared, but I have to try it, you know? To step out of the shadows and tell my friends who I really am. And I betcha it will be good, okay? What would happen if we talked to other people about our fears and scars and burns so that those lies lose their power, and so maybe we give other people the chance to tell us what's *not* written on our labels?"

She glanced at Jake again. He nodded and she kept going.

"Like I said, I don't know what your burns are. I have no idea how long they've stayed hidden. Maybe even from yourself. But I'm still thinking you might have them. So if you're like me, I'm thinking it's time we strip off whatever kind of clothes we've been wearing to cover them up.

"Because I don't care what we've done, don't you think Jake might be right, that we have more worth than we know? Don't you think there's that possibility? I do. I really do. At least I want to with everything inside me. If you're like me, for years we've listened to people tell us about things on our labels that aren't there and were never there, but we believed them. I think it's time to read the biggest true words that are on each of our bottles: We. Are. Worth. It."

The woman looked like she wanted to say more, but she stopped and held out the mic to Jake. He stepped over to her, wrapped the woman up in a massive hug, and whispered to her. "You have not only pulled back the curtain, you've tossed it into a bottomless sea. You said it better than I ever could have. Well done, Beautiful."

She handed the microphone back to Jake and shuffled toward her seat, but before Jake could speak, a man who looked to be in his late twenties stood. He stretched out a hand that fluttered so fast it looked like he was trying to fly. Maybe that was exactly what the man was about to do.

Jake motioned him over. "What's your name?"

"Terry." Terry blinked and swallowed, but his eyes didn't leave Jake's.

Jake lowered the microphone and leaned close to Terry's ear. "You can do this."

Terry nodded, took the microphone, and looked over the crowd. "My name is Terry. Being here today, sitting here today listening to Mr. Palmer and being around all of you isn't where I'm . . . it's not what I'm supposed to be doing. I'm supposed to be . . ." He stared at Jake, who gave a slow nod.

"It doesn't really matter where I'm supposed to be, because now I know that where I'm supposed to be, I mean, without any doubt the place I'm supposed to be right now is right here." Terry jabbed his finger at the floor and Jake could tell he was fighting back tears.

"My parole officer bought me a ticket to this thing two weeks ago. I tossed it on my nightstand in my apartment when I got home that night, thinking it was some stupid cheesy motivational talk thing and I wasn't going to go or anything . . . I mean, I like my parole officer, I mean, he's a good guy, he's been good to me and all that, I mean . . . what I'm trying to say is he's trying to do more than just do the job. I think he really cares, actually, I know he really cares, but I just haven't been in a space . . ."

Terry drew in a quick breath and looked at Jake as if to say, *I'm rambling, aren't I? I'm so totally blowing it.*

Jake took Terry's hand that held the microphone, lowered it, and started to speak, but before he could start, Terry puffed out, "I shouldn't be doing this. I'm sorry. I don't even know how to explain . . ."

Jake raised a finger to his lips and Terry went silent. He again leaned close to Terry's ear and said, "Let me tell you what's on your label right now. In this moment. You are one that opens hearts and souls. The gut-level honesty that I see on your face is about to burst out all over this auditorium, and people are going to be set free. Do you understand me?"

Terry nodded.

"Do you believe me?"

Again, a quick nod. Jake raised Terry's hand, stepped back,

and motioned to the young man. Terry hesitated only a moment and then dove back in.

"So, what happens is the ticket, when I threw it onto my nightstand? It fell off the back but I didn't even know it, because I wasn't looking for it or anything, because like I said there was no way I was going to come today, but the crazy thing is last night I knocked my glasses off my nightstand in the middle of the night, and this is the crazy part, when I went to find them this morning, they're laying on the ticket and the way the lenses are laying, I see the date all clear and big and everything and it's today and something inside me says I have to go."

Another glance at Jake. Another nod at Terry.

"I'm burned too. Just like the lady said. Growing up I always got a double shot of affection." A sad smile played on Terry's face. "Double shot because both my parents beat me."

Terry paused and drew in a long breath. "And just like the lady said, I've been told all my life I'm not worth the dirt I stand on. But . . . but . . . see, this week it all came together, not in a good way though, you know? See, I got ahold of a gun and today I was going to . . ." Terry swallowed hard, bowed his head for a moment, then raised it and clenched his jaw. "Life is worth living, even with burns."

Terry stretched out his arm to give Jake back the microphone. Another huge hug as Terry let his tears come and Jake let his come as well. As Terry made his way back to his seat, Jake moved to the center of the stage, crossed his hands in front of him, and bowed his head. Without question, the audience needed a moment. He needed a moment.

After more than a moment, Jake lifted his head and looked around the auditorium. He'd always had a few people, usually ladies, get misty as he spoke about discovering the strength and glory that were inside a person, about allowing the true label of their lives to be read, but only a few. And only once in a blue unicorn did any guys tear up. But this time more than half were fighting back the water. And some were quietly sobbing.

Jake didn't speak. He simply held the microphone out in front of him as he nodded at the crowd and let God's Spirit do what God's Spirit was already doing. The first one to step from his seat and tell his story was a man who had to be Leonard's age. Then a young woman who couldn't have been more than twenty. Then another woman who looked to be in her forties who was stick thin. More men. Young. Old. In between. Woman of all ages and obviously from divergent walks of life. An hour stretched into two, then three, but no one left.

All of their stories ended with a hug from Jake and words of encouragement from him, but of course he was the one who was buried in encouragement. Finally, the stream of people ended and Jake searched for the words to end a talk unlike any he had ever given.

Jake walked to the side of the stage and spoke to the promoter who had brought him in, who was fighting back his own emotions. "This might be completely inappropriate, but can I pray?"

The man nodded as he blinked back tears.

Jake walked back to center stage and shook his head in amazement. "Thank you, to all of you who were willing to step out of the bottle, to take your masks off in front of all of us. We need to close and I want to do it with a short prayer. If you're uncomfortable with that, no worries, please feel free to leave."

No one in the packed auditorium moved. Jake waited a few more seconds, then bowed his head and rested in the silence for over a minute. Finally he prayed.

"Jesus, we need transparency. We need to step out of the shadows. We need the freedom to live out of the strength and glory you've given us rather than live the lies about ourselves we've swallowed. We need to see that the bottle we all stand in is nothing. We need to see that we have put so much worth on a shell that is dying from the moment we are born. We need to look past the costume we wear to what is inside. We need to see it, and live from it.

"We need to tell others what is on their labels. You've changed me, but there are days I still struggle with what happened to me. There are days where I forget I'm only wearing a costume and that this costume does not define me. Which is why we need to continue to speak the truth to each other. We need to tell those around us about the strength and glory inside them that they can't see for themselves. Bring us that truth, Lord. Open our eyes, and grant us the strength to live our lives with freedom. So be it."

For five seconds there was utter silence in the auditorium. A moment later it erupted with thundering applause as everyone rose to their feet. It wasn't applause for him, but for all of them, for freedom, for the lies that had been shattered and the truth that had just exploded out of every soul in the room.

Jake's watch hit eleven thirty before he hugged the last of those who had a story to tell or wanted to thank him. As he watched the final two members of the audience amble down the middle aisle toward the back of the auditorium, he let himself embrace what had just happened.

He'd simply revealed himself, shown the hidden parts of his soul, but that had not only invited them into his newfound freedom, it had given them hope to find their own.

As silence fell over the hall, the emotion of the day hit him, and Jake yawned deeply. He closed his eyes for a moment, sent up a prayer of thanks, then picked up his laptop and slid it into his briefcase.

Time to head for his hotel. Sleep in till noon if he could, then wake and maybe plan his next trip to Willow Lake. To the house, his house. He smiled. Crazy. And beyond wonderful. Would he ever be allowed back through the corridor? Didn't matter. He saw the world he lived in now more clearly than ever before, and someday, when he slipped free of this body, he would step into a world where all healing would come and last forever.

Jake started to walk toward the building's lobby when a familiar voice stopped him.

"Do you have enough energy left to talk to one more fan?"

Jake knew that voice. It couldn't be. But of course it was. Jake spun and sniffed in a breath of shock. Ari stood five feet away, her makeup slightly smudged.

"Ari?"

"Yes, or is there someone else you know who looks like me?" She winked and her intoxicating smile broke open his soul.

"What are you doing here?"

"It's good to see you."

He took a halting step toward her. "What are you doing here?"

"You already asked that." She took a step closer as well.

"But you didn't answer."

"It should be obvious. I came to see you." Another step closer.

"Why?"

She looked different, but of course she would. She wore black slacks and a dark green blouse, which set off her eyes perfectly. Her hair was pulled back, which made her even more beautiful than he remembered, and the feelings he thought had faded returned in a blizzard of emotions. Hope. Resignation. Love? Yeah, definitely love, the most dangerous emotion of all.

But Jake smiled inside, because even though his feelings would never be returned by Ari, he would be fine. He knew who he was, and that person was far more than enough. He knew what God thought of him. He knew that above all else he would fight for the heart of that kid he met back in the cabin through the corridor for the rest of his days on earth.

"Didn't Peter tell you I left his company?" she asked.

"I asked him not to talk about you."

"Of course." She looked down and nodded. "I understand."

Ari shifted from one foot to the other and something in her countenance shifted. Was that anticipation on her face? Nervousness? She glanced at everything but him. Strange. He hadn't seen her like this. Her evergreen confidence had been replaced by an uncertainty he was surprised to realize she was capable of.

"Are you okay?"

"You probably won't realize how powerful that was just now." She pointed behind her at the stage. "You think you know, but you don't understand the full scope of what happened."

"You're probably right. But it wasn't me. It was—"

"Stop." She held a finger up to her lips the exact way he'd done with Terry earlier in the evening. "It was you. And it was the people who spoke. Yes. All of those mixed together so no one and everyone did it. But you were the one who stepped out of the shadows and opened the floodgates that set a great many people free. And freedom will continue to come as what happened here tonight ripples out into the lives of the friends and families of the people who experienced this moment."

"That you were here is . . ."

"Strange?"

"Yes."

Ari smiled. "I want to help you out, read to you what I saw on your label tonight."

"Okay."

"But first, I need to explain something." She motioned toward the back of the auditorium. "Should we make our way out of here as we talk? Before someone kicks us out?"

Jake agreed, trying to decide if Ari's suggestion was more a function of not wanting to look at him than a desire to appease the building's security team. "Sure. That's fine."

"Back at the cabin, in July, when we talked between the hammock and the fire pit, just before I left?" She glanced at him as they strolled up the middle aisle. "There was something you desperately wanted. Something I could have given you, something you thought you needed. Something you expected. Do you remember?"

"Yeah. It was monstrous. A huge request." Jake held out his hand in front of him and shook it, fingers wide, and spoke in a deep voice. "I wanted to . . . I wanted to . . . wait for it . . . I wanted to have coffee with you."

Ari laughed. "I probably deserve that. But on the other hand—"

"But on the other hand that wasn't what I was asking for. I wanted you to accept me. Tell me I was okay. Reverse the vast ocean of revulsion Sienna had drowned me in, because if you did that, somehow I would be healed. Accept myself. I thought my looks were me. But they weren't. They were the wall I hid behind."

"Yes."

"And it would have been a trap. A false elixir that would have satiated for a time, then turned bitter in my mouth. If you'd agreed to a simple coffee date, I would have read much more into it. It might have even shut me off from the true healing I was being offered."

He glanced at Ari and the upturned corners of her mouth made him smile as well.

"Anything else?" Ari brushed a loose strand of hair back from her forehead as they stepped through the lobby doors onto the street and faced each other.

"Thank you. For speaking truth when you told me to stop hiding. That if I wanted to live, I couldn't hide any longer."

"Something happened to you at the lake after I left, didn't it?"

"It did. I found a place where I was given the thing I wanted most in the world."

Jake looked deep into those green eyes speckled with amber and felt himself falling inside them. He did nothing to resist. Stupid? Yes. Was he about to get his heart bruised? Yes. But not broken. Better to live a life of freedom where his heart was bumped and bruised from time to time than keep it shut in a room where no light ever came.

"I'd like to hear the story," she said. "All of it."

"Sure." Jake nodded. "We'll do that someday."

Ari tilted her head and once again flashed her nova smile. "What if someday were to become now?"

Jake automatically glanced at his watch, even though it wouldn't have mattered if it was three in the morning. "I think that can be arranged."

As they strolled down the street, the warm, late-evening air swirling around them, Ari grabbed his hand and gave it a squeeze. He savored the feel of her hand and gave her a squeeze back. Her touch would only last for a moment, unlikely to ever return.

But she didn't let go.

A NOTE FROM THE AUTHOR

M y friends,

People often ask where my story ideas come from. "It's different every time," is the vague answer. The more specific answer—at least for the story you just finished—is that the idea came directly from my wife, Darci.

Every summer when our sons were young, we took them to a small lake in eastern Washington state. At the end of the lake was a wall of cattails and beyond them, a vast bank of trees. One summer, Darci, Taylor, Micah, and I—along with family friends—punched through the cattails and found ourselves in a huge meadow on the other side. I told my boys we'd entered into another realm, one not of this earth. Every year after that we pretended we were exploring that extraordinary world.

One day when Darci and I were batting around story ideas, she said, "What if you did a story on the corridor? You could make it challenging to find and put something on the other side that will change the life of anyone who gets through."

I loved the idea instantly and dove in to writing the story. As I wrote, Darci offered penetrating insight on the characters, setting, scenes I'd scratched out . . . everything.

So if you liked *The Long Journey to Jake Palmer*, thank Darci. If you didn't, blame me.

Regarding the theme of the novel, it's universal, don't you think? Isn't there a part of you that wonders if you're enough? A part that doesn't think there's much good written on your label? There's a part of me that wonders those things.

The good, no, *great* news is we *are* enough, in Jesus. There is no shame, blame, condemnation at all in him. That's just one of the myriad proclamations written on each of our labels.

My prayer is you gather with close friends and take the time to read each other's labels. That you take hold of those words and phrases and etch them deep in your heart, and that you step into more freedom than you've ever known before.

James L. Rubart
March 2016

ACKNOWLEDGMENTS

Great thanks goes out to my family: Darci, Taylor, and Micah Rubart for their unwavering belief in me. (Double thanks to Taylor for being the first to read the first draft of *The Long Journey to Jake Palmer*, and for giving me excellent feedback.)

Also, thanks to Allen Arnold, Ron DeMiglio, Mick Silva, and Thomas Umstattd Jr. for amazing brainstorming sessions about the paths this story could and should venture down.

Thanks to my editors, Amanda Bostic and Erin Healy, for yet again being absolutely brilliant at what you do. This story would be a shadow of itself without you.

And thanks to Jesus for allowing me to once again enter this playground called telling stories.

DISCUSSION QUESTIONS

1. What do you feel are the major themes in *The Long Journey to Jake Palmer*?
2. Which character in the novel could you relate to the most? The least? Why?
3. Camille isn't the most pleasant person in the world. Do you have any Camilles in your life? How do you make that relationship work?
4. Jake's deepest question is, "Am I enough?" The question is almost universal. Are you one of the many who ask it about yourself?
5. If you answered yes to the above question, where do you feel you haven't been enough in someone else's life?
6. Where do you feel you haven't been enough in your *own* life?
7. Jake gives talks about it being impossible to read the label when you're standing inside the bottle, and we're all standing inside our own bottles. What do you think is on your label? Do you want to find out?
8. Is there anyone in your life who tells you what is on your label? If yes, how do they do it?

9. Have you ever told those close to you what is on their labels? Has anyone ever told you what is on yours?

10. During an author retreat I (James) once led the group in a read-each-other's-labels exercise. It was powerful and uncomfortable, both at the same time. We were all nervous to hear what would be said about us, but when the words were spoken, it brought healing and freedom. Would you be scared to do a label reading exercise? Why or why not?

11. If you're reading *The Long Journey to Jake Palmer* in a book club, or informally with friends, would you be willing to lead a read-each-other's-labels discussion? If yes, when do you think you'll do it?

12. Most of us hide things about ourselves. Are there things you'd be willing to share, like the group at Willow Lake shared with each other? That's a fearful exercise, but do you think there's anything freeing about doing that?

13. Jake talks about "stepping out of the shadows." Where do you need to step out of the shadows?

14. In Jesus, we are more than enough, but that can be a hard message to grasp, and once we grasp it, hard to hang onto. How do you see yourself taking hold of that message and how will you hang onto it?

What if you met your twenty-three-year-old self in a dream? What would you say?

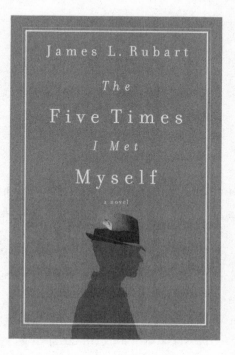

"If you think fiction can't change your life and challenge you to be a better person, you need to read *The Five Times I Met Myself*."

—Andy Andrews, *New York Times* bestselling author of *How Do You Kill 11 Million People*, *The Noticer* & *The Traveler's Gift*

THOMAS NELSON

AVAILABLE IN PRINT AND E-BOOK

An Excerpt from
The Five Times I Met Myself

1

MAY 10, 2015

The dream had come again last night, just as it had sliced into
Brock's subconscious the night before that. A dream now
dominating a significant portion of his waking moments. He had
to talk to someone about it—someone with at least a smattering of psychology. Someone he could trust. His best choice was
Morgan. His only choice, really.

Brock crossed Seattle's 4th Avenue and looked up at the sky
as it surrendered to dusk. Not long till the spring evenings would
hold the light till after nine o'clock. He reached the other side of
the street, strode up to the front door of Java Spot, yanked the
door open, and stepped inside. Three-quarters full. The perfect
number of people. Not so many that newcomers would turn away,
but enough to tell people it was a place to be. Morgan had to feel
good having that many customers at six twenty.

Brock glanced around at the 1940s motif. Posters of Rosie the
Riveter and Ted Williams, an old Coca-Cola sign, and the famous
shot of the sailor kissing a nurse in Times Square hung on the
walls. Definitely captured the hope of a post–World War II pop-
ulace. Or maybe Java Spot simply appealed to those who wanted

an alternative to the corporate giant that had more coffee shops sprinkled throughout Puget Sound than 7-Elevens.

On one side: a cluster of what looked like college students, a few couples, and some solo acts. The opposite side: three people hunched over their Mac laptops, and a large group of midforty-somethings laughed and pointed at each other in rapid-fire succession. What Java Spot put in its drinks was obviously the right concoction, which made Brock smile again, because he'd developed those concoctions being consumed in all fifteen of Morgan's locations as well as the rest of the country and overseas.

Brock took one more glance around the coffee shop, then strolled behind the counter and said, "Not a bad crowd for a Monday night."

"You can't come back here."

"Deal with it."

"Nope. Employees only. Get out. Now."

Morgan Myers lugged his sizable girth toward Brock and grinned. When he reached Brock, Morgan grabbed him by both shoulders and shook him like he was a stuffed animal. Yeah, maybe Morgan had put on more than a few pounds since their college days, but even after thirty-one years, he hadn't lost any of his linebacker strength.

"Amazing," Morgan said. "You actually have the hint of a tan to go with your slightly graying mane. A vacation you call work—but at least you got some sun."

"It was work."

"Uh-huh. A week in Costa Rica sipping coffee and checking out beans. Brutal. How did you survive? What, you were probably slaving away three, maybe four hours a day before you hit the beach?"

"Four and a half." Brock grinned at his friend.

"When did you get back?"

"Five days ago." Brock lowered his voice. "That's when they started."

"When what started?"

"When you get a moment, I need to talk."

"The doctor is in." Morgan tapped his chest.

"A degree in psychology you never used makes you a doctor?"

"I use it every day." Morgan waved his paw of a hand at the crowd. "Spill it. Problems with Karissa? Tyson? Work?"

"A dream. More like a nightmare."

Morgan beckoned with his finger and led Brock to the back room and into the office. After they settled into the small space, Morgan beckoned again with both hands. "Let's go. Tell me about dem cah-razy dreams."

"Strange dreams, not necessarily crazy." Brock glanced at Morgan's office door to make sure it was shut.

"You said nightmare."

"Not exactly. I'm not sure how to describe it—I'd almost call it spiritual but not in an uplifting way."

"Like a God dream?" Morgan's eyes were expectant.

"What do you mean?"

"I mean God dreams, where you know he's trying to tell you something." Morgan leaned forward and opened his hands. "Where he's talking to you through the dream, warning you, or letting you know something is coming, something to get ready for."

"God does that?"

"Um, yeah."

"It's not like that, I don't think. It's more . . . You ever have one of those dreams that's so real you can't tell if it's a dream or not, and when you wake up, you know intellectually it had to have been a dream, but you're still not one hundred percent sure?"

"Yes." Morgan's voice grew softer and he repeated his earlier request. "Tell me about the dream. In detail. And why it's freaking you out so much."

"My dad is in it."

"Oh boy, here we go."

"The dream isn't just a dream." Brock leaned back and focused on the ceiling of Morgan's office. "Yes, it's a dream, but Morg, I know it was more. My dad is young, early thirties I'm guessing, in the days before his nervous breakdown. The days before he started hating me."

"He didn't hate you."

Brock ignored the comment. "The light in his eyes is like fire. And he wears a jet-black fedora straight out of the fifties—so now I finally realize where the name of the company came from. He never wore a hat like that in life, and yet it was more him than anything I ever saw him wear." Brock glanced at Morgan. "You get that?"

Morgan nodded.

Brock paused. "You know how most dreams have elements of fantasy in them? Things that couldn't happen in real life? This wasn't like that. Everything was as it should be. And it would take the push of a feather to convince me it really happened. That I was truly there. It was more real than real life."

"Go on."

The memory of the dream engulfed Brock and he lived it again, for the millionth time.

Brock," his dad rumbled as they sat next to each other in Brock's boyhood backyard on a summer evening, both of them facing west, the sun starting to set.

"Yeah?" He gazed at the Douglas fir tree in the north-west corner. The tree he'd climb to the top when he was nine and ten and eleven and twelve to get away from his father.

"You need to listen to me." His dad held a small rect-angular box wrapped in brown paper, which he tapped on the armrest of his chair. He pointed to the box and raised his eyebrows. "You see this? It's important."

"What is it?"

"Pay attention."

"I am." He turned to face his dad.

"No, not listening with one ear out the door like you always did." Dad beckoned with his finger right next to his ruddy cheek. "Right here. In my eyes. That kind of listening."

"Okay." The air warmed and his father's eyes grew more intense. Brock had the urge to bolt from his chair, but his body wouldn't move. "I'm really listening."

"Good. You need to. Yeah, you really, truly need to." He turned the box over in his hands. "You have to make peace with Ron. Have to."

"Peace with Ron? Yeah, sure, Dad. Peace with a brother who's a year and a half younger but acts like he's three years older? One with a life mission to beat me in every-thing he does?"

"Same mission as yours."

"I'm not as bad as—"

"He's your brother."

"No, he's my business partner." Brock clutched his chair's armrests as anger rose inside. "And you gave him fifty-one per-cent of the company, which he lords over me every moment."

His dad turned away and gazed out over the darkening

horizon. Once again he tapped the rectangular box in a slow rhythm on the armrest.

"It's coming, Brock, turning toward you just like the rotation of the earth. You can't stop it. It won't be easy. Definitely not easy. But good. You probably won't believe me, but it's good."

"What's coming, Dad?"

"Embrace it, Brock, even though it will be difficult. Face the truth, though it will be painful, for the truth will set you free." His dad leaned over and smacked his palm into Brock's chest so hard he caught his breath. "You need to get ready."

Brock pulled back. "Why'd you—"

"If you don't, it's going to bury you. If you don't, *I'm* going to bury you. Got it?"

"What's coming?"

His dad rose and grabbed Brock's shirt with both hands, yanked him out of the chair, and shook him hard. "Get ready!"

"For what?"

"Get ready!"

Louder this time.

"Tell me what's coming, Dad!"

Brock's dad pulled his face so close their noses touched and his voice dropped to a whisper. "For—"

But each time the words left his dad's mouth, the colors around them swirled and buried Brock, and he woke, breathing hard.

Brock stared at Morgan and whispered to his friend, "I have to get control of that dream. Get rid of it. My dad scares the snot out of me every time, and I'm tired of it."

"What's coming, Brock?"

"I don't know. I wake up every time before he tells me."

"You've had the dream more than once?"

"Five times in the past five days."

"Wow, someone wants to get your attention." Morgan leaned back and put his hands behind his head.

"This is God's way of saying hello?"

"What does Karissa say about it?"

"I haven't told her."

"Why not?"

Brock closed his eyes and let his head fall back onto his chair. "I don't want to get into it right now."

"Why not?"

"Morg?" Brock cocked his head and opened his eyes. "Give me a break."

"No worries." Morgan held his hands up. "What did you see and feel in the dream? Not with your mind, with your spirit."

Interesting question. On the surface there was nothing more than what he'd told Morgan. But underneath, there were layers he couldn't put into words.

"Like I couldn't stop whatever my dad says is coming, and yet I have to try."

"What else?"

"It's as if I was higher . . . I don't know how to describe it . . . The dream was clearer than it should have been, if that makes any sense. It gave me hope and fear at the same time."

"Yes." Morgan smiled. "Now we're getting somewhere."

"I was there. I saw my dad, but not only saw him, I saw deeper. As if I was seeing the true self that was buried while he was alive. The dream was the most normal scene you can imagine. But it felt like I was touching the past and the present and the future all at the same time. And what he told me didn't come from me or my subconscious, it truly came from my dad. Do you understand, Morg?"

"It was like he was alive. In the present."

"Yes."

"But he looked young. In his thirties."

"Yes."

"And you're thinking he's talking to you from heaven."

"No. It was just a dream." Brock's head lulled back. "I mean, I don't know. It's why I'm talking to you." He clenched his fists. "So what he said . . . Was that a warning from God like you suggested? Or only a chemical reaction inside my head as I slept? And if it was a chemical reaction, could God have his hand on it? Maybe he orchestrated it?"

Morgan said in a sing-song voice, "'The place where dreams and reality intersect, where the dream is immersed into the reality and is no longer a dream. A place where the infinite reaches us beyond the limitations of our mortal coils.'"

"What?"

"It's a quote from a book I read six months back. Thought I told you about it." Morgan twisted in his chair, stood, and scanned the bookshelves that ran across the back wall of his office. He shuffled a few feet to his left, reached for the highest shelf, pulled out a thin volume, and tossed it to Brock. "Here."

Brock caught it and looked at the cover. *Lucid Dreaming: Turning Dreams into Reality.*

"What's this?"

"Read it. Amazing stuff in there. Keep it, don't need it back. It's yours."

"What's lucid dreaming?"

"Read it. It might help you deal with the dream. Figure out what God's doing."

"Do you know what my dream meant?"

"Maybe." Morgan's eyes narrowed. "If I'm right, you're in for a ride."

"Why do you think that?"

"Just a feeling. Read the book and see where God leads you."

Brock tightened his grip on the steering wheel as he wove through the darkening streets toward home. Why were there always more questions than answers when he talked with Morgan? He supposed it was the price of friendship with a man so well read and probing.

Morgan's intuition was rarely wrong. Which meant the coming weeks would be a roller coaster without any chance to get off. As if he didn't have enough tension pumping through his veins at work, and even more on the home front.

The journey continues in
The Five Times I Met Myself by James L. Rubart